Family Language L

MW00479843

PARENTS' AND TEACHERS' GUIDES

Series Editor: Colin Baker, *Bangor University, UK*

This series provides immediate advice and practical help on topics where parents and teachers frequently seek answers. Each book is written by one or more experts in a style that is highly readable, non-technical and comprehensive. No prior knowledge is assumed: a thorough understanding of a topic is promised after reading the appropriate book.

Full details of all the books in this series and of all our other publications can be found on http://www.multilingual-matters.com, or by writing to Multilingual Matters, St Nicholas House, 31–34 High Street, Bristol BS1 2AW, UK.

PARENTS' AND TEACHERS' GUIDES: 19

Family Language Learning

Learn Another Language, Raise Bilingual Children

Christine Jernigan

MULTILINGUAL MATTERS
Bristol • Buffalo • Toronto

Library of Congress Cataloging in Publication Data
A catalog record for this book is available from the Library of Congress.
Jernigan, Christine
Family Language Learning: Learn Another Language, Raise Bilingual Children/Christine Jernigan.
Parents' and Teachers' Guides: 19.
Includes bibliographical references and index.
1. Language acquisition – Parent participation. 2. Language and education. 3. Language arts.
4. Language and languages. I. Title.
P40.8.J47 2014
418.0071–dc23 2014033090

British Library Cataloguing in Publication Data
A catalogue entry for this book is available from the British Library.

ISBN-13: 978-1-78309-280-2 (hbk)
ISBN-13: 978-1-78309-279-6 (pbk)

Multilingual Matters
UK: St Nicholas House, 31-34 High Street, Bristol BS1 2AW, UK.
USA: UTP, 2250 Military Road, Tonawanda, NY 14150, USA.
Canada: UTP, 5201 Dufferin Street, North York, Ontario M3H 5T8, Canada.

Website: www.multilingual-matters.com
Twitter: Multi_Ling_Mat
Facebook: https://www.facebook.com/multilingualmatters
Blog: www.channelviewpublications.wordpress.com

The policy of Multilingual Matters/Channel View Publications is to use papers that are natural, renewable and recyclable products, made from wood grown in sustainable forests. In the manufacturing process of our books, and to further support our policy, preference is given to printers that have FSC and PEFC Chain of Custody certification. The FSC and/or PEFC logos will appear on those books where full certification has been granted to the printer concerned.

Typeset by R. J. Footring Ltd, Derby
Printed and bound in Great Britain by the Lavenham Press Ltd

Contents

Acknowledgments

I would like to thank Multilingual Matters, in particular Tommi Grover and Dr Colin Baker, who provided expert guidance while still giving me the chance to stand behind my choices.

The foundation of this book was first laid, however, with good parent models. To Mary Alice and Jim Kearley for their emphasis on the value of education and persistence. To Tom and Cheryl Galbreath for reminding me to enjoy life through creative outlets. And Lois and Bob Jernigan for their encouraging cards and emails.

I also thank my husband, Stephen Jernigan, for his selfless and unfailing support of this project from the very beginning.

And to my children, James and Sydney Jernigan, for their patience and trust in uncharted waters. They make me a proud and happy Mamãe.

Preface

When, early in my pregnancy, I told people I was going to speak Portuguese to my baby, they looked at me funny. Maybe it was because of my Nashville, Tennessee accent. Or because I didn't even start learning Portuguese till a few years before. Or maybe because my husband doesn't speak it. Typical responses went like this:

- 'Wow, is your Portuguese that good?' *(Skeptical look of 'Let's be realistic.')*
- 'REA-lly? When are ya gonna fit THAT in?' *(Dubious look of 'You have no idea how much time a baby takes.')*
- 'What does your husband think about that?' *(Eyebrows raised in warning.)*
- 'Why Portuguese?! Why not Spanish?' *(Followed by unsolicited advice on how much more useful Spanish is.)*

These reactions made me doubt myself. Maybe it was impossible to teach a language I didn't know that well. Maybe my husband would feel left out. Maybe I had chosen a less useful language. But added to the voices that nearly made me give up were the voices that made me hang on for dear life:

- 'I only have a little French from high school, so my kids are out of luck.' *(Furrowed brow, defeated shrug of shoulders.)*
- 'My mom's originally from Germany. It's too bad she didn't do that with me.' *(Disappointed look of 'Too late now.')*

Here were people who regretted their parents didn't pass down a language. Here were parents who wanted to share a language, but assumed it was too hard or too late.

The Impetus

So, pregnant as a whale, I decided to get to the bottom of this non-native thing. I turned to every book on bilingual parenting I could find. I looked online, too. Very little mention was made of parents – like me – who were still learning a second language.

I decided to begin my own research, interviewing people from different parenting groups. There were moms who had some experience with other languages. There were dads who wished they had foreign language experience and were willing to learn. And there were parents who were scared of learning a language because somewhere in their past, a mean or boring teacher had bled the enthusiasm right out of them. I published some of the findings in popular parenting magazines. The subsequent emails and letters to the editors sent a resounding 'Tell us more!'

Why Me?

I'm able to write this book for you for two very good reasons. First, professionally, I've taught two different foreign languages, trained foreign language teachers and given talks on language acquisition for over 15 years. My research focus has been on motivation and expectations in second language learning – which has a huge bearing on how successful we are at picking up languages.

Second, and more importantly, I'm living the part. Our household is bilingual by choice, but neither my husband nor I grew up bilingual. Learning Portuguese started during a six-month stay in Brazil, teaching English to teenagers. When people ask if I am 'fluent', I tell them fluency is a project I don't expect to finish in my lifetime. I speak what I can to my children and learn more each day.

All this to say that yes, professionally, I'm well qualified to write this book. Personally, though, I'm not much different from you!

Introduction

The Myths

Back when I was young, I envisioned memory as a mailbox that could become completely full. New memories would crowd out the old ones. Memorizing a new phone number might just bump out the name of a famous president. Unfortunately, this faulty notion of memory is frequently applied to our brains with language learning. Parents fear that if little Johnny learns words in a second language, he might automatically forget or get confused about words in his first language. Though evidence does not support this full-inbox version of memory, the myth gets propagated, even by health professionals and well-meaning educators. This book will help you deal with other people's misconceptions and feel confident about your language choices.

A Book for Non-Natives

This guidebook isn't like other bilingual parenting books. They're written for parents who have spoken a second language from birth, and often include case studies of people who've traveled the world, who've grown up around many languages, or who live in a multilingual environment.

Instead, this book speaks to people who are still learning the second language they want to impart to their child. The case studies include parents who did not grow up speaking two languages, who are not well traveled and who are in a location where mainly one language is spoken. The examples from books and articles on bilingualism cited are ones that are useful to non-native speakers of the language.

This book focuses not only on ways to teach your child another language, but also on how you can improve your own second language skills. You'll abandon the notion that parents and teachers have to know everything. Top-down teaching from parent to child is replaced with a parent–child partnership. And some psychology is included to help you deal with mistakes and uncertainties.

Not an Academic Work

Though this book often supports its claims with books and articles used by academics in areas related to foreign languages, it is not an academic work in itself. If that's the kind of book you are looking for, or if you would like to read this book along with a more academic text, the five below might be helpful:

- *7 Steps to Raising a Bilingual Child* by Naomi Steiner.
- *A Parents' and Teachers' Guide to Bilingualism* by Colin Baker.
- *The Bilingual Family: A Handbook for Parents* by Edith Harding-Esch and Philip Riley.
- *Language Strategies for Bilingual Families: The One-Parent-One-Language Approach* by Suzanne Barron-Hauwaert.
- *Raising Bilingual–Biliterate Children in Monolingual Cultures* by Stephen Caldas.

Other Audiences for This Book

If you are a native speaker of one language and living in a country with a different majority language, this book is also for you. For example, a German mother living in Australia who wants her children to learn German can benefit from this book. It will help you consistently speak your native tongue to your child. The specifics on resources and hints on engaging your child will smoothly guide the acquisition process. And you won't be doing it alone. You'll learn how to enlist the efforts of your family, friends, teachers, coaches and even strangers!

If you have no plans to learn a second language yourself but want to raise your child bilingually – whether it's through immersion programs or a nanny who speaks the second language – this book is for you. You'll learn how to choose from the many opportunities for language exposure. If you are a home-schooling parent, for example, the tips given will show not only how to include a foreign language in your home curriculum, but also how to teach children to excel in and enjoy the foreign language.

Whoever you are on the parenting journey – expecting parent, new parent, parent of a middle or high schooler, godparent, grandparent, aunt or uncle – you're in the right place to share a language with the child you love. Whether you're a language lover or one who nearly flunked freshman French, relax. Read. You're exactly where you need to be.

Other People's Stories

Since we learn best from stories, this book is full of examples from parents in different countries successfully exposing their children to another language. Most are taken from transcripts from interviews with over 80 families and are cited by initials only, followed by the words 'interview' or 'email interview'.

Some of the parents here are new to the bilingual process and others are veteran parents of bilingual children. There are parents who adopted children from other countries and wanted them to maintain their original ethnic language. I also spoke to some bilingual families with one or more parents who speak another language natively. This way you'll see how a more 'typical' bilingual situation plays out.

To get a broader picture of language teaching and acquisition, I spoke with caregivers, such as bilingual daycare workers and foster parents, to see how they shared a second language in the short time they had with the children. What better way to see the many possible scenarios of language teaching!

Some of these parents I found through my website, Bilingualwiki.com, established several years ago to share what I was learning and give parents the chance to talk about their experiences.

The interactions I 'overheard' through these families' voices validated my personal experiences. They offered practical advice. They helped me stay positive. I saw my own struggles and triumphs reflected in their revelations.

My Own Case Study

I've also used my own stories throughout this book. Since my pregnancy, I've kept journal notes on my interactions with doctors, friends, relatives, and my husband and children. I wrote entries in little black notebooks strewn around our apartment, or tucked in diaper bags and purses. Later, when my children were napping, I typed them up. As the kids grew, I started typing my observations directly into Bilingualwiki.com, in the section 'Journal from the Trenches'. The entries detail my children's progress in English and Portuguese, as well as my own efforts to improve my language skills and cultural knowledge. They let me air my frustrations and gush with glee. You'll see them cited as 'journal' and I'll put the date, too. Please forgive the run-on sentences, but I want to keep the entries faithful to the original flow of emotions.

It is perhaps this section that is most different from other bilingual books. I show you how I succeed, but also how I fail. I show you times when my family was amazingly helpful and other times when I cried from feeling weird or wrong in the bilingual endeavor. All this to give an accurate picture of the work and stamina that are needed, but also to show how worth the time and effort each bilingual moment will be.

Anonymity

People who shared their stories sometimes requested anonymity. Therefore, their names, genders, languages, or countries were changed. And then there are times I've mentioned my own family, co-workers and friends. I imagine they'll be happy with what they see. If not, I hope they understand I'm trying to give honest impressions.

Terms and Abbreviations

Throughout these pages, you'll find the term 'bilingual' used to refer to speakers of more than one language. Though 'multilingual' is more accurate in cases where a child speaks more than two languages, most of the examples in this book come from bilingual households and not multilingual ones.

You'll see several technical expressions and abbreviations in this book. To refer to the country that speaks your second language, I write 'target country'. If you're learning Romanian, then Romania is your target country.

For a 'second language' or 'foreign language', I'll write 'L2'. And when I want to refer to someone's first language – the one they've spoken since birth – I'll write 'L1'. For example, I grew up in the United States but learned Portuguese as an adult. That makes English my L1 and Portuguese my L2. The abbreviation 'L1' will also refer to the majority language of a given country. That means English is the L1 of England.

These distinctions get blurred when we're talking about children. If a US family has a father who speaks his second language, Russian, to his daughter, and a mother who speaks only English, their child will technically have two L1s. But to simplify, I'll still call Russian the L2. The idea is to distinguish the second language from the language spoken in the country where they live.

Finally, to show how to search for certain programs or sites online, I will choose a language or a country as an example. I might suggest you search 'children speaking French' or 'playing in France" You would then know to substitute your language and country in place of 'French' and 'France'.

Gender References

As to gender references, I alternate the use of 'he' and 'she' and have tried to be equitable without being distracting.

Come Aboard!

My daughter was just over three when she mentioned matter of factly that she had 'two voices'. When I asked what she meant, she explained that she had one voice in English and one in Portuguese. She recognized her special gift – the one we've worked on since the day she was born. One we wrestle with and laugh about, and one we ask others to come on board with. I invite you along for an amazing ride!

How to Use This Book

Use this book as a springboard, a how-to, a maintenance guide and a cheerleader to help you implement another language within your busy and beautiful life. It's not intended as a textbook, with a final exam looming. It's okay to jump ahead, skip chapters and go back if you need to. That's why so many separate chapters and headings are offered. If your kids are in middle school, you probably don't need to read the parts about infancy. If you're familiar with the benefits of bilingualism, just skim Chapter 1.

Finally, you'll read many examples from families working toward bilingualism, and in the highlighted text you'll find entries from journals I've kept on my own children. Search for yourself and your children in these examples. That's how you'll find advice that fits your particular lifestyle. This book lays a detailed map in front of you, but only you can find the 'You are here' arrow. Only you can decide which roads will get you where you want to go.

1 There is a Free Lunch!
Bilingual Benefits the Easy Way

To have another language is to possess a second soul.
Charlemagne (quoted in Kaplan, 2010)

You probably already know some of the benefits of bilingualism. In your enthusiasm, you might even be tempted to skip ahead to Chapter 2. This chapter, though, describes research that might surprise you. And it'll keep you motivated.

What Are You Doing?

I'm going to take a guess and say you probably have very good reasons for your choices in life. But when it comes to raising children, it can be difficult to describe those reasons, especially when your mother-in-law asks for details. So we'll list the top five reasons why language exposure is good for children and adults. This will help you explain your language plan to curious strangers, friends and extended family.

Free Lunch

Steven Pinker, cognitive psychologist and author of *The Language Instinct*, says of bilingualism, 'One free lunch in the world is to learn another language in early childhood' (Pinker, 1995: 22). We'll use this idea of a 'free lunch' as an acronym for the benefits of a second language:

L Language advantages. Even in the first language!
U Understanding others. Others who speak the L2, and others who are different in other ways.
N New ways of thinking. A variety of ways to solve problems.
C Connections, codes and character. Higher self-esteem through stronger family connections.
H Healthy brains. Handles multitasking, stays more focused and makes better decisions.

Language advantages

Children exposed to a second language have an edge when it comes to language, even their first language. And that's not just for full fluency. Even a little foreign language helps. Developmental pediatrician Dr Naomi Steiner writes,

> One study found that children who knew just a little Italian in addition to their native English had a greater understanding of words and more enhanced reading skills than their peers who spoke only in English.... Children gain cognitive and academic benefits even from just a little exposure to a second language. (Steiner, 2008: 19)

Enhanced first language vocabulary

Some parents worry their kids will be confused by having vocabulary in more than one language. Colin Baker, in *A Parents' and Teachers' Guide to Bilingualism* (2007), found that bilinguals were actually better at using new vocabulary, even in their first language. He found that by knowing there were two words for everything, children paid more attention to word meanings and tended to use even their first language words more accurately.

Essentially, an L2 gives children a built-in point of comparison. Li Wei of the *International Journal of Bilingualism* says that these comparisons help children understand the universals of language. They see how pliable language can be. This helps them pick up on meanings that a monolingual child would miss (Li Wei in Lauchlan *et al.*, 2013). Carey Myles writes,

> Bilingual children often demonstrate a greater sensitivity to subtle differences in meaning than monolingual children of the same age, perhaps as a result of their more sophisticated ability to analyze the nuances of word choice and grammar. They are more skilled at interpreting and manipulating grammar to communicate clearly. (Myles, 2003: 62)

Language awareness

Part of the sophistication gained when a child experiences other languages involves an early awareness of language itself. Researchers in second language acquisition call it 'metalinguistic awareness'. It is basically what makes you laugh when you hear the pun: 'Two cannibals were eating a clown. One says to the other: "Does this taste funny to you¿"' (Upegui, 2008).

Barbara Zurer Pearson, professor of linguistics and communication disorders, says bilinguals' heightened awareness comes from having to choose between languages many times a day. 'They develop a greater awareness of the language and are better at establishing this abstract connection between letters and sounds' (Pearson, 2008: 16).

This more mature connection between letters and sounds means bilinguals understand that words are collections of symbols – representations of things, but not the things themselves. Baker puts it this way:

A bilingual child is … more aware of the arbitrary nature of language. [This] free[s] the child from constraints of a single language, enabling the child to see that ideas, concepts, meanings and thoughts are separate from language itself. (Baker, 2000: 67)

This awareness gives them an edge when manipulating these symbols to express ideas. They end up with more diverse vocabulary and tend to be superior writers. A study in *Science Daily* (2012) found 'a marked difference in the level of detail and richness in description from the bilingual pupils'.

Fascinating research with bilinguals has also shown that since they don't get caught up in the literal meaning of words, they can think 'outside the box'. For example, in one battery of tests given to monolinguals and bilinguals, researchers presented a water bottle and asked about different ways it could be used. 'Instead of stopping at "put water in it", bilingual children had more creative answers like, "filling it with sand and making a paperweight"' (King & Mackey, 2007: 4).

Stronger readers

A wealth of research indicates that bilinguals' heightened awareness of language as symbols makes reading easier and increases the speed of reading. (See p. 125, 'Bilinguals have an advantage'.) Ellen Bialystok (2002), a Canadian psychologist specializing in literacy and bilingualism, found that on reading tests, bilingual children learned twice as quickly to recognize words without the help of pictures. She says they learn more quickly that the written letters on the page carry meaning. From there, bilinguals score higher on word recognition and general reading tests.

More languages

Children who are exposed to one foreign language tend to do well in other foreign languages. Since they are accustomed to hearing unfamiliar sounds, they try harder than monolingual children to decipher languages they hear. Michael Erard, psycholinguist and author of *Babel No More*, writes 'There is no theoretical limit to the number of languages one could learn' (Erard in Okrent, 2013). The limitations are only those placed on our expectations.

One mother who speaks French to her daughter tells me how easily her daughter picks up languages from those around her.

When Mary Kate was almost three years old, a Spanish-speaking two-year-old girl came to visit us…. Soon after this girl's arrival, Mary Kate was saying, *'Cuidado!'* [Careful!] and *'Ven aquí!'* [Come here!]. I think her experience with French helped her to realize that other people speak other languages and that it's not weird, and it somehow predisposed her to picking up foreign phrases quickly, even if they weren't French. (J.F., interview)

Understanding others

Recent research indicates children with more than one language are better at understanding other people. This starts with their listening skills. Since bilinguals can literally listen in two languages, they always have to choose the correct language to listen in. This constant monitoring is thought to help them listen better and pay more attention. Baker writes that bilinguals are 'more aware of what is going on beneath, above and inside the language', making them 'more in harmony with the needs of the listener in conveying meaning sympathetically' (Baker, 2000: 67).

This openness to others extends beyond children's immediate family and friends. Children who learn another language are constantly confronted with different language forms. This makes them less judgmental and more open-minded to other people's differences. The author of *Catching Tongues* said this perspective can be wide reaching:

> As parents, I believe we have a duty to raise our children to be citizens who will ensure that racist, xenophobic ideas are not tolerated in our society, and learning a second language is one way to help our children down this path. (Gibson, 2011: 21)

One father who speaks his second language, English, to his son writes '[One] thing which influenced my decision [to teach my son a second language] was [that] if you are bilingual, you are more of a world citizen and not a nationalist' (K.N., interview).

Raising world citizens means your kids will do better socially They pay attention to the language they use and are more in tune to the needs of others. Kendall King and Alison Mackey, authors of *The Bilingual Edge*, work with children in school language programs. They say,

> These children are more likely to make friends from other language and culture groups, both within their school language programs and beyond. Importantly, they also have fewer negative stereotypes about other groups. (King & Mackey, 2007: 8)

Resources lead to understanding

Children with an L2 are exposed to resources that foster greater understanding of other people and their cultures. The new buzzword in preschool and elementary schools is 'empathy building'. Researchers and educators have realized that children are more empathetic if they read books or watch videos about other cultures. They become familiar with a variety of lifestyles, lessening the judgment and fear that come with the unknown.

Interpretation and receiving correction

Bilingual children tend to make more friends and work better with parents, teammates and strangers. Studies show that's because children who know more than one language understand language subtleties and social indicators more easily than monolinguals. This understanding gives them a social edge when interpreting how someone else feels.

For example, is the teacher really mad at me, or just feeling frustrated? Does the boy sitting beside me feel sad, or is he just concentrating on something?

Studies also find that bilingual children respond more positively to correction and guidance from others (Ben-Zeev, 1977). For example, bilingual children on the soccer field can more readily see their coach's point of view and accept pointers on improving their play. Bilingual children more easily modify their behavior in the classroom setting, instead of getting upset at their teacher's comments.

Understood by others

Not only do bilinguals more easily understand others, they can also do well at being understood by others. Studies on bilingual children indicate that they can better organize and formulate their ideas before speaking. This means their friends and teachers more easily understand them. It also means their parents more easily pick up their thoughts and feelings.

Kids raised around two languages show more interdependence than monolingual kids. This ability to depend on others makes it easier for them to connect with other children and with adults.

Attention and connection

You will see at first-hand how an L2 brings you and your child to the attention of others. As a parent, capitalize on this extra attention. When you see other people watching you speak the L2, smile and make eye contact to encourage their questions. You serve as a model for your children to be open to meeting other people. Meeting other parents interested in an L2 can help you feel more supported in reaching your goals. You might also encounter other people who speak your L2, opening up new avenues to practice and learn.

Below are journal entries from when my daughter was one, two and four years old.

I sort of like speaking Portuguese to Sydney even where others can hear. Maybe I'll meet more Brazilians that way. (journal, 8/3/2002)

Speaking another language all the time has opened up meeting so many new people and it just makes even the trip to the grocery store more interesting. (journal, 6/10/2003)

Another advantage to speaking Portuguese to Sydney is that ... people overhear me speaking to her and they ask, 'Is that Italian' or 'That's not French is it?'... They often share with me their stories of people in their family or friends who are also bilingual. It just makes the whole stay-at-home mom experience more interesting because otherwise it's sometimes hard to start up a conversation with a total stranger at the playground. (journal, 7/17/2005)

New ways of thinking

A different language is a different vision of life.
Federico Fellini, Oscar-winning film director (quoted in Dubey, 2013)

As far back as the 1960s and '70s, research showed that children with an L2 have greater flexibility of thought. Instead of being tied down to one way of sharing ideas, their brains have an openness to alternative routes of expression, called 'mental flexibility':

> Mental flexibility ... helps them be more creative and come at problem solving in new ways. This higher level of imaginative ability stems from the constant negotiation of which name to call which object. Bilinguals less often get stuck on ... 'the boundaries of words' and can therefore 'establish a wider variety of connections and meanings. (Baker, 2000: 67)

With fewer boundaries on their thoughts, children are free to be more creative. Pioneer language researcher Wallace Lambert showed that bilinguals reflect a 'richer imagination and an ability to quickly process a multitude of possible solutions' (Lambert, 1977: 16). Researchers since then have agreed that this advantage means children excel academically: 'bilinguals outperform similar monolingual peers on both verbal and nonverbal tests of intelligence and tend to achieve higher scores on standardized tests' (Marcos, 1998).

Dr Greg Yelland, coauthor of the article 'The metalinguistic benefits of limited contact with a second language', writes 'Even "marginal bilinguals" show more facility than monolinguals with general "working things out" skills' (Yelland in Steiner, 2008: 22). He argues these honed skills mean children score higher in the verbal parts of standardized tests, and on the math. They also have higher IQs and are better at memorizing.

Field independence

The ability to see general patterns, as well as their component parts, is called 'field independence'. Adults tend to have more of this than children. Have you ever wondered why your child gets bogged down in details instead of seeing the big picture? That is because children take years to develop field independence. Bilingual children, however, tend to be more field independent than non-bilinguals (Te Kete Ipurangi Ministry of Education, 2012). This gives them several advantages. Studies show they have higher science and reasoning skills (Martin, 2011: 234). They more easily retain academic information, work well with less direct instruction and solve problems more effectively.

Connection, codes and character

Sharing an L2 at home means parents and children have a code language. It is a code in that parent and child understand what is being said, but onlookers do not. Sharing a language that others do not enter into makes for a special connection that leads to more open communication, a closer relationship and higher self-esteem for children and parents. Let's examine each of these specifically.

The language connection

Even in your first language, you speak different versions of the language depending on who you're talking to. You speak more formally when talking to an elderly stranger, using 'yes' or even 'yes, ma'am' instead of 'yeah'. If you suddenly started talking to your best friend the way you speak to an elderly stranger, she'd feel confused – maybe even offended – at how stilted you were. That's because language also represents the kind of relationship you have with someone. Now imagine speaking an L2 with your child. The L2 builds an even stronger bond because it is so different from the way others around you speak.

I'll share a striking example from a family I interviewed. The father, Ralf, has spoken German for years to his daughter, Sara, now five years old. Ralf is German, but is married to an American and lives with his family in the United States. Ralf was trying to become an American citizen. After much preparation and waiting, he was finally awarded his US citizenship. The day he came home from the awards ceremony, he started speaking to Sara in English, instead of their usual German. He was just joking around when he said 'Okay, no more speaking German with Daddy, Sara. I'm American now!' (R.D., interview). To his surprise, she burst into tears. He had to console her for some time – in German! – assuring her again and again that he was making a joke and that, of course, they would keep speaking German together. Even at a young age, Sara tied the German language to her relationship with her father. To abruptly stop speaking German would mean cutting a cord they'd had since she was old enough to talk.

The bond of extra time

Parents say the relationship with their children is greatly enriched because of the extra time they spend with them sharing the L2. I've found this to be true in my life, as well. (See p. 27, 'Relationships'.) The L2 has encouraged me to continually communicate with my children. This entry was taken from my journal when they were nearly four and six:

I've found another advantage to raising the kids bilingual is that it pushes me to spend time with them, talking to them, not just doing around-the-house chores in silence and such. I get a reminder that I haven't been vocal with them … [when] they struggle to find the word in Portuguese…. Playing Uno and Go Fish has helped a lot…. I think every mom struggles with … rarely get[ing] down on the floor to play because there are always bills to pay or phone calls to be returned or beds to make. (journal, 1/26/2007)

Other parents had similar experiences. They reported that being aware of speaking an L2 made them talk to their children more. This mom speaks French with her infant:

On a related subject, I can't remember if I told you that I really feel I do a better job teaching my infant French instead of English. I talk more often if I am speaking French, because I am conscious of teaching a language. (F.T., email interview)

Code language

Imagine having a code language with your child to express all the things you don't want others to hear. For me, it was great to be able to correct my kids without other people understanding. I love this journal entry from when my daughter was four and very stubborn about apologizing.

> Today Portuguese really came in handy. One thing I cannot get Sydney to do until she's good and ready is apologize. Today she smarted off to my dad. I told her she needed to say she was sorry and could tell Diddy [Daddy] was waiting for an apology. She flatly refused and instead said, in Portuguese, 'I want juice,' so I told her, 'After you apologize.' She said she was sorry right then and there. (journal, 5/19/2005)

Think back to times in your childhood when your parents corrected you in public. It may have been because you did something that embarrassed them: you made a rude comment that other people overheard, or you asked a loud, personal question about a stranger. Parents say it's much easier when no one can understand the embarrassing things kids say. One mom states,

And sometimes Mary Kate says things inappropriate about people and you can explain in French. Once she was in a restroom and a lady passed gas and Mary Kate said, 'She farted Mommy!' [but] in French. (J.F., interview)

In this case, the code language helped not only the mother, but also the stranger to not feel embarrassed. I've had many such situations, one when my daughter was just two:

> This morning ... we were at the mall and Sydney saw a woman who was overweight with bushy black hair going everywhere. She yelled out and pointed at the woman saying, 'Bruxa!' [Witch!] (journal, 11/4/2004)

Of course, parents still have to explain to children why these comments are rude or hurtful, but since no one actually gets hurt in the moment, the intensity is dialed down.

Character: Child's self-esteem, self-concept and self-confidence

Children benefit psychologically from the special parent–child connection that comes through a shared code language. Research shows this bond to be healthy for children's self-esteem, which is defined as how they feel about themselves based on others' feedback. Children feel important when their parents talk to them in a special way. And they reap the benefits of extra quality time from parents.

Sharing a code language has also been shown to be good for a healthy self-concept. This means how children know and understand themselves. Children who understand themselves better can more easily explain their likes and dislikes to others. This helps them make and keep friends.

The Connecticut Council of Language Teachers (2013) emphasizes that learning an L2 builds children's self-confidence in school, even in subjects that are not typically 'language related'. This higher sense of achievement serves as a foundation whenever they feel frustrated by difficult academic subjects.

Parent self-esteem

The stimulation of teaching an L2 can also be good for parents' egos. It keeps their minds active on those long days with young children. When my kids were really little, I felt numb and bored if I was taking care of them all day with little adult contact. Here's an example from a summer day:

> Today I thought, 'If I weren't speaking Portuguese and doing this bilingual thing with the kids, I would be going stark raving mad right now'.... It's just that I get so bored some days staying at home with the kids. I try to plan fun things … but the days are so long.… Somehow knowing that I am teaching her the language makes it more bearable. (journal, 6/30/2005)

The later entry below shows how speaking the language helped me feel smarter and more interesting than if I were 'just' a stay-at-home mom:

> I enjoy being in public and speaking another language to Sydney … it's fun to get the inquisitive looks, to talk to people who ask, 'Excuse me, but what language is that?' … asking me if I'm speaking Chinese or Russian. (journal, 12/23/2007)

Healthy brains: Attention, multitasking and memory

Imagine your bilingual child at her desk at school, seated beside another student who has trouble sitting still. The other student keeps talking and jumping up to get water or sharpen his pencil. Your child is better equipped to handle distractions than her monolingual counterpart. Incredibly, even infants who haven't started talking yet demonstrate this improved performance in the area of attention (Olson, 2014).

That's because she has had to favor one set of language rules in her head while ignoring the rules of the other. Diane Ackerman, author of *An Alchemy of Mind: The Marvel and Mystery of the Brain*, says this 'trains the brain early to focus and discriminate [and] ignore what's irrelevant' (Ackerman, 2004: 201). Neurologists believe this healthy brain training occurs non-stop.

> Both of the languages of a bilingual are always active in the mind. Therefore bilinguals must make a decision about language at some, usually subconscious, level every time they open their mouths to speak and their brains must choose which language to tell their mouths to use. Every time they hear something, they have to determine which language it is in before they interpret it. (Pearson, 2008: 15)

The constant mental juggling bilinguals do also helps them make better decisions outside the classroom (Kroll in Swayne, 2011). Imagine that your child is in high school, old enough to drive. Behind the wheel, she changes the radio station, listens to passengers in the car and checks her phone's navigation. Take comfort in a recent study on multitasking and bilingualism. Driving tests were given to monolinguals and bilinguals. Bilinguals did much better at tuning out extraneous noise and proved to be superior drivers, because they could focus on what was important and ignore non-essential information (Bialystok in Dreifus, 2011).

Show me the money!

If we fast forward a few years, we find that bilingual children have an advantage over monolinguals when they reach the workforce. The Center for Applied Linguistics explains:

> Individuals who speak more than one language have the ability to communicate with more people, read more literature, and benefit more fully from travel abroad. Knowing a second language also gives people a competitive advantage in the workforce. (Marcos, 1998)

American business writer Edward Trimnell (2005) points out in his book *Why You Need a Foreign Language and How to Learn One* that Americans have difficulty competing for jobs in some multinational corporations because few can fulfill the bilingual requirements. These requirements are becoming more popular as higher-level business people see that executives without language skills cannot negotiate with internationals. They may have translators,

> but they could be excluded from conversations their business associates have in their own language (sometimes even in their presence), which will put them at a strategic disadvantage. (Geisler, 2012)

In Canada, research shows that bilingualism has financial benefits even if the bilingual workers don't actively speak the language on the job. Bilinguals earn more money because those who hire them judge them to be 'stronger in unmeasured labour market characteristics such as ability, cognition, perseverance and quality education' (University of Guelph, 2010).

For workers who use the L2 at work, Alister Wellesley, managing partner of the recruiting firm Morgan Howard Worldwide, says 'If you're doing business overseas, or with someone from overseas, you obtain a certain degree of respect if you're able to talk in their native language' (Wellesley in Andruss, 2008). At a round-table held by the *Financial Times*, executives and consultants said they felt corporations 'benefited from the diverse background and skills of multilingual leaders – and would benefit more in the future'. Laurence Monnery, co-head of global diversity and inclusion at Egon Zehnder, said 'Multilingualism will be better valued and better leveraged by companies…. Multiculturalism makes better leaders' (see Hill, 2013).

Where are these jobs and these needs for multilingual leaders? Wellesley says that though any business would need bilingual employees, the sectors most in need are 'finance, sales, technology, manufacturing, professional services and government jobs' (Andruss, 2008). And what are the dollar figures? If we use the United States as an example, 75% of its firms compete internationally. The bilingual edge can come in the form of being hired ahead of monolinguals. Or it can mean higher wages. Salary.com says that the average bilingual pay difference ranges between 5% and 20% per hour more than the position's base rate (Morsch, 2009). In areas with a high percentage of bilinguals (Miami, Florida, for example), fully bilingual workers earned nearly $7000 more annually than monolinguals (Davis, 2000).

Benefits for parents

Speaking another language can also help parents maintain a healthy brain. Research shows that bilingualism delays memory problems in later years. That's because in speaking an L2, you're using different areas of your brain, exercising them with constant activity. The additional effort you expend boosts the blood supply to your brain. That helps keep the neural connections healthy over time.

The extra energy will have a long-term payoff – sharper word recall for years to come. One parent who was interviewed in a bilingual parenting book describes the phenomenon:

> My German has actually improved since I had [my son] Max. Before, I used German very little in everyday life…. It seems that even though my main conversation partner is a two-year-old, just the fact that I speak German every day seems to keep the cogs oiled and I don't forget as many words. (Barron-Hauwaert, 2004: 41)

Foreign language study in adults has also been shown to ward off dementia, since aging brains get the benefit of dual language processing. Ellen Bialystok, a research professor in cognitive development, likens bilingual activity to doing Sudoku or other puzzles, only better:

> Nobody spends all day every day doing crossword puzzles, but everybody spends all day every day talking…. It's a way to get massive doses of this stimulating activity without doing anything special. (Bialystok in Shute, 2012)

Amazing Results

I hope you leave this chapter ready to experience the little extras that made the effort worthwhile. One mother puts it this way:

> I am so grateful that we decided to try this 'German thing' seven years ago…. As I listened to my three-year-old (who's a very late talker) construct his first complicated German sentences, I feel awe-struck … amazed this whole 'German-thing' actually worked … and worked so well. It just proves once again that if you stick with something, you're guaranteed to get results…. Our lives have been so enriched by the whole experience. (S.S., interview)

Advantages of Bilingualism

- Language advantages – even in their first language.
- Understanding others – improved social skills.
- New ways of thinking – more flexible thinking for better problem solving.
- Connections – stronger family connections, higher self-esteem.
- Healthy brains – better at staying focused, improved decision making.

2 Forget the Unicorn:
Why 'Non-Native' is Just Fine

The native speaker remains like the unicorn, inspirational but always a mirage as we get near.
Alan Davies, *The Native Speaker: Myth and Reality* (2003: 85)

There are two things to avoid in dealing with a legend like the unicorn. The first is to make too much of it, the other is to disbelieve it entirely.
Chris Lavers, *The Natural History of Unicorns* (2010: 258)

Non-native speakers may feel inferior when compared to the mystical, ever-impressive 'native speaker' – the unicorn of the language learning world. How can non-native parents tap into the wisdom of native speakers while still feeling confident in their own right?

Who is a Native Speaker?

First, we should determine the definition of the term 'native speaker'. Most likely the first thing that comes to mind has to do with being raised to speak a certain language. The *Oxford Dictionary* (2014) states: 'a person who has spoken the language in question from earliest childhood'. But what is it about earliest childhood that makes a native speaker better than any other speaker? Surely an intelligent person in their twenties could study a language and get to native speaker fluency.

I believe the difference between a bright, adult student and a native speaker comes in what's called 'communicative competence'. It's the combination of word knowledge, grammar and knowing the social cues of how to use the language well. The best example of such expressive ease comes from a study about requests and apologies:

A native speaker's facility with language allows him or her to respond spontaneously, whether orally or in writing, without the need to search for the most appropriate, or the most correct, word or phrase. (Rintell & Mitchell in Davies, 2003: 97)

So, where does that leave those of us who are feeling anything but communicatively competent?

Non-Native Teachers

One starting place is to look at instructors who didn't grow up speaking the language they teach. I've given conference talks for such teachers where the mere mention of the term 'non-native speaker' plays like a racial slur. It smacks of insider knowledge in an exclusive club where they don't belong.

These feelings of inferiority are rooted in how history has viewed language education. The conventional wisdom of the 1960s through the '90s said that if your college French teacher wasn't actually French, you weren't going to learn as well as students with native teachers. But there was no actual research to support the idea that your French teacher should be Madame Dubois and not Mrs Walker. German Professor Claire Kramsch is cited in the book *Non-Native Language Educators in English Teaching*: 'Native speakers do not speak the idealized, standardized version of their language: their speech is influenced by geography, occupation, age, and social status of the speaker' (Kramsch in Braine, 1999: xv). One language specialist states it more strongly:

> The myth exists that the native speaker is the superior teacher. Like all myths, it relies on ignorance and a notorious lack of empirical evidence, no, in this case, a total absence of evidence. (Baker, 2010)

In fact, in my work with teachers, the Mrs Walkers are superior because they had to learn the language, not just acquire it from birth. They're better at explaining how the language works because they learned the rules themselves. They're also more in tune to difficulties their students may have, since they remember the challenges they faced themselves.

Native Speech Ain't Perfect

Not only are native speakers not necessarily the best teachers, they aren't even perfect *speakers*. Researchers studying the speech of native speakers had trouble finding complete sentences that were grammatically correct. Instead, native speakers' language is riddled with 'false starts, hesitations, interruptions, backtracking, sentence fragments, and grammatical errors' (King & Mackey, 2007: 22). Yet, even imperfect speakers end up raising children who are successful communicators. One mother I interviewed describes a man whose German mother had little formal education. He still learned the language perfectly well.

> How would anyone judge if a person's language skills were high enough? As a child I had a friend whose German mother, a somewhat plain woman, spoke very bad German. Well, tough! (K.D., email interview)

Native Speakers in the Minority

Native speakers are not even necessarily the majority speakers of a language. In fact, non-native speakers of English actually outnumber native speakers three to one (Crystal in Power, 2005). According to *Newsweek*, these non-native English speakers don't just passively absorb the language handed down from native speakers, they shape it by adding new words and altering meanings (Power, 2005).

Native Speaker as a Tool, Not a Goal

So, if native speakers aren't necessarily the best teachers, aren't a perfect model of the language and aren't even majority speakers, do we need them in our language plan at all? I would argue that yes, we do. Just as dictionaries or the internet are good tools, native speakers can be useful to parents learning and sharing an L2.

Here's an example. While I was tutoring a Korean student in English, he came to one session with a list of 'anger' words: angry, mad, frustrated, upset, furious, etc. He had looked up the words in the dictionary, but the definitions were all about the same. He needed a native speaker to explain the subtle differences and offer examples.

Let's say you're learning Spanish. You may have questions you can't find the answers to on your own. You don't have to hire a Spanish-speaking tutor. You can strike up a conversation with your co-worker who's from Ecuador. Or that woman at the gym who speaks Spanish to her children. Don't be timid about asking for help. Remember that people are generally happy to be asked questions they know they can answer. If you're worried about reciprocity, look on English language learning sites and find a native speaker to trade language questions with. Chapter 4, 'Be Your Favorite Teacher', suggests numerous ways to find and learn from native speakers.

Validation From Native Speakers

Native speakers can also validate the work you're doing with your child. In my interviews with families, parents said that interaction with native speakers helped them see that 'Wow! Someone can understand my child and me. We must be doing something right!' When parents and children are understood by a native speaker, the foreign language feels more 'real'. One mom writes:

> For the first few months, I didn't know any native French speakers. When she [my daughter] was several months old, I met a French Canadian and a French lady almost at the same time, but separately. I nervously asked each to speak to her in their native French to see if she could understand. She could! It made what I was doing feel legitimate. (J.F., email interview)

But I'm Not a 'Language Person'

> *It isn't how little you know that matters, but how anxious you are to learn.*
> C. Newland, 11th Lieutenant Governor of North Carolina (PBS Home, 1990)

Though it's nice to feel validated, it's not imperative to have the help of a native speaker to learn and teach an L2. And you don't have to be a 'language person'. Enthusiasm goes a long way. I love hearing stories from parents who didn't consider themselves 'language people', but plowed ahead with an L2 and are reaping the benefits.

I have to tell part of my own story here, because while growing up, I thought of myself as language deficient. I hated high-school French. The teacher was crazy as a bat. In college, I signed up for more punishment so I could go to France in my junior year. Again, I hated it. I tried my best in class, with all those pointless exercises and ancient literature. Some days, I'd be so lost that after class, I'd go back to my dorm room and cry.

By nothing short of a miracle, I did get to go to France to study. But even living abroad, I couldn't break the language code. I couldn't keep up in class, I avoided my host family and wondered 'What the hell is wrong with me?'

Then, once out of college, things changed. I got the chance to spend six months in Brazil teaching English. I arrived in Brazil dopey from lack of sleep. Soon, I met some neat people. I went out to clubs and restaurants and hated not understanding what people were laughing about. At night, I came home and poured over my dictionary to learn what I could, because I was lonely and wanted to understand people and make friends. Within a month, I could carry on basic conversations. The more I talked, the more I learned, and that motivated me to keep learning.

The difference between France and Brazil was the motivation. Not that I wasn't motivated to learn French, as I really did want good grades and the chance to study abroad. The difference is that the motivation for Portuguese was personal. It was based on relationships and wanting to make friends.

So if you struggled with language classes in high school or college, learning a language with your child will be radically different. You'll have a new type of motivation that's personal. So start small and see how the more you learn, the more you'll want to learn.

Four Reasons Non-Native Parents Worry

Even with the above assurances, non-native parents aren't always convinced that they're capable of learning an L2 and teaching it to their children. Let's examine four main fears and how parents can get past their anxiety.

(1) This feels unnatural

Some parents reported feeling unnatural, weird or artificial when speaking their L2 to their children. In some cases, these feelings kept them from even trying. One woman puts it, 'My husband decided he felt it was a bit artificial to speak Greek with our son, even though he speaks it absolutely perfectly' (N.S., interview). Similarly, a mom who tried speaking Spanish with her children explains 'The problem was that I felt weird speaking it, not just out in public, but inside my own house, even in the kids' rooms reading in Spanish' (A.H., interview).

For parents of infants, it appears that the second language felt weird because the baby wasn't responding yet. (See p. 40, 'Start small'.) Babies show few signs of comprehension in their early months, so parents feel like they're essentially talking to themselves. And when we speak to ourselves (whether out loud or in our own head), we do so in our L1. So speaking the L2 can feel like we're not being 'real' with ourselves.

The best advice to offer here is to say that yes, it might feel strange. It felt strange for me too, at first. But as Jane Merrill, mother of twins and author of *Bringing Up Baby Bilingual*, writes 'You must become conditioned to speaking a foreign language with the baby before it feels natural' (Merrill, 1984: 4).

If you persist, the newness will wear off. Another mother writes,

> Although we had thought out a careful plan, at first Paul and I did feel very awkward speaking French to Jeremie. After about a year of speaking French to Jeremie, it started to feel strange to speak to him in English. It even seemed strange to speak to *other people*'s infant children in English. (If I'm not careful, I still blurt out French sentences when communicating with other people's toddlers.) We felt more comfortable speaking French to him, even though we often found ourselves hunting through a dictionary for vocabulary. (We still have a dictionary constantly handy.) (J.N., email interview)

It's obvious from this parent's words that even though their French still needed a lot of work, it had become *their* language and didn't feel weird anymore.

All babies understand English, right?

Several English L1 parents said they felt strange about talking to their babies in a language other than English because they assumed that from day one their child would understand English better than other languages. One mother speaking French to her infant says,

> When I first started speaking French to Mary Kate when she was a newborn ... I had to confront my previously unnoticed belief that all infants understand English naturally. For the first few days, I would say something in French and then translate it into English. It took that long for me to convince myself she didn't understand *either* language, but that she could learn both. (J.F., email interview)

New parents need to trust that what they're doing makes sense. (See p. 38, 'Babies' brain data'.) Another mom who teaches French to her infant son describes her journey in an email interview:

Around his first birthday, I noticed that he understood what I was saying. Through-out the awful six months where he barely said a word of French to me, I kept telling myself, 'He still UNDERSTANDS, he knows exactly what I'm saying,' and this in itself was motivating enough to keep me going. (M.G., email interview)

I want to parent, not to teach

Some of the parents I interviewed worked as language teachers. Even they expressed reservations about teaching their children a second language. Some decided not to. One father who was a college professor teaching Spanish and Portuguese explains why he wasn't speaking either language to his son:

I know some families who speak to their children in another language, but I've always felt that it was a little artificial. I'd rather go play ball, fish, fix cars, play with bunnies, catch snakes and lizards, hike, watch sports, and barbeque fatty meats. Somehow, real life takes precedent over language practice at home. (O.P., interview)

I feel he equates speaking an L2 with a pencil-and-paper kind of learning. The acquisition we're talking about, though, is the kind you experience, not the kind you take tests on. The fun activities he lists – 'play ball, fish, fix cars, play with bunnies, catch snakes and lizards, hike, watch sports, and barbeque fatty meats' – can be done while speaking the L2. New vocabulary will be needed with each activity – 'Look at the bunny!' or 'Be careful, it's hot!' Children aren't cognizant of learning an L2 if it is integrated into their playtime.

I'll share a personal example about my own son. When he was six, he overheard me telling someone that I had been teaching his sister and him Portuguese. He corrected me, saying, 'But you're not teaching me Portuguese!' His sister, age eight, understood what I meant by 'teaching' and explained to him that it was not teaching like in school – the talking to them in Portuguese was the teaching. His adamant response was, 'But she's not TEACHING us Portuguese!' The language was integrated into his life, so it didn't feel like teaching.

George Saunders, in his book *Bilingual Children: From Birth to Teens*, had a similar experience of the added language being a backdrop in his children's lives.

What to outsiders might appear to be an artificial situation does not appear so from within the family itself. German is the language naturally used for playing or arguing with me, seeking my advice, permission, consolation, telling me of their ex-periences, and so on. It is what [my son] Thomas once aptly called his *Vatersprache* (father tongue). (Saunders, 1988: 137)

Talking 'through' the baby

Some parents felt their language choice to be unnatural when other adults couldn't understand what they said to their children. In an interview email, one mom tells me,

Another issue that I constantly deal with is that of talking *through* your baby. I mean those situations when people talk to the baby but are really speaking to you. An example of that is the time after our exercise class when the babies are on the floor and the moms tell them what they will do next. In reality, this information is intended for the other moms, letting them know whether you are available for a walk in the park or have to rush home. This is a weird example, I know, but these 'talking-to-you-through-the-kid' situations come up daily. (J.A., email interview)

I know from personal experience what this mom is talking about. Sometimes I was with friends and realized it was time to go home because Sydney was getting fussy. To explain to the other moms why we were leaving, I wanted to say to Sydney 'Oh, you haven't had your nap yet!' But then that would mean switching to English so everyone else would understand. And though that would feel convenient, or more 'normal', it could set up a habit that didn't fit my goals. The best solution was to just say directly to the moms 'She's getting fussy, so we'll head home'.

The new normal

From the early days of speaking another L2, you'll find yourself redefining what 'normal' is. Saunders says that the L2

becomes the language of intimacy between the child and the parent and ... as far as they are concerned, it is their language! Such a situation appears 'artificial' only to the outsider who is convinced that a parent must be a native speaker of a language to be able to transmit it to his/her children. (Saunders, 1988: 41)

I am reminded of my own upbringing. When I was a toddler, my parents divorced – back in the days when divorce wasn't that common. Both parents remarried before I was old enough to know what was going on. Onlookers may have thought 'Poor Christine, the product of a broken home', but really, I felt bad for kids who didn't have two dads – kids with just one home, one pet, one birthday party. Growing up with two families – as growing up with two languages – led to a richness of experience more special than 'normal'.

(2) I don't know baby talk

Another source of anxiety for many parents is that they don't know how to 'baby talk' in another language. Luckily, baby talk is pretty universal. (See p. 41, 'Infant-directed speech'.) Caregivers from around the world talk in a higher pitch to their children. Dean Falk, author of *Finding Our Tongues: Mothers, Infants, and the Origins of Language,* says that, universally, baby talk has words with repeated syllables, like mama, dada and boo-boo (Falk, 2009: 89). Baby talk also includes the lightweight words for baby-related things: baby wipe, dolly or blankie. In interviews with new parents, many reported feeling lost when it came to talking on a baby's level:

I am not a 'native speaker,' but plan to teach my child to speak Spanish in the United States. I learned Spanish through literature and missionary work, mainly dealing with adults. How do I learn the 'baby talk?' I can look up words like, 'diapers' and I think I already know that one, but I wouldn't know how to say, 'Don't touch that!' (D.K., interview)

I remember an area I had difficulty with: I didn't know nursery rhymes or many children's songs or finger plays in French. In addition, I didn't really know French 'baby talk' – the cute way you sometimes talk to kids. (F.J., interview)

At first I had to look up a lot – like diaper – in the dictionary [or] wheelbarrow because it's not important till you have a kid who has one. (F.T., interview)

Solutions for baby talk

So how do parents learn baby talk? Many parents said it helped to be willing to ask even embarrassing questions. One father used his L2, English, in his workplace in Hungary. He had to swallow his pride to get his questions answered.

I use English all the time at work.... So I didn't think it would be odd to speak it to the kids, but it was because I have a fairly good knowledge about business English ... but 'diaper' or 'potty,' I've never had to use. [At work] you're supposed to be an expert so it's embarrassing to ask someone how to say it. Like I don't know what is the children's way of saying 'shit.' So is it 'poo?' (E.O., email interview)

There are a variety of other possible responses to the need to learn baby talk. Here are three main categories of parental advice.

(i) Start by just talking

When you first start speaking to your infant or young child, you won't know all the baby words. What you say may sound like adult talk, but just get started anyway. Tell her 'It's time to eat. I'm hungry!' or 'Bedtime. It's really late.' One mom describes the running monologue/dialogue with her baby:

My Japanese wasn't in baby talk, so I had to look up words like 'playground equipment' and 'baby bottle,' and I didn't know any of this and didn't have the confidence ... but then I started using [Japanese] in my daily life, just giving a run-down on the day like, 'Come on, let's go to the park' so that helped and built up my confidence. That was even before they started talking so it was like a conversation with yourself and it was a while before I could express myself without thinking. (P.R., interview)

Don't worry that you're not a walking dictionary. One mother I interviewed was hard on herself:

Some aspects are my headache, especially colloquial expressions. For example, I said, 'Let mommy apply some lotion on your face' instead of 'put on some lotion,' and I said 'Release it' instead of 'let go.' I am trying to find some baby-talk materials. (M.N., email interview)

I assured her the words she was using were just fine. Her frustration echoed Merrill's as she writes of herself 'I bemoaned my restricted vocabulary, barren especially in the area of household objects and activities where small children substantially operate'. Merrill had a friend, though, who spoke his L2 at home: 'He shoved aside my doubt: "I keep a dictionary by my bed. You can do the same"' (Merrill, 1984: 4).

Many successful parents mention keeping a dictionary nearby.

He [my son] wants to say things in French, like … 'fireworks.' I use a dictionary a lot. I have two lying around the house. I feel fluent in certain adult topics but not in kid-speak or some household stuff. (J.V., interview)

So when I was educating my first child, if I didn't know how to say 'bulldozer,' I had to look it up. To know the vocabulary of the 15 different types of trucks like a cherry-picker truck, I had to literally look them up. (K.C., interview)

Children's books can be more instructive than dictionaries because they show the language that fits the world of children. (See p. 110, 'Where to find books in the L2'.) If you're struggling with vocabulary, choose books that have heaps of pictures. Or use an L2 picture dictionary for reading time. Let your child choose the pages they're interested in and just talk about the pictures. (See p. 112, 'Stair-step questions'.)

(ii) Native speakers on baby talk

To ask questions about baby talk, find a native speaker of your L2 – preferably one who's a parent or regular caregiver. Make a list of the expressions you don't know and ask for help! Or spend time with the native speaker while you're with your child, asking questions as they arise.

When I first noticed my own difficulties with baby talk, I invited a Brazilian woman to work with my baby and me. I paid her for what were essentially two tutoring sessions. I asked for her language input as I cared for the baby. It was especially helpful to learn mealtime expressions like 'Open wide!' and 'Look, all gone!'

Native speakers can also serve as correctors. As they hear you interact with your child, they will teach you expressions that fit young children. It was only when we had a Brazilian exchange student that I realized some of the expressions I used with my children weren't really age appropriate. For example, when I was changing a diaper, she heard me say what I thought meant 'Oh no! You passed gas!' But what I had really said was 'Oh no! You farted!' She taught me a sweeter term, like 'gassy-wassy'.

(iii) Websites for baby talk

If you don't have access to native speakers, you can listen to them online. Search YouTube for 'babies with mothers' or 'babies with fathers', typing the words in the L2. You'll find videos of parents playing with their infants, feeding them, bathing them or watching them take their first steps. Listen to the simplified language and hear the rhythm of the speech. Repeat what you hear aloud.

You can also learn 'parent-speak' by exploring parenting websites in the L2. Search for 'parents and children', written in the L2. If you search for *padres y hijos*, for example, you'll find the site for a popular Mexican parenting magazine. Like parenting magazines in many different languages, *Padres y Hijos* offers advice for new parents, ideas for recipes and games, and children's health information. The many images accompanying the articles make it easy to get the main idea. One way we recognize the power of such images is through government research for language learners in the military: they use the faces of Sesame Street characters like Cookie Monster to teach Arabic (one of 14 languages the puppets speak) (Everyday Language Learner, 2012).

Other exposure to the ways parents speak to children can be found in parenting blogs in the L2. You can usually subscribe for free. If you post a comment, be sure to say you're still learning the L2. You can ask direct questions about the language and culture, such as 'What do you call pacifiers?' or 'What is a good nursery rhyme for bedtime?'

(3) I don't know enough

Non-native families interested in bilingualism often fear their language skills are not good enough. Does any of the worry expressed in these interviews sound familiar?

> Part of the reason I don't speak French with her all the time is that I am afraid of teaching her mistakes…. A native speaker will be able to tell that I make lots of mistakes. (M.H., interview)

> I think I have good verbal skills and can express myself quite well, though I still have difficulty understanding native speakers without them slowing down…. I find it hard to keep up with Spanish TV, for example. Do you think it's the right thing to do to speak Spanish to my daughter? (E.I., interview)

> When our son was born, I had a minor in Spanish – I was a C student…. So, really, I felt there was no way I could have helped Jonathan become bilingual in Spanish, because my second language skills were not that good. (E.P., interview)

These quotes reflect parental anxiety over not measuring up. This book is here to remind you that you are fine to start just as you are. Your child can start learning just a few words and you'll learn more together.

For parents starting out with infants or very young children, take heart in knowing your children won't be ready for developed language skills right away. I was struck by the comical reaction from a stay at-home-dad, Todd Pinsky, in his autobiographical book *Homedaddy: Little White Lies and Tales from the Crib*:

> Many parents are full of stories (among other things) about how their child's first word was 'ratio,' or 'jurisdiction,' and they will tell you these tales with such wide-eyed belief that you will either have to make an awkward excuse to leave or use your pepper spray. (Pinsky, 2003: 22)

Why is it absurd for a small child to say the word 'jurisdiction'? Because children learn words they use in everyday life – words they need, such as 'No!', 'More juice' or 'Dada.' So early on in your introduction of the L2, remind yourself that you need only the basics, not college-level words yet. (See p. 95, 'You are good enough'.)

The words all around you

I once worked with a Vietnamese immigrant family who did not speak English. The first time I met the children was in their home. I brought some textbooks for teaching English as a second language. After five minutes with the children, I shoved the books back into my bag. The best way to teach them was to use what was around them – literally – what was on the floor, what was on the table. We played hide and seek in their house, and each child learned to count to 10. We played games outside, too, where they learned 'Me first' and 'Stop!'

Language lessons can be accomplished by just living your normal life with your kids – reminding them to brush their teeth, discussing which items to buy at the store and playing card games. You don't have to know the word for every single thing you touch. Even in our L1, we have trouble with word recall sometimes. If I can't remember the word 'wrench' in my L1, I can say 'that tool you loosen things with'. It's the same with the L2. You simply need enough language to express your ideas. If you forget the word for 'van', use the words 'big car'. We'll look more at this technique – called 'circumnavigation' – in Chapter 6, 'Marketing Strategies' and Chapter 7, 'Talk Talk Talk'.

You will make mistakes

There will inevitably be times when you think you know the word for something and you get it wrong. One parent who blogged online about his experience with raising bilingual children writes,

> First of all, I faced obstacles deep within myself ... I deeply felt embarrassment, a constant feeling that I am doing something abnormal, something against nature, especially if other people are around and above all native speakers. Then I am ashamed of all the mistakes I make or might make. (K.N., interview)

Parents who wrestle with perfection need to remind themselves that there's no test at the end of the semester and no cruel language teachers listening in. We can even let our children hear us make mistakes, and see us look things up in the dictionary and ask for help from native speakers. This humility helps our children ask for help when they don't know something. And it takes the pressure off us. A father I spoke with notes 'I'm frank with Jonah about my limitations in French. He used to call it Papa's language, but he has long since realized it's not my first tongue' (J.V., interview).

The owner of a bilingual Spanish/English pre- and elementary school would love more people like this papa. She says that many of her students' parents know some Spanish, but doubt their ability to help their kids with school work:

> There's a self-consciousness about their errors. People are worried about making a mistake because they don't speak perfectly, which I think is completely unfounded…. The occasional mistake is so trivial compared to the great gift you're giving your child. (K.C., interview)

One parent expresses how this gift is not just the specific L2 you're teaching, but the love of languages and culture in general:

> We realized that even if he did learn to speak, to some degree, the French we were teaching him, he would also learn the grammatical errors we might use, the non-native pronunciation, etc. We both agreed that whatever we could teach him would be better than nothing. We also felt confident that if he could understand the concept behind multiple languages as a young child, that he might be motivated and more prepared linguistically to study and learn several foreign languages later on. (J.N., interview)

Laugh it off

> *Humor is the spiciest condiment in the feast of existence. Laugh at your mistakes but learn from them.*
> L.M. Montgomery, *Anne of the Island* (1915)

I'll never forget that when I was first learning Portuguese, I confused *coco* (coconut) with *cocô* (poop). Coconut is really popular in Brazil, but I wasn't a fan. One day I went to the bakery and ordered sweet milk candy without *cocô* (without poop)! The baker laughed and said 'But of course!'

As a language learner, these slip-ups are an important part of taking risks, part of learning. One mother writes:

> One time I made a mistake with the masculine and the feminine. A macro is a simple programming term. I thought it was masculine, but lo and behold, it is feminine. When I said the wrong form in front of some native French speakers, they laughed and told me, *le macro* is slang for a dirty old man who likes very young girls. Oops! (F.J., interview)

If we parents can face our errors with an unabashed 'Oops!', we'll be better able to move on and keep taking risks. One American woman living in France said she spent many months afraid to say anything in French because she didn't want to make mistakes and feel like a child. Then finally, one day,

> I had a linguistic epiphany at the butcher's. I thought to myself, 'What do I care what the butcher thinks of me? I just want some meat.' (H.G., email interview)

Learning from language teachers

Part of parents' fear of making mistakes stems from their lofty idea of 'teacher'. They think they can't speak with their kids in an L2 because they're not language teachers. I advise these parents to ask themselves 'Do I sing with my kids? Do I bake cookies with them? Do I shoot basketball with them?' Then I continue 'But are you a professional singer, a world-class chef, or a Globetrotter?' That way, parents realize how often they help their kids in areas they don't excel in themselves.

Ironically, even language teachers have some of these same fears of not measuring up. Peter Floyd, a language teacher trainer, gave a rousing keynote speech at a well-known conference for French teachers. At one point, mid-sentence, he theatrically took off his blazer and held it at arm's length. He said, whether native or non-native, teachers need to 'take off the cloak of perfection'.

> Those who let go of a sense of having to be in control and instead agree to flounder a little, may even look goofy sometimes, but they'll end up not knowing everything, but knowing enough. (Floyd, 2011)

This freedom to not be an expert encourages us to try more, to dare more. Merrill writes,

> Sometimes the mere thought of wording an explanation of a mechanical process or scientific principle in French makes me pass the buck to their father. But must not words be carefully chosen … even in one's native language? And isn't it fun to discover with the children that 'hijackers' in French are 'pirates of the air'? (Merrill, 1984: 5)

Not enough culture

Another point of anxiety parents mentioned was that they didn't know enough about the L2 culture. They assumed they had to have insider knowledge when, in fact, it's fine to teach cultural norms and values as an observer. To some extent, it's more interesting to teach a culture that's not your own because you have your own rich experience to serve as comparison. And depending on how you explain what you know, you guide children to look at other values as different, but not weird or inferior.

Bilingual mom and author Virginie Raguenaud writes,

> As our children learn to integrate different cultural values, beliefs, and assumptions, they naturally develop a broad definition of identity. They learn not to define themselves by a little box on a census form, but rather by the many layers they deem relevant.... [They] learn not to box people in and not to impose limits on how others identify themselves. (Raguenaud, 2009: 47)

Not crazy about the culture

Though a minority, some parents did not want to teach their children about the L2 culture. This was particularly true for parents teaching American English.

> I love English, and speaking the language, but I don't identify at all with the American way of life. (C.E., interview)

> Most Europeans think American culture is an oxymoron, which might be an exaggeration, so I'm not sure I would want my kids to get too deeply involved in what is the current American culture, but I'm not sure Europe is much better, but I don't want them to be like the average American. (A.N., interview)

Other cultures were also frowned upon.

> There are a lot of French culture things that I disagree with because France is very anti-religion and we're religious ... and they are very accepting of sex at an early age. So boys and girls will have sleepovers where they have sex at age 15 and 16 and the parents know this and aren't opposed to it. And in France there are pictures of naked women in stores that sell stamps. (F.T., interview)

> I let my daughter watch a Brazilian channel we had for a while, and she wanted to dress like the women on the channel with short tight blouses and short tight shorts. Finally, we just discontinued the channel. (G.F., interview)

When faced with cultural differences, it's important not to throw out the baby with the bath water. In our own culture, if our children are behaving like people who don't exhibit our values, we discuss how our values are different and why that's the case. Children, especially older children and teenagers, are more receptive to our ideas if we explain our beliefs without criticizing others. When we raise children to make non-judgmental choices, they are more skillful socially in the wider world.

(4) Other people don't get it

Another parental fear about sharing their L2 is the judgment of others. They worry that when they mention their L2 plan to friends, neighbors or co-workers, they'll meet with negative comments or unsolicited advice.

> I'm in Conover in the middle of nowhere in North Carolina near Hickory. People barely speak English.... It's so much less international than Cary [North Carolina] and here [when I speak French], they look at me like I'm an alien. (J.F., interview)

> I get various responses from friends and family, from ... 'Wow! That's brilliant!' to ... 'Are you sure you know what you're doing?' (E.I., interview)

> There have ... been friends and relatives who interfered. They kept, and some still keep on warning me that I might harm the development of my children. Some even quoted pseudo-scientific sources in which it is proven how dangerous it was to raise children bilingually. But they could never show me such books or articles. (K.N., interview)

Even educators may not agree with your decision, as one mom attests:

> I asked several of my friends who are school teachers what would happen if I spoke to my child in Japanese, and they said that since I am a non-native speaker and my husband is monolingual in the majority language, he [my son] would probably just learn some numbers, colors and names of animals. That came as a big disappointment for me. (P.R., interview)

Some of this negativity may be well intentioned. For example, your father's concern may be that you'll be disappointed. A teacher may be basing her advice on ideas not supported by research. Take well-meaning advice with a grain of salt. It's just another opinion that is less informed than yours.

Relationships

Some onlookers to your language plan might not understand what you're doing. One English L1 parent said that misunderstandings sometimes led to negative comments. Let's look at some specific comments. Possibly the most hurtful were those that said that teaching an L2 could damage the relationship with the children. Parents were told they would not make the same emotional connection with their child if they didn't use their L1. These criticisms made parents doubt their motivation, as if they were using their children as guinea pigs. One father speaking Spanish in Ireland writes,

> I think sometimes people have thought it's a kind of a game – that somehow I'm playing out some kind of project, or intellectual exercise, with my daughter. I don't like that thought at all ... and I take the responsibility very seriously. (E.I., email interview)

The question is, how do we handle these negative attitudes? One parent shares how she reacted:

> I worked with a complainer who said that I should say 'I love you' to [my daughter] Becca in English, but I told her I say it from my heart, and that the language doesn't matter. (T.N., interview)

It's important to note that even native speakers of a language meet with similar negativity. A Latina mom residing in the US says of speaking Spanish to her child:

> I have been surprised by the unsolicited criticism. I'm tired of feeling the need to defend my decision to people who don't understand bilingualism and how it works. I even have a few family members who get angry with me.... (Flores & Soto, 2012: 89)

Just like with other parenting decisions, you'll meet people who think they know better than you. This book will help you feel confident enough in your language plans to stand up to others' negativity. Chapter 12, 'Meeting Challenges', gives more suggestions on how to deal with criticism from others, using logical and convincing arguments.

Showing off

Another factor that made people feel nervous about speaking the L2 around others was the stereotypical perception of the language itself. It was hard to speak foreign languages – like English or French – that are considered higher-status languages. Parents were afraid they would look snobby. (See p. 99, 'I feel silly'.)

One Korean father talks about his reticence to speak English in Korea: 'It may cause some people kind of jealousy or showing off' (J.H., interview). His sentiments were echoed by other parents:

> I didn't want to speak English to my son [while we were living in Brazil] because people looked at me like I was being snobby ... of being *chique* because of all the stereotypes of Americans and English and the whole first versus third world thing. (L.A., interview)

I have problems speaking English to him in public [in the Czech Republic], especially in a playgroup situation, as I feel a little 'show-offy' and weird. I find it harder to fit in and start blaming myself for creating such a situation for my son to grow up in. (J.A., interview)

My family would be very supportive [of speaking a second language], but my husband's family are not so education-minded and would probably think we were being snobs. (H.G., email interview)

In many situations, onlookers with these stereotypical attitudes may feel uncomfortable or inferior. Think of someone you are fairly competitive with. It could be a co-worker or another parent who has 'amazing' children. When you're faced with their success – 'Our little Johnny got into Harvard!' – you might feel a little jealous. That's how people may feel when they see you speaking another language to your kids. Their feelings of inferiority could bring out negative comments. If you meet their negativity with a light, self-deprecating remark, you can verbally bring yourself down a notch and show you're not 'all that'.

Here's a personal example. When I feel other people are uncomfortable with us speaking Portuguese, I say something in a humble and casual tone: 'I know! It seems crazy, right? And we don't know a lot of stuff. We make lots of mistakes, but so far, so good.' This humility tends to soften people and they'll see you less as an über-parent and more like a peer who also struggles to get things right.

And as for the high status of the language itself, that may eventually work in your favor. It's a good motivator for you and your family to stay the course. One father raising English-speaking children in Germany writes,

My children like it [the L2] and Philip, the oldest, is even a little bit proud of speaking English by now. This is maybe due to the fact that English is held in high esteem in Germany. (K.N., email interview)

Talk right, Mommy!

Parents sometimes meet with negativity from their children. I interviewed a professor in foreign language education. Even with her expertise in language learning, she wasn't sure what to do when her own child rebelled against speaking Spanish. When she chose a Spanish book to read to him, he would say 'Talk right, Mommy! Talk to me in plain!' (A.H., email interview).

This negativity toward the L2 is similar to children's aversion to healthy food or early bedtimes. When your child doesn't want to go to bed, you probably offer him choices so he feels more in charge. 'Johnny, you can sleep with your yellow pillow or with the blue one.' Similarly, offer him several L2 books and let him choose which he would like to read. Or let him choose whether to stay in bed to read or to sit on pillows beside the bed. In Chapter 12, 'Meeting Challenges', we'll look extensively at how to handle push-back from your children. For now, just recognize that resistance is normal for children of both native and non-native speakers.

Visualizing success

Athletes show us how to persist by vividly imagining themselves achieving their goals. We parents can do the same when faced with people who just don't get it. The following scenarios illustrate situations you might face and how to deal with negativity from yourself and from others. These suggestions encourage you to be assertive, without escalating the tension.

(1) A stranger

You're in line at the supermarket with your 10-month-old daughter. You exchange pleasantries with the woman behind you, whose son is about your daughter's age. Your daughter starts pointing at things in the candy rack and you speak to her in Italian: 'Oh, what do you see?' Supermarket Mom asks what language you're speaking and, during the ensuing conversation, finds out you're not a native speaker of Italian. She looks shocked and says, 'I speak some Spanish, but I could never do that with Luke. I can't imagine not saying "I love you" to him in English!'

Your response. Smile at Supermarket Mom and say with a pleasant voice 'Oh, well, actually, I say "I love you" all the time. It's in Italian and she understands. It *completely* translates.' Then change the subject by asking something about her son.

(2) Your in-laws

Your in-laws find out you're planning on speaking German with your four-year-old son Philip. Your mother-in-law says skeptically 'But I didn't know you were that fluent in German.' Your father-in-law asks 'You never lived in Germany, did you?'

Your response. Try not to take this personally. People frequently seem critical about things they don't understand. Try 'No, I never lived there. And I haven't learned a lot of German before now, but I'm learning a little more each day as I talk to Philip.' If they still look dubious or bring it up again, keep things positive. 'We've learned so much! You'll enjoy seeing how much better we get little by little.' (See p. 164, 'Grandparents and expectations'.)

(3) A co-worker

A co-worker went to Japan with you on an extended business trip. When he hears of your plans to start speaking Japanese with your six-year-old, he asks 'Don't you have to start right when they're born or they'll never really learn it? Plus, that trip to Japan was only a couple of weeks. Did you really learn all that much?'

Your response. Breathe deeply and say 'Actually, you can start later with children. The research that said you *must* start early was found to be overstated. And as for the trip to Japan, I'm adding on to the little Japanese I learned there, using lots of different resources for adult learners. We're working toward language exposure, not total fluency – not yet, anyway.' End the discussion on a positive note: 'I'm glad you're interested. I'll let you know how it goes.'

(4) Your child's teacher

During a parent–teacher conference, you mention your language plan. The teacher says 'I've read research that says you should only speak your first language to your child. It's better for the child. And I think using two languages might confuse her.'

Your response. Explain that you think you know the research she's referring to. 'It was probably for immigrants who've come to this country. For example, a woman from Spain who moves to the UK is encouraged to keep speaking Spanish to her children so they'll be bilingual.' Smile politely and close with 'It seems like a weird experiment, but it's actually well supported by recent studies. Children don't get confused, because their brains have ways of separating the languages. And learning another language actually helps with reading in the first language. I'm glad you're interested, and I can tell you about our progress at our next conference if you like.' (See Chapter 1, 'There is a Free Lunch!', for other helpful responses.)

(5) Your parents

They supported the idea of bilingualism when your child was a baby. But once he started speaking the language, they felt frustrated. Your mother says 'I don't speak French, so I don't understand when he talks to you.'

Your response. Show concern for your parents' feelings by rephrasing what they've said: 'I'm sorry it feels like you're missing out on some things.' Then thoughtfully add 'But this is the language we speak together. I can translate anything he says and will try hard to do that. It means a lot to me that you're supporting us in this.' (See p. 164, Grandparents and expectations'.)

If this continues to be an issue, you can direct your child to speak the L1 when your parents are around. Gentle nudges like 'Talk to Grandpa and Grandma' will help him naturally switch to the L1. If you feel it would be well received, do some research on the L2 classes near where your parents live. Talk with them about what's available.

If they decide to take classes, send letters and emails from you and your children in the L2. Include photos or drawings that will help them understand the letters. You can also make videos of the kids singing nursery rhymes in the L2 or acting in a little play. Videos are better than live performances, because they can be viewed repeatedly.

(6) Your child

Your daughter wants you to play trains with her. When she hands you Thomas the Train, you say in Spanish, '¡Oh! ¡Tomás el Tren!' She challenges you with the English version of the name. 'No, Thomas the Train!'

Your response. The Spanish name may sound strange to her. She most likely heard it on television in English. Try repeating Thomas's name in a silly accent that's fun to her. Then say '*Mamá dice "Tomás el Tren." [Mommy says "Thomas the Train."] ¿Se puede decir "Tomás el Tren?"* [Can you say "Thomas the Train"?].'

Lay Thomas aside and play with other toys. A few minutes later, ask '*¿Donde está Tomás el Tren?* [Where is Thomas the Train?]' Give her a chance to find the train. Then say in that same silly accent, '*¡Ah! ¡Tomás el Tren!*'

Whether you're feeling frustrated by your child's resistance or the negativity of other people, try humor and levity. Give a goofy look, use a silly voice or make a joke. Take yourself off any pedestal you might be on. If you dig your heels in, it becomes a battle of wills. If you lighten up, you're more effective.

Passion and Attention

The non-native speaker's biggest advantage is his passion for the language. For many of you who are speaking an L2, you chose that language – it didn't just get handed down to you from your parents. So you may have a strong affinity for it.

This passion works as fuel. It spurs you on to speak the language with your child and spend extra time with her in the process. Parents offered lots of examples of how sharing the L2 has strengthened the parent–child bond. (See p. 7, 'The language connection'.) One mom states 'It deepened the relationship because it activated my passion' (S.B., interview).

Saunders writes of his own experience,

[it] has enhanced the relationship. Because I, representing virtually the children's only contact with German, feel directly responsible for ensuring the children's continued and unstressed progress in German, it has meant that I have perhaps given them more attention than would have been the case if I had spoken English to them. (Saunders, 1988: 22)

Saunders describes his reticence in speaking German to the children because his career entailed frequent travel. He found, though, that the extra attention he gave his children in sharing the language made up for the time away. When he traveled with work, his wife could tell when the kids were missing him, because they would start speaking German among themselves. He explains 'The lack of German in the home is a tangible sign of my absence, and the desire to see me again and to speak "our" language is given indirect expression through this increased use of German' (Saunders, 1988: 22).

Children may need some extra language input if they've had some time without it, even short periods. For example, my children have trouble expressing themselves in Portuguese after they've been in school all day. When I pick them up, I give them extra language input. 'I know you had that math test and you also were going to play either volleyball or basketball in PE, right?' This little blurb in their L2 helps click their minds over before they're asked to produce anything themselves. It also gives them some of the vocabulary they might need. That way, once I ask them how their day went, they're armed and ready.

Relationship

The extra input you give your children doesn't have to be dull, factual-type language. Just tell stories! Tell them funny things from your past, talk about what you did at work or explain something you found interesting that day. Hearing your stories will make your kids want to share what's happening with them.

Asking open-ended, specific questions encourages more sharing. Ask questions about their friends, their favorite movies or toys, or something weird they saw or heard that day. This is especially easy to do in the car, where your kids are a captive audience. Merrill notes how sharing these moments in an L2 makes them richer. 'As only those who are interested in informal home bilingualism will understand ... I feel how flat and routine relating to my children would be without the added language and culture' (Merrill, 1984: 6).

As you become mindful of talking and listening more to your children, you'll see how much easier it gets to speak the L2. (See p. 7, 'The bond of extra time'.) You'll also love how your relationship deepens.

Myth Busters About Native Speakers

- Native speakers are not perfect speakers of the language.
- Native-speaking teachers are not necessarily better than non-native-speaking teachers.
- Native speakers aren't always the majority of speakers.
- Native speakers can be used as helpful tools without being the absolute goal.

3 Start Small, Start Now: Choosing a Language and Moving Forward

Ah … the magic of making a start.
Steven Pressfield, *The War of Art* (2012: 376)

Often the hardest parts of moving toward our goals is taking that first step. It's especially true if our goals are a little fuzzy or seem too difficult to achieve. This chapter will get you started. It'll also let you know why certain ways of starting will make the road ahead easier.

What's in Your Way?

Bilingualism may sound good in theory, but when you think of what it entails, it may not seem doable. Let's examine some doubts you may have about getting started.

I'm too busy

You may see bilingualism as one more 'project' to try with your children. Parenting magazines promise 'Only a few minutes a day with the periodic table and your future surgeon can skip high school and head straight to med school.' Your parenting group is reading *Infant Literacy Through Cribside Shakespeare*. And you want to start your kids early in music lessons, dance, soccer, etc. How on earth will you squeeze in any more?

Jane Merrill answers this question in her book *Bringing Up Baby Bilingual*: 'The wonderful aspect of bilingual child-rearing, disciplined though it be, is that it meshes with, yet does not add burdens to, an already busy life' (Merrill, 1984: 9). Bilingualism isn't another extracurricular activity. It's an everyday habit that fits into your lifestyle.

My language skills need work

Some parents don't get started because they are waiting for their language skills to improve before speaking the language to their child. But any language skills are a good place to start. You may lack appropriate vocabulary, since you learned very little in your high-school Spanish class. But bilingualism is like math – you don't have to know calculus to count to 10. You just need to use the little bits and pieces of language that you know and pick up more as you go.

I don't have all the details worked out

You don't need to have all the details for the future worked out to get started. If you're pregnant or have just had a baby, you're too busy with doctor visits and diapers to plan very far in the future. Know that you have time later to work through all that.

Similarly, if you have older children and you're worried about the logistics of school and friends, know that it's fine to put off making longer-range bilingual plans and just see how things work out in the present.

Choosing the Language

The Holy Roman Emperor Charles V, king of Spain, archduke of Austria, and master of several European tongues, professed to speaking 'Spanish to God, Italian to women, French to men, and German to my horse.'
Guy Deutsoher, *Through the Language Glass* (2001: 1)

Many parents have difficulty deciding which language to learn and teach their child. Part of the difficulty can be that they are looking at languages as if they are mutual funds. Each one has its merits in cold and calculated market shares.

Which is the best language to learn?

The question becomes 'Is this the best way to choose a language?' King and Mackey, in their book *The Bilingual Edge*, write that deciding on a language requires 'a bit of emotional digging', and taking the time to do that digging at the outset is worth it in the long run (King & Mackey, 2007: 41). I advise parents to imagine themselves speaking a language to their children. What language do they envision? How motivated can they see themselves being to learn and speak that language?

If you choose a language with too many 'shoulds' in mind, you might end up trying to learn something that really doesn't interest you. Carolyn Gibson, in her book *Catching Tongues: How to Teach Your Child a Foreign Language, Even If You Don't Speak One Yourself*, writes 'My theory is that the only way to guarantee any long-term success of your efforts is if you have an interest in it yourself (self-interest rules, I always say)' (Gibson, 2011: 117).

If you love Mandarin because of the culture and because you hope to travel to China one day, great. Go with Mandarin. But if you're just choosing it because it's purported to be an important language for business, you might not have the motivation to continue over the long term. (That is unless the monetary gains are motivation enough – you might become rich!)

Are some languages too hard to learn?

Parents ask if it makes sense to choose an easier language. They recognize that, for English speakers, the vocabulary in a romance language like Spanish is easier to recognize than in languages like Arabic. My advice is to choose the language you are most interest in, even if it's the more difficult language. As far as your child is concerned, know that even if you choose a 'hard language', babies' brains are equipped to learn it. Diane Ackerman, naturalist and author of *An Alchemy of Mind*, writes,

> Babies are born citizens of the world, as linguists like to say. It doesn't matter if they're born into a world of high-rises or tundra, jackhammers or machine guns, Quechua or French. The ultimate immigrants, babies arrive ready to learn [language] with a brain flexible enough to adapt to almost anything. (Ackerman, 2005: 201)

I already know some German, so...

Some parents intend to choose a language they have studied in the past. If they had Spanish in high school or French in college, they might continue with that. One mother asks for advice on this topic:

> Simon [her husband] already speaks French and I sort of remember it from school, so we thought of French, but Spanish, we have been told, is the second world language after English, so that is sort of on our list as well. (A.A., interview)

My next question for this mother would be 'So do you think you would like learning French better or Spanish?' This is important because, again, you will be more apt to continue learning and teaching a language you enjoy.

A family language

Some parents want to teach their children a language like Serbian or Farsi because someone in their family speaks it as a native language. Or they may themselves be native speakers of a foreign language – Thai parents living in Great Britain, for example, may want to speak Thai to their children.

If this language is not a major language, parents may question its value. They worry it may not be offered in middle or high school. I remind these parents that the added benefit of visiting with family and speaking the L2 will make language learning so much more relevant. And, I advise them to speak the language that makes sense for their family, not the one that is most popular.

As far as school is concerned, they can do a third language later, resting assured that the research shows their children will have an easier time with the third language, since they have a second one under their belt.

Defy logic

Your choice of language doesn't have to be logical. If it fits who you want to be, if you think it's interesting, or if you want to learn it because the sounds are funny, go for it!

Barry Farber's book *How to Learn Any Language* encourages this type of choosing. He writes,

> Don't feel frivolous if you feel you want to learn a language but don't know which one. You're part of a movement to correct a weakness that has bedeviled America since the founding of our nation. Do you like opera? Try Italian. Diamonds? Try Dutch. Commercial advantage? German or Japanese. Cutting-edge positioning for the world down the road? Chinese or Arabic…. (Farber, 2000: 49)

Realistic Goals

You may be a goal-oriented person who likes to work out your goals before starting to use the language. In this case, it's important to keep your objectives realistic.

'Bilingual', for example, doesn't necessarily mean that there is equal use of both languages. Even in bilingual regions – Quebec, for instance – people are often more fluent in one language than the other. For example, one person might be better in English for academic purposes but socially better in French.

Take the burden off yourself and realize your goal doesn't have to be complete fluency. Instead, it can be a competency in certain areas. You might want your child to be able to hold simple conversations and you would be okay with some errors. That is a doable goal to work toward.

Another example of a workable goal comes from a mother I interviewed. She is from China and wants to teach English to her daughter.

> As to my expectations, I do not think she will be able to speak English as a native speaker just under my instruction. But it is possible to make English as a tool for story reading, writing and for future communication. (M.N., interview)

Fluid goals

Your goals may be fluid. You may, for example, initially decide you're going to exclusively speak L2 to your child. Later, however, you might decide to speak the L2 only on the weekends, when the pressures of your job are less. Only you know what works in your household. The important thing is to make some sort of loose plan to know your decision is real and well grounded.

Start Early – If Possible

We've all heard that early bilingual exposure is preferred to later learning. Early exposure may not be an option for your family, however. In this case, jump to the section 'Not too late' (p. 39).

In utero

When researchers in childhood bilingualism say to start early, they mean to start really early. Drs Hart and Risley, authors of *Meaningful Differences in the Everyday Experience of Young American Children,* note that most parents begin really talking to their children only when they hit the two-year mark, when, in fact, it is imperative to talk to your children before they reach that age, while the neural connections are especially receptive to learning vocabulary (Hart & Risley, 1995).

Babies recognize their native language and their mother's voice from exposure to her speech while in utero. *Science Magazine* describes several recent studies on fetal learning. These indicate that newborns, particularly those in the third trimester, familiarize themselves with sounds of the languages their parents use. The article's author, Beth Skwarecki, writes:

> Be careful what you say around a pregnant woman. As a fetus grows inside a mother's belly, it can hear sounds from the outside world – and can understand them well enough to retain memories of them after birth. (Skwarecki, 2013)

If you are expecting a baby and already speak some of the L2, talk aloud to yourself. It will familiarize the baby's ears to the sounds and rhythms of the language. If you feel weird talking to yourself, find someone who speaks the L2 and spend time together. If that's not possible, read aloud from a book or magazine in the language, or from a website.

Babies' brain data

Never underestimate your baby's intricate brain. It is exploding with activity due to the extra metabolic activity and blood flow. Barbara Zurer Pearson, author of *Raising a Bilingual Child*, writes,

> Their brains are working twice as hard as adults … to make new connections between neurons. It is through these connections that they learn the sounds and words, and then compute the grammar of what we are saying. (Pearson, 2001: 102)

Research into the acquisition of the first language is constantly indicating that parents should talk to their babies about what's happening during the day, to build the neural circuitry of the infant's brain and speed along babbling and speech (Dougherty,

2001). A play-by-play of a typical Tuesday, say – 'After your nap, we'll have lunch, then go the library' – can instruct parents in the non-native language as well, since they may regularly need to turn to the dictionary.

Childhood and beyond

Jeffrey Kluger, in *Time Magazine*, described the ages from birth to six as the easiest time to pick up a language, because of the extra synapses children have at that stage (Kluger, 2013). That's why adult language learners have more of an accent. Lise Eliot, in *What's Going on in There? How the Brain and Mind Develop in the First Five Years of Life*, writes of the 'certain telltale signs' later learning leaves:

> No matter how hard they try, most adults who learn a foreign language inevitably have certain problems in pronunciation (giving them a distinctive accent) as well as in grammatical usage – like using the wrong pronoun or leaving out an article – that clearly mark them as non-native speakers. (Eliot, 1999: 263)

This idea that the first few years of life (the 'critical period') are crucial for learning a first language began when researchers claimed there was a 'biological timetable' to language development (Brown, 1994: 52). The timetable was later expanded to cover second languages as well, with some well-known researchers claiming that children best learn a language before the age of five (Krashen, 1973).

Not too late

If you, dear reader, are crying out 'Oh, but Little Johnny is already seven! I've missed those crucial infant years!', do not despair. There is what some researchers call a 'second window of opportunity', when children are aged four to seven. Its supporters argue that language acquisition will be 'relatively fast, successful, and … similar to first language [acquisition] … if it occurs before the age of puberty' (Snow & Hoefnagel-Höhle, 1978: 1114). At this stage of development, children are okay with making errors and not knowing exactly how to say things. If they get stuck, they make it up! This attitude makes it easy for them to try new words and experiment with a new language identity.

One researcher, Fred Genesee, in his study with Canadian students, found that older children – specifically seventh- and eighth-graders – were actually more successful than younger children (Genesee in Murphy, 2011: xvii). He offers several reasons why: they have more highly developed verbal skills in their L1, they have more fully developed literacy skills, and they are moving toward more abstract thinking skills. (See p. 45, 'Is it too late?')

And for those who have children outside that range, another window opens from age 7 to 16, according to Jeffrey Kluger's article 'The power of the bilingual brain' (Kluger, 2013). After 16, it becomes more of a challenge, but with other factors – such as attitude and motivation – the age divide can be bridged.

General language developmental stages

Some parents worry that their child will be slowed down developmentally if they are learning a second language. It's helpful to have some framework of what children do developmentally at different ages so you don't constantly wonder if your child is keeping up.

Annick De Houwer, in her book *An Introduction to Bilingual Development*, writes 'Children who hear two languages from birth do not say much in the first year of life' (De Houwer, 2009: 4). Around a year and a half, they begin using single words. In their 'terrible twos' they display another leap, using short expressions by stringing two words together (Dat's mine!). When they hit three years, they can speak in longer utterances and use more verbs. De Houwer writes that they use 'short sentences that have many of the little bits that adults would use' (2009: 5).

Age four brings short sentences, and they might start naming things in books you read to them. They typically begin talking through things as they do them: 'Going in the car' or 'I'm taking a bath!' At around age five, they usually have some foundation for language and can communicate fairly well, with better grammar than before. The big caveat here is 'usually' and 'about', because there's variability in these yearly estimations.

If your child is a little slow developing in both languages, fear not. A delay about the length of time that a boy is behind a girl may appear for children of two languages. It will even out soon.

Start Small

If you start speaking the L2 while your baby is very young, she obviously won't be responding at first. That can feel a little weird, but if you plow through the oddness and speak to her anyway, she will reap the benefits of early exposure. (See p. 16, 'This feels unnatural'.)

I used to do what I called 'breastfeeding monologues'. In my journal notes, I write,

> I've been having daily monologues with Sydney since her birth (in Portuguese of course). I tell her what day it is, how old she is, what we're planning to do, etc. Often times I have to look words up in the tiny Portuguese dictionary by my bed (had to look up 'seal' when I told her how we were headed for the Aquarium). (journal, 5/2/2002)

Part of the reason these monologues felt odd is that I was used to speaking to adults in Portuguese, not babies or children. I eventually started feeling comfortable using that sing-songy voice we all use with children (see p. 19, 'I don't know baby talk'.)

Infant-directed speech

There is a lot of science behind the practice of babbling to babies. Some researchers call it 'motherese', though a more technical term is 'infant-directed speech'. It's different from talking to adults, or even young children, because of the higher tone and the more up and down nature of the pitch. The enunciation is more precise and pauses are longer between words and sentences. And there's a lot of repetition. Communications expert Dr Kathy Reschke writes,

> Although infant-directed speech isn't used in every culture, it is present in many, many languages around the world.... Scientists have discovered that babies pick up an amazing amount of knowledge about language and communication just from hearing 'baby talk'. (Reschke, 2002)

Start small with infant expectations

It can feel strange to talk to an infant or child who does not yet respond in the language. The authors of *Bilingual Is Better* quote one parent as saying, 'Talking to my babies in my second language feels like talking to the house plants' (Flores & Soto, 2012: 88).

For infants, consider the ways they are responding – eye contact, little grunts, different facial expressions that indicate they are engaged. And then, around three or four months, they start making more verbal sounds. They grab your attention by gurgling or offering little baby shouts. So when you speak, leave room for their responses. Imagine this encounter:

> You: Time for a bath now.
> Baby: [Squeals.]
> You: You like the warm water!
> Baby: [Starts to cry.]
> You: Oh, you don't like the water? Oh, I'm sorry. You will feel so clean after this.

Through these simple interactions, babies are learning turn-taking skills. They are also picking up components of vocabulary. Virginie Raguenaud, in her book *Bilingual By Choice*, writes 'The number of words a child hears throughout the day is directly linked to the child's intelligence and vocabulary size' (Raguenaud, 2009: 30).

Embroidering their speech

As your children age and start to give one-word answers, you can do what Jane Merrill's book *Bringing Up Baby Bilingual* recommends: you can 'consciously embroider' children's speech (Merrill, 1984: 79). So when your baby makes a sound that resembles the L2 word for 'no', you want to add on to that utterance. For example, you could say 'Oh, no? No, you don't want more apple sauce? No apple sauce?' Once you ask a question, pause for the response. Continue the conversation, if possible. 'But it's so good!'

You can continue this embroidery even as your children get older and begin speaking in fuller sentences. When your three-year-old says 'I want ice cream!' You can say 'I'd like some, too – a really big scoop! What kind of scoop do you want?' Children are taking all this in and storing words for when they need them later.

Expectations for older children

Starting an L2 with older children is trickier, but doable. The key is to be very visual, especially in the beginning.

Visual springboards for language

Before you expect children to use the L2, you've got to give them lots of input in the language. One easy first step is to read children's books. The bright pictures and the soothing words from your mouth are a rich input of words, tones and expressions which your children can build on each day. Early on, the books don't have to be written in the L2. You can look at the pictures and tell your own story, or just say the names of the things on the page. If you don't know the word for something, look it up and pencil it in beside the picture. And just as you do with children in their L1, ask questions as you go. If you have just read the word for rabbit, ask a question about the rabbit so your child has to point to it.

Books with verse are particularly useful because the rhythm and rhyme help children remember the vocabulary. Poems and nursery rhymes give clues to pronunciation. (See p. 101, 'Rhythm and rhyme'.)

Start with pointing

There will be times when you speak to your child in the L2 and he does not understand. You may need to give him visual clues as to what you mean. You may also start by saying the bulk of the sentence in your L1 and just one or two words in the L2. For example, 'Do you want some of this *manzana* [apple]? It's delicious!' When he responds yes or no, ask him to repeat the word, *manzana*. Be sure to ask your questions in an animated tone and offer enthusiastic praise when he repeats the word.

Body talk

I speak two languages, body and English.
Mae West (Language Lens, 2012)

It's easy to forget that body language is a way to talk. It is imperative to give children the tool of body language as another way to express themselves – especially when they don't know certain words in the L2. Movements reinforce memory. Think of times you learned songs with motions. If you've spent any time in preschool or elementary classrooms, you've seen how quickly children pick up song lyrics when they are accompanied by motions. (See p. 119, 'Motions to music'.)

There are skills to acting out things that we assume are inherently known, but these are actually learned. Children find through experience that a raised finger can mean 'No!' and that a smile can mean 'Yes', Overtly teach your kids a variety of signs and symbols to later connect them to L2 words. For example, show them how to point to things when they can't think of the word. Use gestures when you talk and help them use simple hand motions when they speak.

Ask questions, even in their L1, such as, 'How many ways can we show we mean "no"?' They will probably come up with a shaking head. Show them another option by doing a *tsk tsk* motion with your index finger. Encourage them to use facial motions by showing them how pursed lips or a furrowed brow also might mean 'no'.

This early work in body language may feel like a roundabout way to acquire a language, but it's crucial. When children can't remember a word, they can use their body language skills and be understood.

Children who use body language in the absence of a word should be mightily praised. For example, 'I love how you used your body all shivering to show me the word "cold!"' And parents should react to body language accordingly: 'Let's put on some PJs to warm you up!'

Just start now!

More important than how you get started is that you get started. Discuss which language makes sense for your family and make some general goals for language learning. Then set a date to start, or, better yet, just start now!

How to Start Small

- Talk to your infant even if it feels silly.
- Embroider the speech of young children.
- Use visual cues like pictures in children's books.
- Introduce the sounds of the language through poems and rhyming songs.
- Point while you talk and encourage your child to point too.
- Use body language like gesturing or making motions to songs.

4 Be Your Favorite Teacher: Learn What You Want, When You Want It

Why Teach Yourself?

In this chapter, you'll discover tricks of the trade that help you pick up a language. And you'll see that you're not alone in the endeavor.

But I'm not a teacher

If you're not a professional teacher, you may feel overwhelmed by the task of teaching yourself another language. But imagine your favorite teacher in high school or college. What about him or her did you like? Perhaps you were drawn to characteristics like her patience, creativity, kindness or sense of humor. Now ask yourself 'Do I have any of these qualities?' Most likely, you have at least one of the characteristics that you feel make a good teacher.

Emphasize this personality trait in your mind. Imagine that part of you being the teacher.

But I'm not a language person

The traditional model we all grew up with is obsolete.
Jim Stengel, global marketing officer, P&G (2013)

You may worry about teaching yourself another language if you weren't good at learning languages when you were in school. My friend, Traci, told me that after finishing her last high-school French class, she had an aversion to foreign languages. She grew up in a small town in North Carolina and was terrified of her French teacher – a native speaker of French. On her last day of class, Monsieur Bernard told her, 'Trazzeee, I will geeve you a C eef you promeez nev'r to speak Français again.'

If you fear you were this kind of learner, it's important to recognize that the beliefs about your abilities may be outdated. You now have new outlets for learning an L2 – ones that you get to choose. You can have a completely different learning experience when you have less class time and more real-life learning.

Is it too late?

Toss out the limiting adage 'You can't teach an old dog new tricks'. You're not a dog, for one thing. And research abounds that, yes, adults can learn languages. In fact, the adult mind has some advantages. Tracey Tokuhama-Espinosa, in her book *Raising Multilingual Children*, writes:

> While children have the edge over adults in one way when it comes to learning language, adults have advantages in other mental realms. As shown by numerous studies, humans never lose the capacity to learn a foreign language. Adolescent and adult learners are actually better than small children in grasping abstract concepts of syntax and grammar. (Tokuhama-Espinosa, 2001: 20)

People hear about the 'critical period' and think that, as adults, they have missed the window of opportunity. (See p. 39, 'Not too late'.) But this period isn't definitive. Human development specialist Dr Diane Bales writes that 'a language and its sounds … may require more time to learn, but the adult mind is capable of learning another language and its pronunciation' (Bales, 1998). Likewise, John Bruer notes 'One of the dangers of the emphasis on [the] critical period is that it prompts us to pay too much attention to when learning occurs and too little attention to how learning might best occur' (Bruer, 2002: 142).

So, let's get started.

First Steps

Getting yourself motivated

As you start improving your language skills, ask yourself 'What will make me want to learn more?' Do you learn better with people, or alone? Is it important for you to be organized with books and papers, or do you like a looser type of learning? Keep these traits in mind as you make your goals.

To put yourself in a good position to receive language input, tell people you're learning the language. It'll give you a level of gentle accountability, since people will ask how the learning is going. It'll also open up avenues for meeting native speakers or other people who are learning the language. You never know when a friend or co-worker will connect you with an L2 speaker.

Lower anxiety

Anytime you're undertaking something new – whether it be learning a new language or starting a new job – it's perfectly normal to have reservations about your decision. A touch of anxiety can be helpful. Use it to push yourself to do well. Research shows that one of the main fears language students have is that they will misrepresent themselves.

Let this fear fuel you to learn more so that you will offer an accurate portrayal of yourself.

If your anxiety is too great, however, it gets in the way of word recall and fluency. That's because the feelings of nervous frustration trigger a release of fight-or-flight chemicals that interfere with the memory and learning part of your brain.

The first step to avoiding these feelings is to identify them. What physical sensations are in your body when you feel anxious? Do you feel fluttery in your stomach? Do you feel somehow 'knotted up'? These emotions can come from what is called 'negative self-talk'. The Mayo Clinic defines self-talk as 'the endless stream of unspoken thoughts that run through your head'. Much of your self-talk, according to Mayo representatives, 'comes from logic and reason. Other self-talk may arise from misconceptions that you create because of lack of information' (Mayo Clinic, 2014). Recognize those feelings for what they are and try what you normally do to calm yourself down. For example, take five deep breaths.

When you're trying to recall a word, try to maintain the L2 in your brain instead of berating yourself in your L1. To keep the thoughts positive, have a quick little mantra in the L2 to recite to yourself. Mine is simple: *Está tudo bem* ('All is well').

Warming Up

Let's examine how we get our brains ready to acquire a language.

Just listen

Our brain is more prepared to learn if it has a chance to warm up. An amazing study out of the University of New Zealand found that just listening to the sounds of another language gives you a huge boost when it comes to learning new vocabulary. It's true even if you don't understand what you're hearing. The hypothesis is that 'Neural tissue required to learn and understand a new language will develop automatically from simple exposure to the language – which is how babies learn their first language' (Sulzberger in PhysOrg, 2009). This means that just listening to Spanish radio or to streaming French television prepares your brain to learn, even if you aren't consciously catching what's being said.

Reactivation of a long lost language

If you've decided to speak a language at home that many years ago you took in high school or college, you are not starting at zero. You still have a skeleton of the language lying dormant in your brain. This knowledge can be reactivated.

Start with some passive contact with the language, such as watching movies in the L2 with subtitles in your L1. Television rentals have subtitles in languages you'd never imagine. Sitcoms are especially helpful. The sentences are shorter, so it's easier to follow the subtitles. Sitcoms are also great in that they give you exposure to how people really talk day to day. The subtitles for the show *Modern Family*, for example, describe the goings on of three households, which is useful for learning vocabulary around the house.

It's important to do this activation a little each day. You can listen to music in the language for a few days. Then, for the next two or three days, do some reading of websites or magazine articles with very familiar content (something like world news, of which you already know the gist). Try this for two weeks, and you'll feel a difference in how much you're remembering of the language.

Learning the Words

I am a firm believer in learning language as needed. That means not memorizing vocabulary lists. Instead, do what children do as they acquire language – learn the words as you need them in the real world.

The little notebook

Learning vocabulary as you need it can be tricky, since you don't always have time to look words up in the moment. Or you might not have the resources you need right then. For example, you may be in mid-conversation when you get stuck on a word, and there's no time or no dictionary to look it up. The solution? The Little Notebook.

Get a pack of little spiral notebooks at a discount store or office supply place. Distribute them in your purse/laptop bag, car, bedroom, near your favorite armchair and in the kitchen. That way, when a word comes up that's unfamiliar, jot it down and look it up later.

When you do have time to focus on learning, practice rewriting a word you're trying to remember. Write it with different types of handwriting (cursive, print and bubble letters). Or try writing different forms of the same word. For example, if it's a noun, write it in the plural. If it's a verb, try conjugating it with different nouns. Make up a simple sentence with the word. And, of course, something silly is preferable to help it stick. This practice will be more effective than just copying it over and over, because you're doing more actual manipulation of the word.

Attach words to habits

The hard part about learning new words isn't looking them up, it's remembering them. One way to remember new words and their meanings is to pair some practice time with already established habits, like brushing your teeth. Write the words on sticky notes and place them on your mirror, say, or on the window where you wash dishes. You can then give them a quick glance while you dry your hair, or while waiting for water to boil.

Calendar testing

Put your calendar to use. If you have a calendar agenda book (or an electronic calendar), when you learn a new word, write it alongside its L2 translation on the day you learn it. Then skip ahead a few days in your agenda and write just the word. Beside it, write today's date. For example, if on March 1st you needed the word for 'niece' in Spanish, you'd write in that day's agenda, 'niece = *sobrina*'. Then on the agenda page for a later date, say March 5th, you'd write 'niece = — (March 1st)'. On March 5th, when you come across the word in your agenda, try to remember the L2 translation. Write it down. Then check the date beside the definition to see if you're right. If you're wrong, write the word again on a later calendar date to try again. You might keep up with the dates of the definition in the back of your calendar to check your progress over time.

Paper and online flashcards

You may be the kind of person who responds well to learning with flashcards. Your preference may be paper flashcards. Write the L2 word on one side, with an L1 translation on the other. Or, to use the L2 exclusively, write the L2 word on one side with an L2 definition on the other side.

To streamline this activity with technology, try an online flashcard site. General sites for memory, such as Ankisrs.net, make it easy to generate flashcards and quiz yourself on the computer or your mobile phone. These sites let you rate each new word with a difficulty level that later determines the number of times you'll be quizzed. Sites like Quizlet.com are specifically designed for language learning and offer help with symbols and accent marks.

The funny and the strange

Humans tend to remember funny stuff. Think of all the dollars spent on humorous commercials. Advertisers know viewers remember their products better when they laugh.

Recent research shows the universal the link between what's funny and what's remembered. Middle Tennessee State University showed, for example, that undergraduates' memory in recalling information from silly sentences was much better than for regular sentences. Much higher memory recall was noted for such sentences like 'There are three ways a man can wear his hair: parted, un-parted, and departed' (Jokes All Day, 2014). Sentences having the same information, but without the humor, were less apt to be recalled.

The brain also tends to remember strange things. Any self-help book on memory tells you to associate something weird with a new name you're trying to remember. For instance, if you meet a woman named Carol Reines, imagine her singing a Christmas *carol* in the *rain*.

To make use of these tools, when you hear a new word in your L2, breathe deeply and try to see it in a different way. Does it have a funny pronunciation? Can you imagine someone saying it in a silly situation? Does it mean something odd in your L1? The more you use your brain to label a word funny or strange, the more you'll reap the benefits of memory.

Hanging memories

Hang memories on things you already know. Memory studies give us another way to remember someone's name – thinking of someone you already know with that name, whether a personal acquaintance or a famous person. Then form an image of the new person standing with the familiar person. I cement this image even more by imagining the two interacting in some way. So the new guy I just met, Charles, would be getting an autograph from Prince Charles.

Employ this technique to learn vocabulary. If you learn that the word *parfait* in French means perfect, imagine the dessert we call 'parfait' in English. See yourself taking a bite and exclaiming 'Perfect!' The new connection in your brain is formed.

Cognate languages

You've heard that kids have an easier time learning a language than adults. What you might not have considered, though, is that adults have something kids don't. They have a large vocabulary in the L1 to draw from. There are overlaps in many languages.

If you are learning a cognate language – meaning a language with similarities to your own – you already have thousands of words in your L2 vocabulary. Any of the Latin-based 'romance' languages – Spanish, French, Italian, Portuguese or Romanian – have words similar to each other and to English. Other languages have cognates as well – Asian languages, for example, and languages like Hebrew with Arabic.

In the case of native English speakers, they do well to recognize that romance languages like French were, centuries ago, spoken by the wealthy, more learned people. Laura Lawless, author of 'How French has influenced English', writes 'French took over as the language of the court, administration, and culture – and stayed there for many years. Meanwhile, English was "demoted" to everyday, non-prestigious uses' (Lawless, 2012).

This typically makes French cognates and other romance language cognates fancier than English. Let's imagine you want to say the word for 'right' in French, as in 'my answer was right'. If you can't think of the word for 'right', think of a fancier way to say it. The word you could use in French would be *correcte*.

Oh No! Grammar!

Just knowing vocabulary isn't enough to express your ideas. You have to know how to put the words together. Grammar is the infrastructure that holds words in place, telling them what their function is. One easy site to navigate, Grammar Notes, helps with parts of speech (Shoebottom, 2014). These include nouns, verbs, adjectives, adverbs and others. If you learn the word 'slowly', you'll need to know it's an adverb. That way you'll make it describe the verb: 'He moved slowly'. Otherwise, you're liable to say 'He is slowly' and sound kind of silly.

When to use little words like 'in', 'out', 'to', 'by' is important. Get them wrong, and you can convey a very different meaning. I remember an international English student of mine who wrote me a card at the end of the year: 'Christine, thank you for everything you have done *to* me.'

Learn grammar as you need it

There is no need to learn more grammar than you're going to actually use. When you conjugate verbs (meaning you put them together with nouns), don't bother learning all the subjects: I go, he goes, we go, they go. Instead, just learn to use the 'I' and the 'you' forms, since you'll mainly be talking about yourself or asking questions of the person you're talking to. Some people prefer buying a book listing the verb conjugations in the L2. Search '201 <L2> verbs' for books that devote a page to each verb, giving the meaning and all the many ways the verb is conjugated.

I would suggest, though, that if you're just starting with the language, you get your verbs from a beginning textbook in the language. It will most likely show you the basics of verb conjugation and will also list common verbs (see p. 59, 'Language learning books', and p. 65, 'Textbooks with tutors').

Go through the grammar sections looking for things you can imagine yourself saying. The grammar of commands like 'close the door' or 'sit down' will come in handy while talking to your child. Find the verbs that mean 'to be' so you can say things like 'You are sweet' and 'I am ready'.

Grammar explanations

For specific explanations on grammar you find difficult, search online for things like 'Teach word order <L2>' or 'Teach plural <L2>'.

Or to check the specific grammar of something brief you want to say or write – an expression of just four or five words, for example – type it into Google in quotation marks. If it's a correct expression, someone will have already said it and you'll get several hits. You can see how it's used in context and decide if you're on the right track.

Talk About Yourself, Ask About Others

The first thing to learn in another language is how to describe yourself and explain why you do what you do. That means you need to focus on verbs that conjugate with 'I', such as 'I am, I do, I like'. You also need specific vocabulary that describes who you are, what you do for a living, where you're from and why you're interested in the L2.

First conversations: Memorize your script

Imagine you've met a native speaker of the L2 you're learning. You'll want to have some descriptions of yourself ready. Have them in your head, like a script, so that you can be understood as the interesting person you are. Make sure you know how to say that you're learning the language to help your child learn it. I can almost guarantee that people will want to know more.

Have a general question in mind that you can ask to keep the conversation going. For example, 'Where are you from originally?' Pay attention to the native speaker's ways of showing interest and use them as you converse. In English, for example, as other people are talking to us, we say 'Oh, really?', 'That's interesting' and 'Wow!'

Listen to parents' L1

For parents who are unsure which bits of language to learn first, I suggest listening to other parents speaking their L1 to their children. Can you express the ideas they're expressing? Is the mother telling her child how to get out of a swing? What grammar or vocabulary would you need to say that in the L2? As you listen, make a mental note or use your notebook to remind you what to look up later.

The din in the head

Once you've looked up certain vocabulary, you can practice using the words and expressions without even opening your mouth. We know from brain plasticity research that people can learn to do tasks, such as playing an instrument, by rehearsing in their minds. Dr Elisha Goldstein studied people learning to play the violin and found 'similar shifting in the motor cortex of the brain whether they were actually playing the violin or just imagining playing the violin' (Goldstein, 2012).

Stephen Krashen (2008), language acquisition guru, named this phenomenon the 'din in the head'. It's rehearsing the language by forming dialogues in your mind to practice 'speaking', even without someone to talk to. The rehearsal is particularly important to do right after you've learned a new word or expression. Your brain is trying to fit what Krashen calls a 'new language chuck' into what we already know – to make sense of it and to remember it.

When you first learn a new word, imagine saying it to someone in a short conversation. See yourself being understood and invent a response from the other person. This can take just one or two minutes – just enough to work with the new utterance to fit it in with your past knowledge.

Or, if you're on a long drive or waiting in a lengthy line, invent longer conversations in your mind. What would you say if someone complimented your clothes? How would you ask for help with directions, and what would you say if you had trouble understanding? If you were talking to someone about what's going on right now, what would you say? And how would the other person respond? Jot down any words or expressions you're missing, to look up later.

Write it in the L2

Think of things you could write in the L2 instead of your L1. Could you write your grocery list in the L2? (See p. 137, 'Grocery lists' and 'Recipes', and p. 145, 'Grocery list'.) What about writing events in your calendar or making your 'to do' list in the L2? That way, little by little, you'll integrate into your life new vocabulary of foods, household items and action verbs (for example, 'pick up Granny at the airport' or 'take snack to school').

Label to rehearse

Another way to rehearse language is to label it. (See p. 48, 'Paper and online flash-cards'.) When you learn the name of a thing, give it a label. For example, in learning the Portuguese word for cranberry, I wrote the word on a sticky note and stuck it on the cranberry juice jar. This approach fits well with the idea of learning words as you need them and making varied interconnections and associations. There was no need to learn the word in the past because I didn't have the juice in the house. (See p. 55, 'Google Images'.)

Computer Programs

There are many well-organized and interesting computer programs for self-teaching language. See if any of the following fit your needs and goals.

Rosetta Stone

One of the most popular language programs on the market today is Rosetta Stone (2014). It's snazzy and pricey and offers 33 languages. Rosetta Stone uses an immersion method by showing images alongside the new vocabulary instead of providing transla-tions.

Rosetta Stone can be frustrating, because it involves so much guesswork. Its attempt to have students *acquire* instead of *learn* means that its students can't use many of the logical prior knowledge adults have at their disposal.

Each unit has sections of 'learn, practice, and play'. Unlike most of the programs on the market today, once you complete a unit, you have class with an instructor via video feed. The teacher speaks only the L2.

Pimsleur

Another popular method, Pimsleur (2014), includes eight languages and is based on the idea that humans learn language by hearing, not by reading or writing. It emphasizes learning a subset of language that is 'most commonly used'. Pimsler facili-tates comprehension by working on skills for anticipating what people are going to say. Grammar lessons are disguised so that you learn structure subtly, not with overt repetition. Each exercise builds on what you've previously learned to mimic how you learned language as a child.

Berlitz

Berlitz (2014) is similar in theory to the Berlitz courses offered worldwide. Instruction focuses on communication mostly in the L2 and grammar is not overtly taught. Offered in over 20 languages, Berlitz has CDs for hearing native speech. Since Berlitz appeals to business travelers, it emphasizes learning efficiently, with 'on the go' instruction that can be learned in the car or on your iPod while taking a run.

Fluenz

Fluenz (2014) offers only seven languages, but is growing in popularity and is advertising it will offer more languages over time. It differs from programs like Berlitz that try to mimic how children acquire language and instead focuses on having adults use the tools they have at their disposal. The recorded teacher explains how the L2 differs from the L1, shows videos with subtitles of the language and offers brief grammar explanations when the constructions get tricky.

Which is for you?

To determine if any of these programs would work for you, go to the websites for demos of the software, or check for demos on YouTube. Some of these programs cost hundreds of dollars. If you take the risk of buying on eBay, make sure the program is a new, unopened copy. Alternatively, there are some free computer programs.

Free computer programs

Mango

Public libraries often have, as part of their websites, computer programs to learn a foreign language. Mango Languages (2014) has over 30 languages and helps with useful communication, like getting someone's attention or asking for help. Grammar is discussed only with respect to real communication needs. Mango would be helpful in writing your script for telling who you are and for asking about other people.

Little Pim

Adults can learn from children's software hosted by public libraries. Little Pim (2014) is free of charge around the United States. It can help parents learn household language through its videos of children sipping from cups, putting spoons on their noses and making messes – all while repeating the vocabulary to help it sink in.

Online Resources

Audio magazines

Online sites that have an audio component to practice vocabulary and pronunciation are called audio magazines. They also have a visual component which mimics the format of a magazine. The idea is to have input about a country and its language in a relaxed setting. Audio magazines are usually produced every month or every other month, so you keep getting fresh material. The price is considerably lower than a traditional language learning computer program (less than $10 per month).

The advantage of these magazines over programs that emphasize only the language is that the focus is on the target country, giving insight into the L2 culture. The language is conversational. For example, you'll hear dialogues of native speakers in typical situations – going to restaurants or talking about their day. Some audio magazines have native speakers available for questions. Search '<L2> Audio Magazine'.

The British Broadcasting Corporation

The BBC (2014) offers some phenomenal free websites that use quick video clips specifically for learning language. If you're a beginner, start by searching 'learn a language BBC' for information on 40 languages. It has motivating facts about the language, key phrases and videos with native speakers teaching greetings and cultural norms. Subtitles are offered, since people are speaking at their natural rate.

For other free resources, search '<L2> online free'.

Online translators

If you search for 'free online translator' you'll discover several options for looking up words in over 50 languages. Google Translate (2014) is the most popular and, arguably, the best. For most of these sites, there's a box on the left where you enter the word you'd like to know and a box on the right where the translation appears.

These sites are great for pronunciation. Most have a clickable icon to listen to the word as many times as you need. To check your own pronunciation, listen to the word, then say it aloud, then listen again to hear the discrepancy in your pronunciation and the one offered. Repeat the process until your pronunciation is similar to the actual pronunciation.

Good translators will offer several translations for the word you're searching. Usually the best one is listed at the top. If, however, you're unsure whether this is the translation you're looking for, choose another of the options and place it on the left side to do a reverse search. For example, if you want to say that something is 'funny' in French, the translator might give you *marrant*, *risible* and *louche*. If you take *louche* and put it on the left side to find the English translation, you'll get 'shady'. If you try *risible*, you'll get 'ludicrous'. Only *marrant*, when entered on the left side, actually gives you the translation 'funny'.

Translators can help you learn through writing. Use them to write to your children. If they are school aged, put brief notes in their lunch boxes. If they have email addresses, send them L2 emails.

Google Images

Google Images (2014) holds a wealth of information for language learners. Let's say you look up the translation of a word and even after cross-referencing it you still aren't sure of its meaning. Go to Google Images and type the L2 word. For example, I looked up the Portuguese word *estojo* in Google Translate. The translation was 'case' and I wasn't sure which type of case – a briefcase, a case of apples? I entered *estojo* into Google Images, and saw pictures of small pencil cases and little purses. I had my answer.

Research shows that the image will stay with us longer than a word or definition (Carlson, 2009). So try this method even when you understand a word's meaning but want an extra memory device. (See p. 52, 'Label to rehearse'.)

Using favorite topics online

You don't need every vocabulary word in the language, but you will want words that describe activities you enjoy. If you're learning Dutch and are interested in basketball, search in the L2 *basketbal in Nederland* (basketball in Holland). You'll find sites with information about games and rules. These searches allow you to use the target language as a vehicle for learning more about a subject, skill or cultural area of interest.

Similarly, you can learn from the news of the target country. It will hold rich language and cultural content. Search *hírek Magyarország* (news in Hungary). You'll learn the different section names – food, entertainment, etc. And even if you're reading only the headlines, you're exposing yourself to the L2 in real situations.

Look for interesting headlines. Once you've found one, imagine telling someone what you've read. How would you ask them a question about the article and how would you answer the question? An example of a question is 'Do you know much about fracking in Germany?'

To find out about more sites in the L2 on your topics of interest, open a Twitter account with all the profile information in the L2. Follow some L2 Twitter accounts that grab your attention and start tweeting about sites you come across.

YouTube

One of the best places to learn language is YouTube (2014). By searching for a topic in the L2, you can hear and watch anything that interests you. It might be dance, scuba diving, piano or tennis.

Search the name of a famous person in the target country. You'll hear clips from interviews. Need to know how to do something like tie a necktie? Search in the L2 and hear the different steps from a native speaker. (And if you aren't sure how to write 'Tie a necktie', head to Google Translate.)

To work on your pronunciation, try the same technique you used with Google Translate. Listen to what someone says, then pause the video while you repeat. Listen again to see how close you were to the native speaker.

Language learning social network sites

It's risky to put specific names of sites in a book like this one, because language websites come and go. The ones outlined below, however, have been around for some time and boast millions of users. They can be downloaded to your phone for practice away from home.

Livemocha.com

Livemocha (2014) is a site for language learners interested in acquiring conversation skills through active participation in a social network. The site is set up much like Facebook, but is designed to connect language learners of the same language, also offering opportunities to interact with native speakers. For example, after you've completed some language-based exercises, you can ask native speakers to correct the work for you and give you feedback. Livemocha.com has beginning courses for free in 38 languages and offers higher-level courses at a reasonable price, or free, through public library systems.

Babbel.com

Babbel (2014) is an online language learning software for 12 different languages. It has some features that social networking sites have, such as chat sessions and ways to leave messages. Parts of their courses are free and teach grammar for conversation using tongue twisters, music and popular sayings. I like their quick quizzes, offered within the first five minutes of learning, to check for comprehension. More in-depth study can be purchased for around $10 a month.

Busuu.com

Busuu (2014) is a European-based site. Like more traditional social networking sites, it houses profiles and lets users befriend other users. It also encourages users to 'like' other language-related sites. Busuu.com is unique in that its students help each other through language exchange. For example, if I'm learning Urdu and speak English natively, I'll help people learning English and they'll help me with Urdu. You may not like the idea of teaching your L1, but remember the old adage 'To teach is to learn twice' (Twombly, 2012). Explaining your own language gives you insight into how languages work. And you may meet native speakers of your L2 who want to maintain contact. Courses have some free features, with monthly fees of around $15 for others.

Xihalife.com

Xiha Life (2014) is a multilingual social network for exchange students, expats and people living in multicultural families. Its user interface has been translated into 42 languages and it supports communication in 60 languages. Users can make friends with over 750,000 other users worldwide. They can also upload videos and pictures, share travel tips, play games and maintain blogs.

Palabea.com

Palabea (2014) is a large international language learning community where you can improve your language skills by video chatting with native speakers. Users choose target countries and topics to chat about and discuss the topics with natives of that country. Speakers help each other by correcting each other's speech and teaching new words. The site also helps users find native speakers in their hometown for face-to-face interaction.

Lang-8.com

Lang-8.com (2014) is a language exchange social networking site. Users create a profile and then select from 19 target languages. They visit different sites that house topics of interest. Visitors to the topic sites write journal entries in the target language and have them corrected by native speakers. In return, the user corrects the users who are learning his native language.

SharedTalk.com

SharedTalk (2014) has typical networking features such as a profile and mailbox but focuses on having language partners in the target country. You share emails with each other and use voice and text chatting to practice conversation skills. The site is an extension of the 33 languages covered by Rosetta Stone, but it is free and can be beneficial even without buying the commercial program.

Facebook equivalents in the target country

Many countries have a Facebook equivalent. Find the social networking site popular in your target country and open an account. For a list of these sites, search 'social networking foreign countries'. You'll see, for example, that Orkurt.com is popular in India and Brazil, QQ.com is the leader in China and Hi5.com is favored in many Latin countries, as well as in Europe.

Don't be shy about friending people on the site and letting them know you're learning another language. Since you can 'like' pages and recommend them to others viewing your page, you'll be reading more in the L2. You'll also get more practice reading as your L2 friends post their activities, interests and opinions.

Blogs

Look for blogs in your areas of interest and join a few. If you like French cooking, search for 'blog de cuisine Français [French cooking]' and try to understand what's written by looking at accompanying pictures. Think of something to say and contribute to the blog. Mention that you are an L2 learner. Work on your comprehension skills by commenting on what other people have said.

Other Resources

The high and low tech we use every day can open up a second language for you. Let's examine a few that are affordable and easy to access.

Universities and foreign films

Foreign films offer an alternative way to hear the language while enjoying a good story. University language departments often show foreign films that are open to the public. Check the department's website where your L2 is being taught, or call the department reception desk.

There will likely be people at the film who are learning the L2 and some native speakers as well. Stay after the credits to meet people, discuss the movie and ask about other upcoming events.

Videos in the L2

An alternative to live showings of films are videos in the L2. They let you watch at your own pace. You can see 30 minutes at a time and rewind if you're confused about something. If you are just starting in the L2, search for films with more action, less talk. That way, if you see a car go up in smoke, you can guess that the bystander is yelling 'Help!' Use subtitles in your L1 if that helps, but eventually move to subtitles in the L2, or none at all.

You can find videos of international films from mail-in and streaming video chains like Netflix.com. Read any written description of the film beforehand to get a general idea of the plot. Remember that you will not understand everything. Give yourself some credit for just getting the gist.

Television in the L2

Cable television and satellite networks have subscriptions to channels from all over the world for around $30 a month. You can also stream television via the internet by searching 'free TV in <L2>'.

Find shows that you would watch in your L1, since your background knowledge in the topic will help you guess meanings. For example, if you watch political shows, you'll have an idea what they're saying about elections.

You don't have to be sitting down with full attention on the television to reap the benefits of this input. Having the international channel on while you're doing other activities can be beneficial. You're getting the rhythm and sounds of the language, and your brain is still processing the input.

Songs

Why and how

Songs help you learn language for many reasons. First, their repetition gives you time to learn specific phrases or words you might miss in conversation. Second, the rhythm and rhyming of the lyrics help you remember pronunciation and new vocabulary. And finally, when you listen to music, you are often in a relaxed state. Your mind is more open to – and less nervous about – learning the language.

You can learn from music by doing nothing more than listening to native speakers use the language. If you want to be more active in your learning, read the lyrics and try to sing along. If there's a persistent word you aren't familiar with, look it up. Try singing the song without the music, perhaps in the shower or in your car.

Where?

To find up-to-date music, ask a native speaker where he buys his music. Also try large bookstores, since they often have music you can listen to before you purchase. Music stores that sell second-hand CDs are also a good bet.

To find music online, search 'MP3s in <L2>' or 'Music CDs in <L2>'. Often websites have a bestsellers list, which will give you a good place to start. Many sites let you listen to the music a bit before you make a decision. Get something you really like, or you won't end up listening to it.

Streaming radio

The radio fills a room with music and other rich language. You can learn from the songs, as well as those sound bites between songs. You'll hear information about the music, get news updates and hear local announcements – all from a native speaker. Even the advertisements teach you everyday language about products and services.

Talk radio offers a variety of voices, accents and regional dialects. You can get accustomed to the speed of native speaker's speech without having to respond. Search online for 'streaming radio from <target country>'.

When you first start listening, just work on getting the gist of what's said. Listen as you go about your routines of cleaning or packing lunches. Even when not getting it all consciously, your brain is still working on what it hears.

Books

Language learning books

If you're the type person who can pick up an owner's manual and understand the directions, you might consider getting a textbook for your L2 and doing some work on your own. If you're just starting out, I would suggest getting one that has your L1 in the explanations, as opposed to one that's exclusively in the L2.

To find textbooks, you can try the library, though buying is preferable so you can write in the book. You can search for new or used textbooks at college bookstores. Or look online for 'teach yourself <L2>'. Check if it has an accompanying CD to help with pronunciation. Then read the reviews! You should see descriptions such as 'clear instructions', 'simple explanations' and 'excellent for beginners' (or whatever level you're looking for).

If you can look inside the book, find out if it's more communicative in its approach. You're trying to avoid rote grammar exercises. In other words, does it teach numbers, days of the weeks and verbs in real contexts like dialogues or brief news or magazine articles? If so, you'll learn things you need in real life. If the book has long vocabulary lists with L1 translations and few ways to practice, you won't learn much and will probably not be motivated to continue. Answers in the back of the book are also really helpful.

Phrasebooks

Phrasebooks are generally made for people making quick trips to a country. They offer basic information on how to get around. You can find them at your public library by searching the library's site for '<L2> language phrasebook'. Some even have accompanying CDs or web versions that allow you to hear audio of popular expressions.

Phrasebooks are full of pre-made sentences to get you through customs and order in a restaurant. The chunks of language usually have little to no explanation as to how the components fit together. This means there's little room for any changes to fit your specific circumstances. Some people still find them useful for building their script. My favorite series is *Lonely Planet*, for its 'Must Know Grammar' and colorful teaching style, but I also like Rick Steves' phrasebooks for their easy to follow pronunciation guides (Steves, 2014).

Recipe books

Just by reading bits and pieces of books in another language, you learn an amazing amount of vocabulary. If you like to cook, recipes and recipe books can offer real language you can put to immediate use. To find book titles, search Google Images for *livre de recettes Françaises* (recipe books in French). Then check which titles are carried by international booksellers. The first book cover picture gave me *Pâtisseries Maison*, which I found on Amazon.com.

Recipe books can get pricey because they are heavy to ship. If you know someone going to the target country, ask them to bring you back a cookbook. Or, for free options, search online for 'recipes in <L2>'. That way you can print the recipes. If you're baking, you'll be highly motivated to be exact in your understanding, since a teaspoon and a tablespoon can make a huge difference in the taste.

Short stories

Reading short stories isn't just for children. If you are crazy for plot but are still a beginner, short stories might be just the ticket. Search 'short stories in <L2>' or 'folk tales in <L2>'. These tales give you the chance to follow a storyline without committing to a full novel. Some short stories come with pictures that help you guess what's coming up next. Others have basic plot lines you will recognize since they're based on ubiquitous folk tales.

If you want help from your L1, look online for 'dual language <L2>'. They have one side of the story in your L1 and the other in the L2. To fully enjoy these stories, try to read at least a paragraph before looking at the L1 side. That will keep you from feeling interrupted at every turn.

Novels

You may have tried to read a novel in your college French class and had a difficult time. It's possible you were trying to read at a level too difficult for you. For this reason, I would advise you to avoid buying classics in the L2, even though they are easiest to find. Their vocabulary is elevated and can be frustrating. Additionally, the language doesn't show you the way real people talk today.

As counterintuitive as it may sound, consider obtaining novels originally written in your L1 and then translated into the L2. So for a Brit learning Turkish, a British novel translated into Turkish would be easier to read than a Turkish book by a Turkish author. That's because in the translated book, the Brit recognizes the cultural context – the places are recognizable, the subway familiar and the ways of life alike. A British reader would also be accustomed to the style of writing and the conventions of British dialogue. The other plus side to a translated book is that the L1 version can serve as a dictionary when you get stuck on a word or a concept.

Be sure to get books that aren't overly complex in their sentence structure and their message. I began by reading translated Harlequin romance novels, because they were written for a low reading level and had stories that were predictable and easy to follow. Just search 'English books translated into <L2>'.

If you think you're ready to purchase a book – on Amazon.com for example – and can 'Look Inside' it, get a feel for how well you're understanding. Read some of the first chapter. You should be able to glean the general gist without a dictionary, looking up only unfamiliar key words that are often repeated. If you get stumped on more than one word per every two or three sentences, the book is too hard for you.

Non-fiction and self-help

If you want to read non-fiction, choose topics of interest and/or topics you know a lot about. These could be on subjects like parenting, travel, relationships, health, history or spirituality. You might be interested in biographies or autobiographies. These don't necessarily have to be about people from the target country, since many such books can be found in translation.

Non-fiction can be easier to read than fiction if you're already familiar with the topic. Background knowledge makes you more successful at guessing meaning. It can also be very motivating, since you genuinely want to know more about the topic.

Dictionary clues

Beware of using a dictionary too much as you read. You're better off guessing unfamiliar words than looking up every single one. Think of opening your dictionary as an interruption to your reading, as if someone were tapping you on the shoulder every few minutes to distract you. If you really don't know what a lot of words mean, find a book on a lower level – even if it's a child's picture book. You'll be more likely to stick with reading if you choose books at your level and move up as they get too easy.

For times when you do want to use a dictionary, consider a dual language dictionary. In one half of the book it has the L1 with translations into the L2, and in the other half it has the L2 with translations into the L1. A pocket-sized dictionary is often enough for beginner learners.

If you've purchased a small dictionary but find that it doesn't have many of the words you need, get a more extensive one. Your local used bookstore is the first place to look, as these dictionaries change hands often. You can also buy them used online.

If you prefer to automate your dictionary use, try an online translator on your computer or cell phone.

Magazines and Newspapers

Magazines and news stories in the L2 are an excellent place to learn, especially if the topic is one you love. You can order them online or find free online magazines like the French *Le Point*, the Spanish *Caretas* or the German-based *Amica*.

Try searching 'Online magazines in <L2>' to find magazines in your areas of interest – fitness, business, fashion. The level of writing in a magazine is generally less complex than that of a novel or work of non-fiction. And the context of photos is so rich, they will give you many clues as to what the writing's about.

Outside Help

Befriend the Korean grocer, the Italian waiter, the Albanian at the pizzeria, your dentist's Romanian secretary … your informants will usually love being asked to help you learn their language.
Barry Farber, *How to Learn Any Language* (2000: 62)

Find and learn from other L2 speakers

Native speakers are invaluable to your learning the language. Even if you are learning a less commonly spoken language, native speakers will be close by. One of the best ways to find other speakers of the language is to keep your ears open. If you hear someone at the grocery store speaking your L2, try to say a few words to them. Even if you just say 'Hello, how are you?' and have to eventually switch to the L1, you've shown your interest. This brief encounter can be a foot in the door to getting to know a native speaker.

You will most definitely have questions that are best answered by native speakers. Be ready to ask them questions when you get the chance. Keep a little notebook on hand or have a sticky note with questions in your wallet. I have a running list of questions in my purse: things that are difficult to find in a dictionary, colloquial expressions that are hard to understand, or ideas I want to express but just can't seem to. I have a few native speakers who I impose on only briefly. Some are friends. Others are people I know from a local grocery, and I can get in a quick question as we bag the groceries.

Whether you met someone from hearing them at the checkout line or in a Meetup group (see below), don't be shy about asking a brief question or two. Also try to ask for people's email addresses to get to know them better. Email correspondence can lead to meeting for coffee and spending more time together.

Meetup.com and other associations

Sites like Meetup (2014) can help you find others interested in learning your L2. Search Meetup.com with the language name and the word 'language'. I searched for 'Portuguese language' in my area and found the Raleigh/Durham Portuguese Language Meetup Group that boasts of Brazilian expats, university students and others interested in learning the language.

Or, to find an association of expats from the target country, search 'association of Filipinos in London', but write it in the L2. Or try 'Chinese group Sydney'. Call their contact number to explain that you're learning the language and would like to get involved in the community. People in these groups can give helpful clues on free newspapers in the L2, upcoming gatherings/concerts connected to the target country, or ideas on hangouts for meeting native speakers.

You may also find groups of speakers of your L2 clustered around a common interest, such as a type of music or specific way of cooking which is popular in the target country. You could, for example, search Meetup.com for the name of a popular dance from your target country and get the benefits of the language and the cultural component as well.

You may feel shy about joining, for example, the 'German Language Meetup Group of Philadelphia' if you're not German. I assure you, people will be so impressed you are trying to learn their language that they will welcome you with open arms. Also remember that not everyone in the group will be German. You may meet other L1 speakers who are interested in learning the L2. You can share resources with them and tricks on how to better learn the language.

International students

If you have a spare room, consider renting to a university student who speaks your L2. For information, call the international house of your local university.

You might also consider hosting an overseas high-school student. There are dozens of sites on how to get started: http://www.ciee.org/highschool/, http://www.afsusa.org/, or http://www.ayusa.org/families/what-is-hosting. Understand, though, that the students are in your country to learn your L1, so you'll need to clearly express your language learning goals to them before their arrival. You can make an agreement to speak in the L2 at certain times of the day or certain days of the week.

Tutors

If you have the resources to hire a native-speaking tutor, give it a try. You can save money by hiring someone who isn't necessarily a teacher or trained tutor. If you go this route, you will have to be in charge of the learning process, because your tutor may lack the training to actually take the lead. This set-up should work out if you plan to arrive at sessions with a list of questions.

Language exchange tutor

You can also consider a language exchange for tutoring. That's where you get together with a native L2 speaker who is learning your L1, and trade language help. For example, I met with a Brazilian, and for half an hour we would work in Portuguese, then we would work half an hour in English. Research shows, as does my own experience, that sessions will be more regular if money changes hands, as people place a higher value on time they're paying for. So both of you can put money into a kitty to be used for office materials, coffee or snacks.

Learn some basics

There are certain basics you should cover with your tutor. You'll need to be able to describe things you don't know the word for. Learn the word for 'thing' in the L2 and other slang words for it: 'thingy', 'thingamagig' and 'whatchamacallit'.

Learn how to say the nice words: 'please', excuse me', 'I'm sorry' and 'thank you'. Repeat them often.

Find out how to slow down people's speech: 'I'm sorry, I'm still learning Russian. Would you speak slowly for me?'

Learn how to ask for the specifics of what you don't understand: 'I'm sorry, I don't understand the word —'. This works better than a general 'I don't understand'.

'What I need to know' list

Keep a running list of 'what I need to know' sentences that you can go over when you are with your tutor. Think of times you were unsure in the L2 because of the vocabulary or different cultural norms. Do your best to write sentences ahead of time that you need in everyday life, for instance things you have to say to your children: 'Fasten your seatbelt' or 'Quiet down a little'. Go over the list with your tutor, letting her correct your mistakes in grammar and pronunciation.

Most importantly, ask your tutor to speak to you only in the L2. If this isn't a possibility, ask that she speak most of the time in the L2, moving into your L1 only when it is really necessary.

Interviewing as an activity

A good tutoring activity is interviewing. Interview your tutor, asking simple questions about what she does for a living, what she does in her free time and what she likes to eat and drink. Make sure you are corrected for errors as you go.

You'll learn vocabulary by listening to your tutor's responses. Practice new words you learn by asking follow-up questions. If he gives, for example, 'parasailing' as one thing he likes to do, ask 'When do you parasail?' and 'What do you enjoy about para-sailing?'

It's important to know how to talk about yourself and your interests. So switch roles and have the tutor interview you. If being corrected as you speak is distracting, ask your tutor to write down corrections on a notepad and help you with them after you're done speaking.

Textbooks with tutors

If you prefer more structured tutoring time, find a good introductory textbook. It should look like fun, with lots of pictures to give you context. Avoid texts that suggest all grammar.

Buy yourself a nice notebook to hold exercises you complete and notes from tutoring sessions. Learn only the language you need from the text, skipping over what doesn't apply. For example, most introductory texts will begin by teaching classroom vocabulary. Some of these words will be useful to you, like 'pen' and 'pencil'. You will need these things during your tutoring lesson and around the house, too, perhaps. But words such as 'chalk' and 'desk' you can skip for now.

Ask your tutor to assign homework for the next lesson. That way, she can offer feedback on your work. You and she can discuss new words that come up and practice using them. You might also bring to the session any magazine articles or books you're reading and ask questions about unfamiliar words or expressions.

Letter writing with correction

Letter writing is an excellent way to learn the language. Write a draft of a letter or email to a native speaker and read it aloud in the tutoring session for correction. Rewrite the letter after the session.

If you don't have anyone to write to, make the letter to your tutor. You might write about what you learned last week. Not only are you practicing writing, but you are recapping what you went over in the previous lesson. Or, write a letter to your tutor about something you enjoy doing. That way you are using vocabulary relevant to your daily life and building your script of self-description.

A tutoring format

I have done a bit of language tutoring over the years and find a good format is a weekly one-hour session that begins with a brief review from the last session. Highly motivated students type up the main points from the previous week. That way we can quickly go over them and clear up any misunderstandings. They then have a list of questions that have arisen since the last class. Or they have some homework to correct. The rest of the session can be used for practicing speaking on topics of interest. Some students record the sessions on their cell phones to listen to again while driving, cooking or working out.

Classes in the L2

You may be more inclined to take a language class than get an individual tutor. Classes are a good option, as they help you learn from a fluent speaker while making friends with people interested in the L2.

Some preliminary questions

If you're considering taking a class, ask yourself some questions.

What am I looking for?

Choose communication skills over a grammar-oriented class. The description should mention things like 'conversations', 'daily language', 'common expressions' and 'step-by-step learning'. If the class description is heavy with words like 'grammar', 'structure' and 'linguistics' you may not learn what you need to speak to a child.

What's my level?

To know if a class fits your level, read the course description carefully and don't be afraid to contact the school or teacher ahead of time. Arrive early to say a brief word to the teacher and let him get a feel for your abilities. Remember that if you enter a class and realize it's not the right level, you can discuss with the teacher other classes that better fit your stage of learning.

What's the teacher's training?

The actual number of years your teacher has trained isn't as important as the level of comfort he shows. Does he have a lesson plan? Is he giving students a chance to participate? His language skills don't have to be native, but he should be able to answer your questions.

How much time can I put in?

Find out early if homework is involved and decide how much time you're willing to spend outside of class.

How does this class fit with my finances?

If money's an issue, I would recommend either a community college or a class that might be free at a university or a house of worship.

Relax

This is not your high-school Spanish class where you had to worry about your grades and your teenage peers. Relax, make mistakes and allow yourself to do your best in the moment, even if you sound silly or feel inept. Think of how many errors there are in children's speech. They don't worry about their mistakes and, over time, their speech improves.

Make alliances

It behooves you to make friends in your language class. Choose them carefully, though, so you're with people who really make the effort. Sit in the front of the class, with people who seem excited to be there.

After class, find out about other students. Why are they learning the L2? Does anyone have a spouse who's a native speaker of the L2? Has anyone has been to the target country? Ask your colleagues out to a local bar or restaurant after class to practice the L2 and have some fun.

Hold High Expectations

Being your own favorite teacher means that you'll want to be an instructor who gets good results. Figure out what tricks will encourage you to work harder. If you love interesting notebooks and pens, invest in those for your language practice.

Find ways to build in language practice before or during things you like doing. If you are a chocolate addict, have some chocolate while you do your homework. If you enjoy spending time on the phone, challenge yourself to write an email in the L2 before you make the call. Before you sit down to watch television, push yourself to look over your class notes, write questions for the native speaker at your office, or look up words in the dictionary that you know you'll need with your children.

Cut yourself some slack

That said, discipline taken too far can de-motivate. Whether you plan to learn through commercial computer programs, social networks, methods like the 'din in the head', native-speaker contacts or formal classes, remember that what you're doing may be hard, but it can still be fun.

That's because you set your own goals and learn in ways that work for you. D. Deubel's article 'Four ways to learn English' says that adult learners 'notice language. They are no longer fish in water but fish that know they are in water!' (Deubel, 2011). So as you navigate the waters of being your own teacher, keep in mind that your favorite teacher probably cut you some slack from time to time. Give yourself some breathing room and remember that with language, as with other areas of life, today you may be floundering, but tomorrow's an exciting new day.

Seven Steps to Teaching Yourself an L2

- Get yourself motivated. Tell your friends, buy your materials, find easy online resources.
- Reactivate any past language study you've done by listening to music or television or by reading familiar topics on websites.
- Lower your anxiety. Identify your fears. Remember that fear from the past can stay in the past, and find a helpful mantra.
- Just listen. Even if you don't understand it all, listen to songs and watch films in the L2.
- Keep a little notebook for questions and answers.
- Learn new words while you do daily tasks like teeth brushing or hair drying.
- Write a script that discusses who you are and why you want to learn the L2.

5 Many Methods: Flexible Approaches to Fit Your Lifestyle

Do whatever you do intensely.
Robert Henri, artist and teacher (Goodreads, 2011a)

Nothing is more contagious than example.
François Duc de la Rochefoucauld (1613–80), teacher (in Melvill, 2009: 213)

Previous chapters explained how to get started, and you know it's okay that you're not a native speaker. This chapter shows you how easy it is to find a teaching method that fits your lifestyle. You'll learn to expose your child to an L2 in fun and unique ways. And you'll see how to keep their curiosity piqued and motivation high!

Forget Your Old Language Teachers

In your lifetime, you've already learned a lot of language. When you were a young child, your parents modeled words and grammar by speaking to you. You also learned language by hearing your parents speak to each other. They probably did a good job of teaching you to understand and speak, even though they were not professional language teachers.

Now remember your model for learning a second language. Your Spanish teacher may have been impatient or boring. Your German teacher may have been completely unintelligible. You may still have night sweats over French dialogue memorization and verb conjugations. It's important to put those old, negative models behind you! Let's move forward by using our parents as a model instead of our scary language teachers.

Making a Plan

Some parents find it helpful to make a specific language plan. Just like a birth plan gives a pregnant couple a sense of control over their baby's delivery, a language plan empowers them to make language changes.

To formulate a plan, either on paper or in your head, ask these questions:

- Who will speak the L2? You, your partner, a nanny or au pair, a babysitter, relative or friend?
- When can you imagine yourself using the L2? During mealtimes, at bedtime, on weekends, every day?
- How will you or the other L2 speakers improve your L2 skills with time? Reading, online language sites, movies, music? (See Chapter 4, 'Be Your Favorite Teacher'.)
- What challenges do you foresee? How can you imagine handling these challenges? (See Chapter 12, 'Meeting Challenges'.)

Discuss your plan with someone who can offer feedback. And, just like with birth plans, be willing to modify your language plan when real life happens.

Organization and Examples

In all the methods we'll discuss, there is one common thread: each has a logical organization that children and adults can understand. Una Cunningham-Andersson and Staffan Andersson, authors of *Growing Up with Two Languages*, say, 'A child will find it easier to sort out the two languages if there is some logic behind the choice of which language is used' (Cunningham-Andersson & Andersson, 1999: 111).

Each method is outlined with specific principles and examples. One may resonate with you, or feel free to mix and match to create your own eclectic approach.

Method: One parent one language (or one person one language)

In the past, conventional wisdom said that both parents had to speak a language to a child for him to learn successfully. But this view fell by the wayside as research showed that children can learn a language solely from one parent or from one caregiver.

This method, called 'one parent one language' (OPOL), involves one parent speaking the L2 and the other parent speaking the L1. It's also called 'one person one language' to include language providers who are not parents, such as nannies or grandparents. The method also works for single parents who speak an L2.

Children exposed to this method learn to separate languages based on the people who speak them. Children growing up in England might have a father who speaks to them in Japanese and a mother who speak to them in English. Linguist John Lawler notes:

Children soon learn that there's a daddy language and a mommy language, and that others speak them too, and they will learn them both and keep them straight. There may be a period when the child gets confused or mixed up, but that doesn't last long. (Lawler, 2001)

One woman who speaks English to her children instead of her native German shows how natural OPOL can feel:

> The OPOL method has worked very well for us and I believe that, for their ages, they are at the developmental level they should be. In fact, if I began speaking German to my children now, I think they would have a heart attack! It would be an unnatural situation for us. (N.L., interview)

Testing the languages

Children in OPOL households test out their different languages on different people. Your job as a parent is to gently guide them toward the correct separation of person and language. One American man who resides in the United States and speaks French to his son says,

> When Jonah was under two, he said something in French to my mother, and I had to tell him 'Nana doesn't speak French' and it was a learning moment, and he's still working all this out, that there are two languages. For the grown-ups [who overheard], it was riotous that he was speaking French to my mother, but to me, it was just normal. (J.V., interview)

The language separation of OPOL can come so naturally that some young children believe that the L2 parent speaks only the L2. They believe this even though they hear the parents speaking the L1 with other people. Language specialist Suzanne Barron-Hauwaert writes 'The child, especially the first-born, may well believe that the other parent simply doesn't understand the others' language' (Barron-Hauwaert, 2004: 78). I saw this phenomenon with my nearly four-year-old. Here's an entry from my language journal.

> Tonight I wanted to look at a book from the library with her [Sydney]. It was a book in English that Stephen [her father] had read with her. I planned on just translating it as I read. I asked her if she wanted me to read it, but she told me [in Portuguese], 'No, you don't speak English yet.' (journal, 9/14/2004)

Fortunately, even when children grow older and know that the L2 parent actually does speak the L1, they tend to accept the language arrangement that's been put in place. It becomes a tradition – like believing in Santa Claus – so they suspend their disbelief and play along. One mom writes,

> My children are perfectly aware that I speak German [the L1] as they hear me converse with neighbors, speak to people at the supermarket, bank, etc. on a daily basis. However, they know that I do not speak German with them, and so far they have accepted this. (N.L., email interview)

What if both parents are around?

OPOL couples must decide how to use the L2 with both parents present. Let's imagine an Irish family with a father who speaks his L2, German, with the kids while the mother speaks English. To make things easier, some families would switch to English when both parents are with the children. One mother I interviewed says that's what they do in her family, though it's not ideal for learning the L2:

> It helps if the husband speaks the language, too, but mine doesn't. If he did, we would have much more progress. With respect to him, I don't want to speak a language he doesn't understand with our children, so I speak Russian *only* when we're by ourselves, because it's not fair if he doesn't understand. (O.F., interview)

Other parents argue that switching back to the shared first language feels 'weird' because they've gotten used to using the L2 with the kids. Here's an example. When I first decided to use Portuguese with my daughter, I thought I would only do so when we were alone together, mainly because I worried my husband would feel left out. My experience, though, was that it felt strange to switch languages with her. I was used to speaking to her in Portuguese during the day. When my husband came home from work and I tried speaking English to her, it felt fake. It was like I was showing my husband what I was saying to her instead of really talking to *her*.

So I decided to use only the L2 with her, even when my husband was around. This meant that he has learned a lot of Portuguese, simply because he's exposed to it day after day. He got his feet wet by hearing the simple language of babies and toddlers. Little by little, he heard more complex language as the children grew.

People ask me what we do at dinnertime when we're in a shared conversation. 'How do you know when to switch languages?' In fact, my kids do exactly what researchers say kids will do, utilizing eye contact as a switch signal. If they turn their eyes to me, they switch to Portuguese. When they catch my husband's eyes, they speak English. Knowing that there's no reason to speak English to the children, even with my husband around, helps me be consistent.

One mother who spoke her L2, Japanese, to her children explains her struggles with consistency and her passion to stick with it.

> I try to be as consistent as possible with sticking to the OPOL method. Often, when I'm tired or angry, I find it easy to just yell out 'Stop it!' [in English] or something like that, but I always stop myself and say it in Japanese. Consistency is not always necessary, I hear, many families switch back and forth, but I find it necessary for our family. I feel that this is especially true since there is only one bilingual parent. (P.R., interview)

OPOL and other people

Consistency is useful outside the home, as well. The L2 parent may worry about speaking the L2 in public because people might stare or feel excluded. There are ways to handle this, though. One mom writes,

I speak only in Japanese to the kids and my husband speaks only in English.... I realize that it can seem exclusive and rude to others and I am sensitive to that. However, I have been very consistent and usually explain to friends and relatives or passersby that I am speaking another language to the kids and excuse ourselves. Generally, people are supportive. (P.R., email interview)

Chapter 12, 'Meeting Challenges', describes specific cases in which parents use the L2 around friends, strangers and extended family. It uses dialogue examples to illustrate how to handle a variety of reactions.

Non-parent caregivers

For some families, the L2 adult is not the parent. She could be a relative or friend who consistently spends time with the child. If you choose a relative or godparent, be sure he is a genuinely willing participant. Delve into Chapter 7, 'Talk Talk Talk', for ways to choose and support this caregiver.

International adoption

OPOL is useful for monolingual parents who adopt a child from another country. Parents can employ a nanny or au pair who speaks the language of the child's first country. Or parents can find a friend who speaks the language and is active in the child's daily life. Again, Chapter 7, 'Talk Talk Talk', offers suggestions on choosing this important speaker in your child's life.

It is enormously helpful if one or both parents learn at least a little of the child's first language. See Chapter 4, 'Be Your Favorite Teacher', for helpful hints on self-study. If another caregiver speaks the L2, parents can also learn by paying attention to the interaction between their child and the L2 adult. They can ask questions, repeat the language they hear and experiment using the words they learn.

Is there time?

Some OPOL families worry about whether they'll have enough time to teach their child an L2. These fears are often expressed by non-parent caregivers, parents of international adoptees and parents who have demanding careers. Parents in the last group may spend time with their children only in the evenings and on weekends. One father writes,

I can't spend as much time as I would like to with my children during a regular working week.... If the language is taught by the one who is working – in our case, myself – the exposure to the second language is just a short period of time per day and hardly enough to keep them on the level of their mother tongue. (K.N., email interview)

Thankfully, this father reported that, over time, his children were successful in becoming bilingual. His worries about having enough time with his children are important, and not unique. They're the same ones we ask in other non-language areas of life. Working parents do a balancing act in bringing home the bacon, taking care of their children's basic needs, making it to dance performances and spending quality time alone with them.

Just as a parent who travels on the weekends may not be able to coach Little League, he may still be able to attend some of the games. What can happen with a busy L2 parent, though, is that the child may show less fluency in the language during periods when they spend less time together. This is temporary, though. One father lives with his two children in Hungary, where he speaks his L2, English. He explains how quickly things change:

> It's easy to tell even if I spent one full day with Dominik, especially I can tell that he says more in English. I went off on a ski trip with him ... and after a week, his English had really improved. (E.O., email interview)

Some working parents say that because they spend less time at home, they tend to be more lenient when their children don't respond in the L2. This same father admits 'I work crazy hours.... I don't push it too much when he responds in Hungarian.... When I have the time I ask him to say it in English' (E.O., email interview). My advice to him was 'Do what works in your situation'.

Is understanding enough?

Some authors of bilingual guidebooks don't sanction a relaxed approach to language exposure. Instead, they warn parents against 'passive' bilingualism, where children understand their parents but don't respond in the L2. The judgment of this warning is that only 'active' bilingualism is valid – meaning only when children can speak are they truly learning the language. With this as the only alternative, expectations are unreasonably high and may force parents, particularly working parents, to abandon their bilingual goals altogether. I would argue that, yes, it's more desirable for children to actively speak the language, but some is better than none. (See p. 151, 'Passive to active'.) Edith Harding-Esch and Philip Riley, in their book *The Bilingual Family*, write about passive bilingualism:

> Outsiders might criticise it ... because the children 'don't speak the language', but one might just as well emphasise the positive aspects and say that the children do understand the language – and that the family as a whole has adopted an efficient system of communication. (Harding-Esch & Riley, 2003: 37)

Passive bilingualism can also turn into active, when your child reaches a different developmental stage. (See p. 186, 'Teenagers' passive bilingualism'.) It can also happen when your child perceives a greater need for the language. (See p. 151, 'Passive to active'.)

It can happen small steps at a time, when your child is ready. One parent who spoke his L2, English, to his daughter, was careful not to push her to respond in English. She did, however, begin to add English phrases to her speech little by little, in her own time. Note that though this father's English is not perfect, he is still able to teach his child:

> Today Cecelia told me for the first time 'Papi, come back.' She hear me using 'come back' in her everyday life when I talk to her and I've never pushed her to say it and I got gladly surprised when I heard it! Also because the emotion on her requirement of me coming back soon. (V.L., email interview)

Try to observe when your child is more willing to actively use the language. You may find that you can take steps to continue the progress, even if it's something as simple as reading a little more at night, or talking more when you're riding in the car.

Method: Two parents, child-directed speech

Another effective method for language learning is 'child-directed speech.' It involves both parents using the L2 with their child. There is a lot of flexibility with this method. Imagine two scenarios. In the first, you and your partner met while working on a one-year project in Turkey. You are back in the States now and want to speak Turkish to your son. You and your partner decide to speak it to each other, too, at least when your child is around. That way, he hears Turkish directed at him from the two of you. He also overhears adult dialogue in Turkish when you and your partner speak to each other. Learning progresses in the home just as it would in the home of parents speaking their native language.

Now imagine a second scenario. You and your husband both speak a little Italian that you learned in college. His language skills far surpass yours, but you still want to speak it to your two children. You can't imagine speaking Italian to your husband, because he'll want to correct you and tell you the word for everything. Plus, you've tried it and it feels ridiculous.

One mother who was the better speaker of the two parents writes 'I feel that speaking [our second language] English changes our relationship for the worse. It often puts me in the position of a teacher, which is a role I don't want to take on in the relationship with my husband' (J.A., email interview).

Other parents who tried speaking the L2 to their spouses said they felt they were pretending to be someone they weren't. They reported feeling they couldn't communicate on a deeper level. In these cases, parents address the children in the L2, but speak to each other in their L1. Over time, the parent with weaker language skills will improve his L2 through listening and practicing.

Remembering to switch

Parents who spoke an L2 to their kids but spoke their L1 with each other sometimes reported difficulties making the language switch. Some who found it too laborious to switch decided it was easier to just speak the L2 with their partner. One native Romanian speaker who started out speaking her L2 (English) to her son while speaking Romanian to her husband says 'I realize that speaking English between the two of us [my husband and me] makes it easier to stick to the only-English rule with my son' (S.C., interview).

Parents who do not want to speak the L2 with each other, however, may need a reminder to switch back to the L2 when addressing the children. For example, if the mother forgets to switch to the L2, the father can use a quick, non-intrusive prompt like 'oops' (saying the word 'oops' in the L2). Then the mother would remember to switch gears and get back into the L2. Children are encouraged to give a prompt as well, helping them build language awareness.

Start now

It's important for the parent who is learning the language to start speaking it to his child, even if he speaks only a few words. Learn to say 'hello', 'bye bye' and 'I love you'. One father, interviewed in the book *7 Steps to Raising a Bilingual Child*, showed how early you can start. He read German children's books to his kids, even though he didn't understand a word he read.

> I could do this because German is quite a phonetic language. The kids understood though, and it still amazes me that they went along with this. Now I am studying German, and I can finally understand those stories! (Steiner, 2008: 35)

Method: Time-based bilingualism

Research shows that children can learn an L2 even if they are exposed only during certain times of the day or week. This method, called 'time-based bilingualism' or 'one day one language', appeals to parents who know a bit of the L2 but do not wish to speak it exclusively to their children. It's popular among working parents who prefer speaking the L2 just on certain weekday evenings, or on their days off. It also fits well with parents who are divorced and use the L2 on the days they have the children.

The main precept behind this method is that some is enough. A Hungarian father writes,

> I'm not worried about him learning the language. I know of a family here [in Hungary] where the wife is Hungarian and the man is Australian and the guy said they started at age 4.5 and his son didn't speak English, but then from Monday to Tuesday he started speaking English ... so I know that in the proper environment he [my son] can learn. (E.O., email interview)

A woman in the United States describes the effects of L2 exposure, with just a little each week:

> We had a foster child with us. From his birth until he was 18 months [old], we kept him two days a week and spoke only Swiss-German to him, as we only speak Swiss-German to our own children. He understood and spoke some as well. Other foster parents noticed that he was using German instead of English. (B.V., interview)

Examples of time-based learning

Let's look at some examples of using this method. You might choose a day of the week, like Saturday, to use the L2. To get the maximum benefits, you'll want to pick activities for the day that involve communication. So instead of a movie, choose a hike, an outdoor festival or a museum.

Use a map app or program like Google Maps. If you're going somewhere new, get the driving or walking directions in the L2 by searching the words 'Google Maps' beside the name of the L2, written in the L2. For Norwegian, if you search 'Google Maps Norsk', the directions from your house to your destination will be in Norwegian. Once you're on your way, map in hand, talk about the directions as you drive – 'turn left' and 'go straight'.

Google Maps taught me the term 'traffic circle'. When we approached the circle, I said to the kids 'Oh, here's the traffic circle. I love traffic circles!' Then I asked them 'Should we go slow or fast in the traffic circle?' The question encouraged the kids to use the new vocabulary.

The trip home is a great time to engage kids in discussing the outing. Ask them what their favorite part of the outing was and their least favorite part. If you went to a museum and they learned the word 'painting', ask 'What was your favorite painting?' Or if you went on a hike, ask about their favorite plant, tree or insect. To keep them talking, ask them why they chose what they did: 'What did you like about that beetle?' For car rides when you're not talking, play L2 music. It's best to choose music that has strong, clear vocals.

If you're spending a Saturday at home, read books in the L2 and listen to music in the language. If you have to go online for anything, go to sites in the L2. For example, when my kids want to bake, I search for L2 recipes by putting the food name and the word 'recipe' in Portuguese. If you're teaching Spanish, for example, you could search *recetas chile relleno* (chili relleno recipes). If you use certain spice bottles for these recipes, put a label on it in Spanish, like *pimentón* for 'paprika'. Use a marker to write harina on the bag of flour.

Remember that you don't need 'official' activities to use the L2. Here's an example. One Saturday my daughter needed a bun in her hair and I didn't know how to make one. I also wasn't sure what the word for 'bun' was in Portuguese, so I went to Google Translate, chose 'English to Portuguese' and entered 'make a bun'. After getting the terminology, I could go to YouTube and search *fazer um coque*. The videos showed Brazilians explaining how to make a bun. After my daughter and I watched the video, I tried following the directions while saying aloud what the video taught: *Agora fazemos um rabo de cavalo, etc.* ('Now we make a pony tail, etc.'). We both learned relevant vocabulary. There were also related videos on the right side of the screen. My daughter sat happily listening to other examples of haircuts and hairstyles, all in Portuguese. They were easy to understand because actions accompanied the words. And she was motivated to watch because the topic was interesting to her.

How much time?

How much time do parents need to expose their kids to the L2? The actual unit of time is negotiable. Just think through the time you've chosen – mornings, Sundays, etc. – to discover how to incorporate the L2 as much as possible. You might use it for a specific part of each day, like evenings after work. Make a list of what you usually do in the evenings. Then decide how things will be different in the L2. Bath time, changing clothes, teeth brushing and reading before bed can all be done in the L2.

Possibly the best advantage to this method is that it's easy to get started. You're not committing to full-time L2 speaking. You're fitting the L2 around your life. Chapter 3, 'Start Small, Start Now', and Chapter 8, 'The Play's the Thing', offer many examples of how to use the L2 in your daily or weekly routines.

Method: Situational bilingualism

You may decide to use the L2 in certain activities instead of basing language use on a parent or a time. This flexible strategy, called 'situational bilingualism', fits well with busy schedules.

Imagine using meals as the L2 situation. To get the most bang for your buck, try doing meal preparation in the L2, too. Introduce typical kitchen vocabulary – knife, oil, pan and refrigerator. Ask your kids, in the L2, to set the table. Label items that are hard to remember the word for, like 'napkin' in the napkin drawer. Use the L2 to ask about preferences for such things as milk or juice. If you're asking about things that involve unfamiliar vocabulary, hold up the actual object – a spatula or the orange juice carton. Learn dinner questions like 'Would you like more peas?' Make sure your children learn the 'magic words' such as 'please', 'thank you' and 'May I have more?'

During the meal, give everyone the chance to talk by throwing out a question. One that kids really like is the 'high/low question'. Each person shares what were the high point and the low point of their day. Answers can be very simple, such as 'I liked lunch'. Or they can be more complex, depending on language skills.

Understand that the activities themselves don't have to be educational in a traditional sense. Just find something you enjoy! For example, you may choose to watch a video in the L2. (See p. 115, 'Videos'.)

Watching a film may require some warm-ups to get your brains ready to understand new vocabulary. Look at the DVD cover, read some of the description and discuss what you think might happen. If the children have already seen the movie (in their L1 or in the L2), encourage them to remember what they liked, or what scared them or made them laugh.

After the movie, ask questions. 'What was your favorite part?' 'What surprised you?' 'What would you change about the ending?' If you have younger children, an artwork project can be used as an extension. Draw characters from the film. Have cartoon bubbles showing what your child would like the characters to say. None of this should be teachy or preachy. Just be interested in your child's perspective.

Is situational bilingualism enough?

Some families worry that progress using situational bilingualism will be slower than 'full-time' methods. My response continues to be that even degrees of exposure are a good goal. If you want to do situational bilingualism but feel your child isn't getting enough L2 input, come up with additional situations to use the L2 in, for example playing language-rich video games. And, board games and card games like Uno will work in any language. (See p. 120, 'Card games' and 'Board games'.)

Be sure you're giving your child adequate language input during the situations. This may mean talking about an L2 activity beforehand so your kids become familiar with the vocabulary. That way, when they're in the L2 situation, they'll have the tools to actually use the language. If you're doing bedtime reading in the L2, look though the book first, just talking with your child about the pictures and repeating new words when possible. Then ask your child to make predictions: 'What's he thinking?' and 'What's happening here?'

Remember that you're teaching a new habit. It takes exposure and practice. You'll also need a little discipline in using only the L2 during your planned situations.

Method: Locational bilingualism

Another way to divide languages is by location. This method, called 'locational bilingualism', has parents and children speaking the L2 in some places and the L1 in others. Often, the locations are split between the home and the outside world. Pearson describes a perfect example, an adult learner of Norwegian. She writes 'the threshold of his parents' home became his cue to switch from English to Norwegian' (Pearson, 2008: 186). Parents can model this 'switch' for their children by literally moving from one language to the other as they enter the home or the alternate location.

This method is often chosen by parents whose L1 is not the language of the country in which they live. A Spanish family living in England, for example, may speak English when outside the home but Spanish once they're in the house. It simplifies the question of when to speak which language, because the perimeters are so tangible.

Why choose locational bilingualism?

Some families choose the locational method to avoid being judged. They fear being met with negative stereotypes about the L2. They may worry that onlookers will think they don't speak the L1.

Parents also verbalized feeling nervous about speaking a language to their children that other people didn't understand. And they didn't want their kids to feel 'different'. One mom explains why she doesn't speak the L2 outside the home:

> The reason for this was to teach our children to be polite and speak the majority language when others could not understand … also [so that] I didn't make them [my kids] feel singled out and different from their peers. (J.N., interview)

Choices within the home

The choice of L2 at home and L1 outside the home still leaves some issues to be addressed. For example, how will you handle guests in the home who don't speak the L2? You actually can continue speaking the L2 even when non-L2 speakers are visiting. You just have to employ smart communication skills. Let's say you have a neighbor over for the first time and your son asks you a question in the L2. Before responding to him, explain the situation to your neighbor. 'We speak Hindi together. He was just asking about his soccer ball.' Then respond to your child in the L2. With this brief explanation and translation, guests are let in on the 'secret' and will most likely be supportive. And you'll preserve the home as an L2 haven.

When it comes to your children's peers coming to your home, you'll find that different kids have different tolerance levels for hearing a foreign language. My son has a friend who listens eagerly to our Portuguese and later asks about words he thinks sound interesting. My daughter, on the other hand, has a friend who interrupts even the briefest communication in Portuguese with 'TRANSLATION, PLEASE!' In this case, I give a brief translation before I talk to my daughter. It doesn't have to be word for word, just something general: 'I need to ask Sydney about her book bag.' The key is to be sensitive to other people's comfort levels while being true to your language decisions. As one mother puts it, 'Normally with adults it's okay [to speak the L2], but with other kids, we speak a bit of English [the L1] to connect more' (D.B., interview).

More Than Two Languages

If you are interested in implementing more than two languages, the four basic types of methodology still apply. Decide where, when, and who will speak which languages. Then work at being consistent. (See p. 102, 'Be consistent'.) I interviewed one family in the United States whose children were exposed to English in school, Urdu at home and Arabic in religious classes. Yes, the brain can handle it! In fact, bilinguals learn a third language faster than monolinguals, as shown by higher scores on oral and written tests (Cenoz, 2003).

Separating the Languages

Just as children learn to separate languages based on which parent speaks them (OPOL), they also find ways to know when and to whom to speak the L2 in the other methods. These language decisions are very complex. (See p. 90, 'Code-switching'.) Psychologist Janet Werker states that babies start separating language at seven months of age. They use cues like the pitch of the voice or the duration of the sounds (Werker in Lewis, 2013). As children get older, they come up with other differentiations. They may be flawed at first, but children will eventually figure them out. They may, for instance, separate language along gender lines.

In one American family, the mother spoke German to her young son and the father spoke English. The son had never heard anyone besides his mother speak German. One day they met a German man visiting the United States and the man started speaking German to the mother. The boy cracked up laughing and said to his father 'Daddy, that man talks just like Mommy!' (R.C., interview).

Children may also separate language according to age. A young child raised in Italy by Australian parents grew accustomed to hearing his Aussie parents and their expat friends speak English while the Italian children in his neighborhood spoke Italian. He was shocked, therefore, to visit Australia for the first time and hear children speak English – he assumed that children spoke Italian and adults spoke English.

Your children will eventually separate the languages along more conventional lines. In fact, children learn to do this even before they're old enough to have any meta-awareness about language. George Saunders described his own children learning German and English through the OPOL method. His son asked 'Daddy, what language am I speaking now?' (Saunders, 1988: 22). The question was asked in the right language, showing that the young child already knew which language to speak to which person.

Getting Kids on Board

Before expecting your kids to start using these methods, particularly if they are older, you'll need to create some initial interest, or 'intrigue'. Move your child away from feeling threatened by the new language and toward feeling curious about it. It helps to familiarize their ears to other languages in general. It doesn't even have to be the L2 you want them to learn – any foreign language will do. It's particularly helpful if they hear other parents and children speaking a foreign language together. One mother explains how this interaction normalized second languages for her son:

> I've noticed he got really a lot more open to speaking the other language when he found out I had a friend who's Chinese and spoke Chinese with her son, and then he [my son] wanted to speak more and he was more confident…. It's not so strange if others do it. (L.A., interview)

Keep your eyes out for speakers of other languages. If there's a mom from preschool who speaks Turkish to her son, strike up a conversation. Start with something simple, like 'I love how you speak Turkish with your son'. Or, if you're unsure of the language, say 'Excuse me, I'm so curious as to what language you are speaking'. Ask them to teach you and your child words and phrases like 'Hello' and 'How are you?' Or, if you're in line at the grocery and overhear another language, bring it to your child's attention and listen to the sounds. Later, discuss which language you think you heard. Also keep an eye out for kid-friendly activities and festivals with the words 'international', 'Asian', 'Latino' or 'Middle Eastern'. These festivals attract crowds who speak different languages.

Keeping Kids on Board

Even after your kids show interest, you'll need some strategies to keep them on board. Kids aren't interested in using language for language's sake. They want to get their message across as fast as possible. One example comes from a mother who was beginning to speak her L2, Spanish, with her son. She was frustrated that he would respond only in English. She states 'Martin responds in English because of the economy of the language' (C.O., interview).

Parents have to make the L2 the more 'economic' language. Let's say you decide to use situational bilingualism to learn Spanish. Your son keeps forgetting to say *cuchara* for 'spoon'. If you hand him a spoon even when he asks in English, you've made English the easier language. Instead, if he speaks in English, ask him a question in Spanish: '*¿Qué? ¿Qué te gustaría?*' ('What? What would you like?') If you think your child doesn't know or has forgotten the word for spoon, show him one on the countertop along with other utensils. When he points to the spoon, respond enthusiastically '*¡Ah, la cuchara!*' ('Oh, the spoon!') as if the mystery is finally solved. Ask him to say the new word: '*Diga "cuchara"*' ('Say "spoon"'). With this quick interaction, you've made it more efficient for him to speak in Spanish. (See p. 176, 'The efficient brain'.) And you've reminded him of the body language skill of pointing to things when he doesn't know the word in Spanish. The next time he needs something, he'll be less likely to ask in English, because using English took him longer to get what he wanted.

The more consistently you insist on Spanish, the more consistently your child will respond in Spanish. (See p. 102, 'Be consistent'.)

Your Commitment to the L2

There will be ups and downs in your own motivation level. Have you ever gone on a diet and then found yourself binging on your favorite dessert? Diet gurus say the biggest danger in cheating on your diet isn't that you take in some extra calories: it's that you might give up on your diet all together.

So avoid all-or-nothing thinking. You may have a period when you find yourself slacking off on speaking the L2. Instead of throwing up your hands and giving up, take a deep breath, think of what you'd rather do and forgive yourself. If your kids are old enough to understand, explain how in the last few hours or days or weeks, life circumstances got in the way of speaking the L2. Tell them you're starting anew. Then do something to mark the new beginning, like going bowling or going out for ice cream – all while speaking in the L2.

Fluid Methods

If you feel that you're trying hard but your strategies aren't working, try another method or a combination of methods. Or, if you feel that time-, location- or situation-based styles of learning aren't allowing enough input, increase the amount of time or add more places or more situations. For example, parents who speak the L2 only in the home might start speaking it on weekend outings. Parents using situation-based methods could add in 'car time' or enroll kids in L2 summer camps.

The most important thing is to relax and enjoy each other's company in the language. Know that you don't have to be stellar all the time. To quote the great philosopher Voltaire, 'Don't let the perfect be the enemy of good' (Jaquith, 2013). You are good enough! You can do this!

A Variety of Methods

- One parent one language (or one person one language) –one parent speaks the L1 to the child while the other speaks the L2.
- Two parents, child-directed speech – both parents speak the L2 with the child.
- Time-based bilingualism – one or more parent(s) speak(s) the L2 during certain times of day or days of the week.
- Situational bilingualism – families speak the L2 during certain situations – mealtimes, for example.
- Locational bilingualism – families speak the L2 depending on where they are at a given time. For example, they may speak the L2 at home, but not outside the house.

6   Marketing Strategies: Finding New Ways to Increase Motivation

The best marketing doesn't feel like marketing.
Tom Fishburne, Marketing Cartoonist (in Nelson, 2013)

This chapter is about more than just ways to advertise the L2 to your child. It's about more than bribing your kids to speak the language. It's about the whole child – what makes her tick and what will make her interested in the L2. You'll learn ways of interacting in the language that will leave your child wanting more.

Motivation

Before we can talk about marketing, we have to look at its building blocks. Mainly, motivation. What makes your child want to do something? What makes the L2 look appealing?

Creating is motivating

To motivate your kids, don't always be the boss. Researcher Dan Ariely, in his book *The Upside of Irrationality: The Unexpected Benefits of Defying Logic at Work and at Home* (2011), says that to motivate someone, you have to let that person create. Change won't come readily from a top-down decision. If you let your kids create part of the learning plan, they're more likely to stick with it.

What would that look like? Let's say you think time-based methods would be best for your family. Talk with your child about which times of day would work best. Let's say you have a four-year-old. She may think of snack time and play time. Be prepared, because a child that age may surprise you with responses such as 'time in the garden', even though you don't have a garden. Don't edit, since part of creating is brainstorming. Show her how important her answers are to you by gathering paper and pens to document her input. Let her do the illustrating. Hang the work in a prominent place.

Try to initiate some of your child's ideas straightaway. Take a walk in some green space near your apartment (the 'garden'). Point out things you notice and say them in the language, asking her to repeat. Help your daughter say the words for things she notices. This may mean taking your pocket dictionary with you, or Google Translate on your phone, since she may notice things you don't know the word for. (See p. 110, 'Where to find books in the L2'.)

Novelty is motivating

Children are motivated when you keep the ways you teach fresh and new. Our brains are hardwired to seek out novelty, so if something is new, it's often times considered more interesting and worthwhile. That's why paying attention to the same thing for a long time can be so arduous. It's why commercials pitch 'new, improved' versions of the same old products.

An example: instead of showing your child all five of the new Spanish books you bought, show her just one and bring out the others incrementally. If you're using situation- or time-based methods, change the ways you're spending time. Instead of eating at the table for lunch, move the meal outside for a picnic. The vocabulary surrounding you will be different, so you'll learn a different vocabulary set.

Even if you just make slight adjustments and eventually go back to the old way of doing things, these little modifications feel like novelty and will keep your kids (and you) more engaged.

Storytelling to create novelty

A fun way to create novelty is through storytelling. Even older children enjoy hearing stories, especially if they directly relate to them. Try inventing stories about people your children know and places they love.

Consider telling a three-word story. Ask your child for three words in the L2. If this is difficult, encourage him to look around and name objects in the room. Then tell a story that includes all three of the chosen words. The stories can get pretty weird if the words are ones like my kids choose: 'dustball', 'sports' and 'moon'.

Make-believe stories are new experiences in the L2. They employ vocabulary and expressions you might not be using in regular life.

Storytelling can also prepare children for an upcoming event. If you're going to a museum or aquarium, invent bedtime stories about a child in a museum or aquarium. Use the vocabulary you'll need when actually walking through the rooms – 'sculpture', 'sharks' and 'Don't touch!' After the visit, encourage children to tell stories about what they saw. The positive sense of ownership children receive from inventing their own stories will become associated with speaking the language.

Extra attention

It's important to offer extra attention when your child is working hard to respond in the L2. If it's breakfast time and your son is struggling to find the right word in the

L2, give him constant, eager eye contact. Offer words in the L2 that might be the ones he's searching for: 'Do you want milk¿ Butter¿' Or ask 'Can you show me by pointing¿' Stay with this as long as it takes to know what your child wants – investing all your energy and attention.

Another way to skillfully use attention is to offer extra feedback when your child speaks the L2. That way, the positive behavior is reinforced. Imagine your daughter has just used the L2 to tell you about a picture she drew. Point out how well she used the language: 'That makes sense because you explained it so well'. Encourage further L2 use with 'Wow, yeah, I see. Tell me more!' Over time, your child will connect speaking the language with the extra positive feedback.

Quicker response

If you want to make using the L2 worth your child's effort, respond more quickly to the L2 than to the L1. She'll learn that when she really wants something, the L2 is her best bet.

I'll give you a personal example. A boy in our neighborhood, Marco, had a Brazilian mother who spoke Portuguese to him. The mother repeatedly complained to me that, though he understood Portuguese, he would respond to her only in English. One snowy day, my kids and I were sledding and Marco, having no sled of his own, came out to join us. I decided that while we played, I would speak only Portuguese to him. Whenever he responded in English, I paid no attention. Things went on this way for some time until we found a great sledding hill. He quickly yelled out to me, in perfect Portuguese, '*Posso ir primeiro¿!*' ('Can I go first¿!').

Rewards

Reward is another strong motivator. If you've taken any psychology classes, you might remember B.F. Skinner's insistence that rewards encourage new behaviors: 'the consequences of an act affect the probability of its occurring again' (Association for Behavior Analysis International, 2013). If parents set up positive consequences for speaking the L2, children are more likely to use the L2 in the future. One mother discovered the carrot of positive reward quite by accident. She spoke French to her daughter and was sure she understood. Unfortunately, her daughter answered only in English. One day, when they were with some French-only speakers,

> A lady who only spoke French … was giving out cookies to kids who spoke French. And suddenly Mary Kate was able to put a sentence together to ask for a cookie. (J.F., interview)

Of course, we can't give a cookie to a child every time she speaks the L2. Not only because it would rot her teeth, but because we know rewards work best when they aren't given too often. But luckily, just the promise of a reward can be motivating.

I'll give an example. My kids love ice cream. I use it as a reward for speaking Portuguese when it's hardest for them – right after school. But I don't want to reward them with ice cream every afternoon. So I gave them each an empty tea box. For each afternoon they speak Portuguese after school without complaining, I give them a card to put in the box. After a certain number of cards, we hit the ice cream shop.

Some parents use money as a reward to speak the L2. It can be just a small amount of money. B.F. Skinner writes 'The way positive reinforcement is carried out is more important than the amount' (Skinner in Manitoba Government, 2013). An added bonus is that children learn the vocabulary around money itself. They learn words for 'penny' and 'dollar'. They learn math words such as numbers and 'more' and 'less'. If you're using situation- or time-based methods, you can distribute the money during and after the situation or time. You can also give it just before the time or situation and take money away when kids speak their L1. Avoid the punitive subtraction, though, if it stresses your kids out. The money should feel like a reward, not a punishment.

Create situations

There are a variety of ways to market the language to your children. One way is to create real situations where they use the language in fun ways. For example, if you're getting dinner ready, set your kitchen up like a restaurant. You could be the waiter, while the kids order food. Or let one of them be the waiter. Bring out paper and markers to write or draw the menu, and put prices beside each item.

Taking on these roles helps kids and adults *play* at using the language without any real repercussions from making mistakes. The distance you gain from playing make-believe helps kids work through their fears of saying something wrong. If they struggle with a word, encourage them to doodle a picture of the word on the menu. You can also ask them to act out the word. If they mimic someone slurping from a bowl, give them the vocabulary naturally: 'Oh! You'd like soup!' And tell them, 'Say, "I'd like soup"'.

Make it play

Your communication scenarios don't always have to be so involved. It's mainly important to have a mindset of fun. If L2 communication feels like play, you'll get more cooperation. Think about what you do when you're trying to motivate your kids to do any task. If you want them to help in the yard, you can use a non-fun approach: 'Rake the leaves or no TV this afternoon'. Or you can invent a game. 'Let's rake leaves into piles and see who can make the biggest pile.' In this same way, if you keep language learning positive, your kids will associate the L2 with enjoyment. For more ideas on making learning fun, see Chapter 8, 'The Play's the Thing'.

Correction

Parents I work with sometimes ask 'Is it all fun and games, or should we at some point crack down on errors?' They seem particularly frustrated when their children make the same mistakes over and over.

Lightweight correction

My advice is pretty straightforward: try to keep your correction 'lightweight' or you'll decrease your child's motivation to speak. (See p. 185, 'Correction: No nit-picking'.) One mother from Korea wrote me for advice. She felt she came down too hard on errors:

> There were some times I pushed them [my kids] hard because I wanted them to learn it SO bad. The methods of teaching I grew up with included great demands of hard work and perfectionism, not much of giving rewards or praises, if not any, but harsh punishments when children didn't meet the expectations. I know it sounds very mean, cruel, and weird, but that was how I was taught in Korea about 35 years ago. Maybe it was in my blood.... [Now] I believe teaching in my old fashion ways harmed my children's ability to learn another language more than it did good. Please help! (S.A., email correspondence)

In responding to her email, I mentioned how children have the goal of being understood, not of speaking without errors. (See p. 145, 'Errors are part of the process'.) So we parents have to balance our goals of correct speech with kids' goals of quick and easy communication. Baker writes,

A constant focus on language correctness and form is unnatural for the child, who is more interested in facts and ideas, stories, and activities. For the child, language is a means to an end, not an end in itself. Language is a vehicle to help move along the road of information exchange and social communication. (Baker, 2007: 64)

Organic correction

If we want children to learn from their mistakes, we have to let our teaching be as organic as possible. Let's start with an example of correction that might be misunderstood. It's of my husband and son speaking English. My husband gives a fairly direct correction to our son, James. It's misunderstood because James is attending to meaning, not grammar.

James: I <u>root</u> my name, Daddy, look.
Daddy: I <u>wrote</u> my name.
James: No, *I* did it, Daddy, not *you*!

A less direct, more organic correction would be:

James: I <u>root</u> my name, Daddy.
Daddy: You <u>wrote</u> what؟
James: I <u>wrote</u> my name.

In this case, James gets asked a real question, with the correct form embedded in it. Since the indirect correction is subtle, it may take some repetition and emphasis. Here is another example:

James: I <u>root</u> my name, Daddy.
Daddy: You <u>wrote</u> what؟
James: I <u>root</u> my name.
Daddy: You **wrote** your name؟ [Emphasis on the word 'wrote' by pronouncing it more slowly and using a higher-pitched voice.]
James: Yes [unspoken, '… I <u>wrote</u> it'].

You see in this last sentence, James still may not come out and say 'wrote' but he heard it repeated more than once, which should help him the next time.
One mother I interviewed takes a similar route in teaching her L2, English:

I avoid any outright statement that they have said something incorrectly. I fear they may feel constantly reprimanded and then refuse to speak English if they are made to believe they are always saying something 'wrong'. If one of my children says something incorrectly, for example 'Today at school Auntie *teached* us a new song', my response would be, 'She did؟ She taught you a new song؟ I would love to hear it!' (N.L., interview)

Code-Switching

Be prepared to see your child doing what's called 'code–switching'. That's when they mix the L1 and L2. François Grosjean, author of *Life with Two Languages*, says that children who code-switch have a 'shift completely to the other language for a word, a phrase, a sentence' (Grosjean in Navracsis, 2003: 4). You might assume this is happening because you are a non-native speaker, but, in fact, bilingual children with native-speaking parents exhibit the same phenomenon.

It may appear your child is confused when he combines languages, but, actually, it is quite normal. Dr Steiner notes,

> Just because a child cannot immediately 'find' a word in one language and then makes the decision to insert the correct word that he knows from another language, does not mean he's confusing the language or that he's confused about which language that he's speaking. It's merely a matter of expedience. The child is doing whatever he can do to get his needs met. (Steiner, 2008: 115)

It's important we see code-switching as a valuable tool for expression. Baker writes that code-switching 'does not happen at random. There is usually considerable reason and logic in changing languages' (Baker, 2000: 53). For example, sometimes a word in the L1 is shorter than the one in the L2, or the L2 doesn't have an equivalent word, just an expression that would take longer to say.

Children also code-switch to show emphasis (Baker, 2007), with the L1 being used as a flag to say 'Look, this is important!' It can be used by children to try to change the mood. Researchers W. Low and D. Lu (2006) write 'Code-switching may be used to ease tension and inject humor…. If discussions are becoming tense, [the switch] may signal a change in the "tune being played"' (Low & Lu in Baker, 2011: 109).

Children can also switch to the L2 to give what David Schwarzer calls 'not only the facts of the event, but also the taste of it' (Schwarzer, 2001: 7). When speaking Portuguese, my children tend to use the English word 'Halloween' instead of the Portuguese equivalent. Though there exists a translation, the actual word 'Halloween' holds for them the memories – sights, scents, tastes – that make up the holiday.

A study from the *Journal of Child Language* suggests that even children as young as two years recognize they are speaking two languages and are making choices about which to use, based on the context (Lanza, 1992: 633). If an English-speaking child is learning French, she may still use English to describe a cookie, even if she knows a French translation. So she might say '*Je veux un* cookie'.

As your child gets older, code-switching rules will become more complex. Edith Harding-Esch and Philip Riley write that code-switching is used

> in very subtle ways to express their feelings, emotions or degree of involvement in a conversation, or simply to show that in their family setting they can, if they are tired, use both languages interchangeably and still be understood. (Harding-Esch & Riley, 2003: 63)

Parents must decide how much they're going to encourage code-switching. If you feel it helps your British child feel competent if he can switch to the L1 to discuss cricket, then it may be worth it to let him switch without correction. Every family is different in what they encourage. I don't correct my children if they are giving a quick quote of something an L1 speaker has said. If you find, however, that switching for one topic encourages switching back to the L1 for many topics, you might discourage the switching.

One step you can take is to guide them to the L2 on the words they say in the L1, emphasizing the L2 word.

Your child: *Il était sur une* [He was on a] motorcycle.
Parent: *Il était sur une motocyclette*? [He was on a motorcycle?]

If you find you are having to intervene too much, try giving less language and asking more.

Your child: *Il était sur une* [He was on a] motorcycle.
Parent: *Il était sur un quoi*? [He was on a what?]

Another action you can take relates to your own code-switching. It is tempting to mix languages, especially when discussing certain subjects. Myles writes,

My husband and his cousin generally use Farsi to speak with each other, but when it comes to discussing home improvement they usually shift to English. Why? It's because they both entered the home-owning phase of their lives in the United States, and in the US the folks at Home Depot usually don't speak Farsi. (Myles, 2003: 49)

But if your children are with you, it might be worth making the effort to speak only in the L2, even when it is inconvenient. Finally, you can heed the advice of Edith Harding-Esch and Philip Riley: give your child multiply occasions when they are in contact with people who truly understand only one of the languages (Harding-Esch & Riley, 2003: 155).

The most important thing to remember is not to demonize these changes in language. Dr Ofelia Garcia uses the term 'translanguaging', whereby the change from one language to another is 'what a key change in the middle of a symphony is to music' (Vinson, 2014).

Staying in the L2

Sometimes children switch from the L2 to the L1 for reasons that wouldn't be classified as code-switching. They may stop speaking the L2 in mid-sentence when they aren't sure of a word. Or they may start speaking in the L1 for no apparent reason.

Parents have different approaches to handling this. Some are quite direct. One Brazilian woman who lives in Australia and speaks Portuguese at home states,

> When Nina had two and a half years we didn't correct with her if she wanted to speak the wrong language with us, but now [that she's three years old], we're harder in this. We say, 'it's not wrong, but we want in Portuguese'. (D.B., interview)

Other techniques are more indirect and may better suit sensitive kids. Let's look at some specifics.

Gentle trigger

One technique is called a 'gentle trigger'. That's a word or expression that redirects your child into the L2. You could ask *'In Italiano?'* (In Italian?). Or you could hum a couple of notes from a song like 'Frère Jacques'. Any interruption that's noticeable, but not overly intrusive.

When my children were really young, I tried using a sound – *peep* – in a squeaky voice. When they'd say a word in English, I'd *peep*. This strategy worked for a while, and the children even started peeping each other. Eventually it lost its effectiveness, and we moved on to other strategies.

Feeding

Another way to move children from their L1 to the L2 is called 'feeding'. If your child seems to be stuck and unable to find the word, give him bits and pieces of the language as he needs it.

This doesn't mean that you become an instant translator, giving him the word in the L2 whenever he says it in the L1. If you play translator, he'll have no real reason to use the L2 on his own. (Remember how we try to make the L2 the more efficient language?)

A better option when your child is searching for a word is to get him to show you the meaning. We've already discussed some simple ways to do this. Ask him to point to the object he's trying to say. Or encourage him to gesture the word. Then, you guess the meaning and feed him the L2 word. Right after 'feeding' the word, ask your child to repeat it.

Ask questions that have the word they're searching for in the answer. Here's an example. In this dialogue, the child speaks Spanish as a first language and is learning English. He's saying the word for 'spider' in the L1 and the parent is guiding him toward using the L2.

> Child: In that video game, an ant crawled on me and an *araña* [spider] tried to eat me.
> Parent: Who tried to eat you?

Child: An *araña*.

Parent: Show me it with your fingers. [Child makes the 'Itsy-bitsy spider' hand motion.] A spider, wow!

Child: Yeah.

Parent: So, which one was bigger? The spider or the ant?

Child: The spider!

The parent reminded the child of the miming strategy: 'Show me it with your fingers'. The parent may even have to start the 'Itsy-bitsy spider' motions, but just enough to give the child the idea of using gestures as tools. It needs to look as though the parent didn't understand *araña* and is getting the idea for the word 'spider' from the child. (See p. 119, 'Motions to music'.)

Once the parent guessed 'spider', she could have followed up with 'Say "spider"'. Instead, she chose to ask a very specific question, 'So, which one was bigger? The spider or the ant?' This question leads the child to use the word 'spider.' Be sure when asking a question to make it as real as possible, as if you don't already know the answer. You want your interactions to feel more like communication and less like education.

Feeding forward

There are simple ways to do some pre-emptive 'feeding' when you know your child will need certain words before she actually needs them. Let's say you're giving your son a yellow truck as a birthday present. Think of words he'll need to talk about the gift. While he is playing with it, say 'Wow, look at that truck. It's so big and yellow. Do you have any other cars or trucks with big wheels like that one?'

This feeding technique is helpful with my kids' after-school talk. To share their day, they need vocabulary like 'recess' and 'art project'. Their school schedules are posted on the fridge so I can ask questions that use the vocabulary they'll need. In the afternoon, after school pick-up, before they even have to talk, I ask some specific questions that are loaded with vocabulary:

- You had music today, right? Did you sing or play an instrument?
- In recess, did you play basketball or soccer?
- Did you have your math test today? Was it hard or was it easy?

If your L2 skills are less developed, your questions might be:

- Was music good? Piano? Singing?
- Was art fun today? Drawing? Painting?

Feeding can also take the form of personal stories that include useful expressions. If you know your child will need to talk about a math test, you could share 'When I had math tests, I had to be careful to check my work…'. In this way, you are naturally feeding forward. If children have the vocabulary before they need it, they are empowered to communicate more independently in the L2. They'll talk more!

Reinforcing

If you've just fed your child a word, you'll want to reinforce it so she'll remember it next time. Just like with the spider example, reinforcement takes the form of simple follow-up questions. It also involves working to keep the conversation going so your child can practice the new words on her own.

I'll give an example from my journal, but I'll swap the languages and use English as the L2. I feed Sydney the word 'own'. I am trying to get her to say the word in English. You'll see that it took a few tries for Sydney to actually say 'own'.

> Sydney: See, I have my _próprio_ pillow.
> Me: What?
> Sydney (shows me her pillow): My pillow, see?
> Me: Oh, you have your <u>own</u> pillow?
> Sydney: Yeah.
> Me: Do you think Granny has her <u>own</u> pillow, or does she use Paw Paw's?
> Sydney: I don't know.
> Me: Hmm … maybe she has her <u>own</u> pillow.
> Sydney: James doesn't have his <u>own</u> pillow. He's just a baby.

In this example, I was grabbing at straws to come up with questions that would elicit the word 'own' in English. Eventually, though, it worked. You've just got to keep at it!

Non-reacting

If you feel like your children know the words in the L2 but aren't using them, you can try another technique I call 'non-reacting'. It's also called 'pretending'. (See p. 181, 'False monolingual strategy'.) When children are very little, pretending can be a bit of a trick whereby children really don't think the L2 parent speaks the L1. As one author puts it,

> Children may believe it for a long time. I have heard of children informing mono-lingual teachers or other adults that there isn't any use trying to talk to the parent because he or she doesn't understand the majority language [the L1]. (Myles, 2003: 100)

As your children get older and realize you do actually speak the L1, you can use the fact that you know both languages to help them when they get stuck. For example, if your daughter asks for a cookie in the L1, you ignore the request. Show that you heard her by saying 'Excuse me?' Let's say that when she repeats her request, she puts some of the words in the L2. React only to the L2 part of what she says. For example, if she asks 'Mommy, can I have a *galleta*?', ask her 'A what?' If your child genuinely seems to have forgotten the word 'cookie', give the first syllable: 'A coo…' That's usually enough to jog her memory.

I didn't realize just how accustomed my kids were to non-reacting until I heard them talking to an acquaintance of mine. She asked how the kids learn Portuguese with so much English around. My daughter replied 'My mom acts like she doesn't understand, even though she does'. My son added 'She won't do what we say unless we say it in Portuguese'.

Is non-reacting cruel?

It may appear cruel for parents to pretend not to understand their children. I would argue two points. First, if your child is upset, that's not the time for ignoring what he says. You want him to feel loved. So, parental discretion is advised.

Second, we must realize that parents already practice non-reacting, particularly when it comes to teaching acceptable behavior and good manners. (See p. 181, 'Eat your peas, speak the L2'.) These corrections can be done in a loving way, with positive results. Imagine a father whose daughter says to him at dinner 'Give me the potatoes'. He may decide not to pass the potatoes until she makes a more polite request, such as 'Please pass the potatoes'. Just as we give prompts in the L2, he might give prompts: 'Use the magic words' or 'Try that again'. Only after she uses the right language does she get the potatoes. So even in our L1, we expect children to use certain words and expressions. Having expectations for the L2 is not much different.

Paraphrase and Postpone

When you don't know the word for something, resist the urge to switch back to your L1. It's understandable that you won't always have a dictionary at your fingertips, but that doesn't mean you leave the L2. What do you do, then, when you're in mid-conversation and you need a word? Saunders (1988) suggests using a brief paraphrase. When talking with his children, if he doesn't know a word, he acknowledges he's in doubt. He and his children agree on a paraphrase until he can look up the word. After he looks up the word, he is careful to teach it to the children. In doing so, he shows them that they don't have to know everything and that they don't have to resort to the L1 when they're in doubt.

You are good enough!

To keep your child motivated and consistent, try to be motivated and consistent yourself. (See p. 102, 'Be consistent'.) If you find your motivation lacking, do what the best-selling motivational writer Dale Carnegie suggests: '*Act* enthusiastic and you'll *be* enthusiastic' (Goodreads, 2013). If you genuinely think bilingualism is worth the effort, this 'fake it till you make it' attitude will get you over the hump until you're feeling genuinely enthusiastic again. (See p. 22, 'I don't know enough'.)

If you're *frequently* feeling unmotivated or frustrated, your current methods might not fit your lifestyle. In this case, consider redefining your goals, reassessing your choice of methods or making changes to your environment.

Fun Ways to Increase Children's Motivation

- Put your children in charge. Encourage them to choose the game to play or to decide how to spend the afternoon.
- Seek out novelty. Keep your plans new and offer fresh materials like books and music.
- Tell stories. Let children tell part or all of the ending and include their friends and pets in the stories.
- When your child expresses energy and motivation, pay extra attention. Offer extra feedback like 'Wow, I like that you're getting so excited about this!'
- Offer positive consequences for speaking the L2. Anything from sweets to monetary rewards.
- Make role-plays in the L2, like setting up your kitchen as a restaurant.

7 Talk Talk Talk: Strategies for When to Talk and What to Talk About

For the things we have to learn before we can do them, we learn by doing them. –
Aristotle, *The Nicomachean Ethics* (in Sacred Text Archive, 2012)

The idea of speaking a language to learn a language is counterintuitive. I remember as a child not knowing how to spell a word. My mother suggested I look it up in the dictionary. 'Look it up in the dictionary!?' I thought. 'But I don't know how to spell it!'

That's how you learn a foreign language. You must talk if you want to learn to talk. This upside-down way of learning can cause frustration, but it gets results. Author Elizabeth Berg, in her book *Joy School*, writes:

> My French teacher … wears French things like a scarf … and she smells like good perfume. But her problem is that she never speaks English to us and sometimes we just need to know something. It is only beginning French. So what I want to know is where does she get off from the first day rattling on in French, French, French? But here is the most surprising thing: I am learning French. (Berg, 1998: 15)

Who to Talk to?

Some parents worry they don't have anyone to speak the language to. I tell them to open themselves up to meeting international people. They don't have to be speakers of your L2. Spend time with speakers of any second language. Ask them to teach you and your child how to say greetings in their language. Or ask how to express something silly. This will show your child that language is fun. It sparks curiosity about language in general. This also has the positive side-effect of easing those feelings of 'Are we the only ones who speak something different?'

Limited Vocabulary

Having a limited vocabulary in the L2 can be a concern to parents as they try to build their child's word base. It is, though, usual for children to have a smaller vocabulary in their L2, and it by no means indicates a linguistic deficit. Recognize that even with fewer words in the L2, your child's vocabulary overall is superior to that of most other children. Studies show that 'a child's total combined vocabulary in two languages will far exceed the monolingual's in one language' (Baker, 2000: 66).

Non-Native Worries

Some parents worry about talking to their children with their non-native accent. Ana Flores and Roxana Soto, in *Bilingual Is Better*, write 'As long as you are not the ONLY Spanish [as a second language] model the child ever has, he will be very unlikely to pick up your accent' (Flores & Soto, 2012: 91).

Sometimes, being a non-native speaker can be a plus, if it makes you more committed to finding L2 resources. Pearson's book *Raising a Bilingual Child* presents a case study of two parents who used sign language and Spanish with their daughter, Sophia, even though neither parent learned these languages from birth. The author writes:

> The lack of native skill on the part of her parent has had little effect on [11-year-old] Sophia's language development. If anything, it has made the parents more willing to make the effort to find other language experts. (Pearson, 2008: 182)

Early-Morning Talk

To build vocabulary, consider the morning time golden. Studies show our brains are better prepared for learning after sleep. And one recent investigation showed that morning study is more effective than evening study with regard to memory. So the vocabulary boosting you do in the morning will tend to stay with you longer.

At the beginning of each morning, discuss different times of day. This gives children exposure to different verb tenses. Begin with talking about the past. Tell them what you dreamed about and ask what they dreamed about. Ask what stuffed animal they slept with. Offer them the chance to create in the language with 'What did your animal dream about?'

From here, start talking about what's happening in the moment. Just a running commentary – 'Such a pretty morning. It's cold in this house. Are you hungry? I'm really hungry. Let's make something warm to eat today.' For older children, ask 'How are you feeling this morning? Are you looking forward to the day?'

As your child eats, discuss the day ahead, building the vocabulary you'll need later to talk about the day's activities. Keep a dictionary near the table and look up words you don't know – like 'park' or 'science quiz'. (See p. 62, 'Dictionary clues'.)

Regardless of when you talk, use every opportunity to teach words like numbers ('three more bites'), times of day (afternoon, night) and emotion vocabulary ('Are you happy/sleepy/sad?'). You are doing what any other parents do for their kids' development, just in another language.

I Feel Silly

You may feel silly, as I did, talking to an infant or very young child in another language. It gets easier with time. One mother I interviewed recognized how important it is to keep talking to your child:

> When our son, Jonathan, was born, we found that it felt strange and unnatural to speak German to him. It wasn't until Jonathan started responding a little more, around 8–10 months, that we started to feel more comfortable with the German. I memorized German lullabies and nursery rhymes, which helped significantly. By the time Jonathan started talking, we felt extremely comfortable speaking German with him. In fact, it felt very unnatural to speak English to him. (S.S., interview)

Another mother said she was fine talking in her home, but when she was in public, she felt like other people saw her as a show-off. (See p. 28, 'Showing off'.) Her persistence, however, paid off:

> It has got MUCH easier now that we are actually having conversations and it's not just me talking to myself. When he was younger, I did feel incredibly pretentious in front of people I knew … but now that he replies in full sentences, people are criticizing me less and less – at least to my face. (M.G., email interview)

Striking a balance between believing in yourself while at the same time not taking yourself too seriously is the key to getting past feeling silly.

Puppets Make Learning Play

Puppets make it easy to use the L2 and to take yourself less seriously. They let you talk about things you don't normally talk about. And since you can use your imagination and invent stories, a whole new set of vocabulary comes up.

You don't have to buy puppets. You can make them from something as simple as a sock. You can even just use your hand as a puppet with your top four fingers as the top of the mouth and the thumb as the bottom. Use dots of pen for eyes at your ring and middle finger knuckles. And *voilà*!

Puppets and dialogue

Puppets also give your child exposure to dialogue in the language. Your child will get to hear simple, fun communication between you and the puppet. She will want to talk

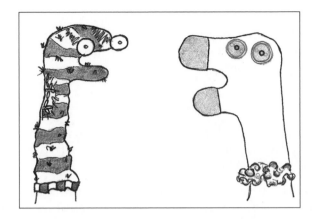

to the puppet, too. You might ask her to choose things around the room that she thinks the puppet would like. A toy teacup, for example. The website of the Newfoundland and Labrador Department of Education and Early Childhood Development (2014) notes 'Puppet play is open-ended and provides students with opportunities to be supported in situations that are unfamiliar or challenging'.

Imagine this dialogue in the language you're teaching.

Monique the Puppet: Oh, a cup of tea. Thank you! I love tea. Would anyone else like a cup of tea?
Parent: Oh, I'd love a cup of tea, please. [Asking child.] Do you want a cup of tea?
Child: Yes.
Parent: Tell Monique.
Child: Cup tea.
Parent: Say, 'A cup of tea, please'.
Child: Cup of tea, please.
Monique the Puppet: Ohhhh, you want a cup of tea, too? Good! Here's your cup of tea.

Monique can go on to ask if anyone would like sugar, cream, etc. Having the puppet as the third speaker lets so much more conversation practice take place.

Another advantage of a puppet is that it's easy to transport. On long trips, for example, it can go in the car with you. The passenger-side parent can make long trips fun by pointing through the window and discussing what the puppet sees. You can take the puppet outside and talk about what's around in nature.

Monique the Puppet: I want to climb a tree.
Parent: You can't do that. You don't know how to climb.
Monique the Puppet: I can learn. Can you teach me, please? [Looking at the child.]

Child: I climb.
Parent: What do you climb?
Child: Tree.
Parent: Tree? Oh, trees, you climb trees!

Once your child's gotten used to having the puppet around, just pulling it out serves as a trigger to speak the L2.

Your child – the puppeteer

Give your child the freedom to be the puppeteer. You'll see how much more imaginative things become with her playing this new role.

Older children may be able to remember lines and put on a little puppet show. If you don't have a readily available audience, record the show on your phone or camera. That way it'll feel more important. It also gives you a way to reflect on it later, extending the learning with your child by asking 'Why did Monique do that?' 'Was she sad/mad/being silly?' You can help children plan subsequent shows based on what you learned from the first ones. (Consider starting a private YouTube channel to house the videos – you can send the link to friends and family.)

And remember, the sillier the better. Laughter helps make the connections between the left and right brain. That will aid with how memory works and store the new learning for later use.

Sing!

Take a moment to think of songs you remember from childhood. I did an informal study asking people which ones they remember, and the ABC song was at the top. Some of us are still using that song when we need alphabetical order. Add singing to your repertoire of learning strategies. Your children will remember lyrics, adding to their vocabulary.

Rhythm and rhyme

Rhymes in songs help us know how to pronounce words. And they teach us the rhythm of the language. Lyrics are fun to sing along to, and that motivates children to learn them. When we have a certain block of lyrics in our heads, we're taking in the grammar of that chunk of language. The repetition cements those chunks into our brains.

Music can help children learn grammar. If a child knows, for example, the lyrics to 'I'm a little teapot', then she's got the framework to extrapolate to 'I'm a little girl'. Or, if a child knows 'I've been working on the railroad', he can extrapolate to 'I've been playing in my room'. Children aren't conscious of these connections, but it gives them a foundation on which to build additional, unique bits of language.

What to do with songs

If you can learn some of the popular L2 kids' songs, sing them around the house and in the car. Try to change the lyrics around to sing about your child. Let's say you're singing that oddly violent French song 'Alouette', where each line talks about plucking another part of the *alouette* (lark). Once you've gotten through the head, the neck, etc., add in some more human body parts, even if they're silly ones, like 'fingernail'. The more you expand on that structure, the more your child sees how universal and useful the expressions are.

Here's an odd trick for using singing to teach vocabulary:

> I went to the opera last night ... it gave me an idea. I started singing in a silly opera voice to Sydney. She always has trouble remembering the expression, *papel hygênico* [toilet paper], so I sang a silly song about it and repeated the words and sang her questions like 'Will you be needing toilet paper?' in an operatic voice. She got into it after a while and sang to me what she preferred for breakfast, etc. (journal, 12/17/2005)

Be Consistent

Though learning is fun, it also requires some work to keep children using the L2. Parents insist that certain behaviors (e.g. speaking at an appropriate volume) have a time and a place (e.g. in a gallery) by using particular expressions (e.g. 'Inside voices!'). The same should be true of which languages children speak to which people. Be consistent with which language you speak, even when it's tiring, even when you don't feel like it and even when you're in a bad mood. Just as you have to discipline a child when you don't necessarily have the energy, that level of consistency is important to help your kids see the order in your language choices. One mom writes,

> I have persevered speaking exclusively to him in French ... even when he replied to me in English for 6 solid months (around 2.0 to 2.6 years). However, since last summer, something clicked and he now addresses me in French I'd say 98% of the time. (M.G., email interview)

Circumnavigate

Some parents wonder how to be consistent in the L2 when they don't always have the vocabulary they need. If this is an issue for you, it's important to think of what you do in your first language when you don't know a word – you find another way to get your meaning across. It's called 'circumnavigation' and it's reminiscent of the early explorers – having to sidestep and go out of the direct path due to unforeseen difficulties.

Let's imagine you forget the word 'hammer'. Think of an alternate way to get the information across. You can do the motion of hammering with your hands. If that doesn't work, you can say 'It hits things into the wall'.

Teach your child the general words and expressions like 'thingy' and 'thingamagig'. (See p. 64, 'Learn some basics'.) Help her learn categories for circumnavigation. If she knows descriptive words like 'tall'/'short', 'flat'/'round' and color words, she can easily get her message across. If she forgets the word 'cherries', she can say 'the little red round things Daddy likes'.

One mom states she is sometimes tempted to just use the word in English, if she doesn't know it in Spanish, but 'I work hard to – even with Cheerios – make up a little word like … "little circles"' (K.C., interview).

When you notice your child negotiating meaning and inventing expressions in the L2, be attentive and excited to guess what she's saying. It can be a real confidence booster for your child to successfully get her meaning across even when the exact word escapes her.

Playgroups

Another language boost for children comes from communicating with other children in the L2. Myles writes,

> One study of sixty Spanish, German, and Vietnamese-speaking bilingual families notes that one of the most effective strategies parents could use to support their children's bilingual language development was to find children their own age and have them play together. (Myles, 2003: 52)

A wonderful way to find these children is to search for playgroups in the L2. Search 'German playgroups Atlanta' or ask native speakers you know if they've heard of a German expat playgroup. You may feel reticent at first to attend a gathering, since you're not German. But parents I interviewed said these groups welcomed them and were flattered that someone wanted to learn their language. One mother who speaks her L2, English, to her child says the playgroup helped speaking English make sense:

> Jan [her baby] and I went to an expat playgroup with two other moms, one from Austria and one from Canada. It made so much sense to speak English to Jan then! I hope to become a permanent member of such a group, especially for when Jan is older and can interact with other children. (J.A., interview)

Not only will your children be speaking the L2 with other children, you'll be talking to adult native speakers. You'll learn the language you need to talk to your children by overhearing other moms talking to their kids. And you can share resources like books and music.

If there isn't a group of your L2, consider starting one, even with just three or four parents. Many native speakers of a language would welcome time with other moms, and being able to speak in their own tongue makes it all the more inviting. The meetings need not be complicated. Gather in a park, in someone's home, a public library or a café. Avoid mealtimes if you want to keep preparation simple. Use the time together to share the joys and challenges of parenting.

Part-Time Babysitter Who Speaks the Language

Another way to get L2 exposure is to hire a babysitter who speaks the L2. Having someone come on a regular basis – on a certain day of the week, for example – is particularly helpful because they form a rapport with your child.

I did this with a Brazilian woman who lived nearby. She came twice a week for two hours each time. Not only did the kids get exposure to the language, but I did, too, and the kids overheard L2 dialogue when the sitter and I spoke.

It's important, just as with a nanny, to establish that this is more than a babysitting job. There should be language exchange taking place. To facilitate language use, leave books on hand for her to read to the children and card games to play (such as 'Go Fish', or a regular deck of cards for older children). Model some of the interactive play you'd like her to do with the children.

Make your expectations known. No television or radio – this time should be active. Speaking, reading and music should all be in the L2. Have a casual debriefing with your child after the time with the sitter. This will reinforce what your child has learned. Instead of vague, 'What did you learn?' questions, ask specific questions: 'What did you do first?' 'What did you eat as a snack?' 'Which books did you read?'

In these debriefings, I learned that the sitter was taking the children to visit her mother-in-law (who doesn't speak the L2). She was also doing her laundry at our house. I had a conversation with the sitter to discuss language goals. I asked her to help the children make a poster or card during each of her visits with words and pictures to describe their time together. This was a means to hold her accountable and also a way for her to 'get credit' for her work. Eventually she became more like an aunt to the kids and a friend to me. She stills serves as an anchor to the target country.

Long-Term Babysitter or Nanny

If you're interested in a long-term babysitter who speaks the L2, know that she can provide a very strong foundation for later learning. This is particularly true if she and your child bond emotionally. The connection will translate into loving the way that person talks, infusing the language with positive associations.

The best way to find a sitter is word of mouth. If you know a native speaker, ask if they know of an L2 speaker interested in babysitting long term. If you do not have a personal connection to a potential babysitter, carefully vet candidates through background checks to make sure they are safe.

In your initial contact with the sitter or nanny, make your expectations about the L2 known. Be clear that in your household, and even outside the house with your child, the L2 is to be spoken. If you have a contract, the language component could be explicitly described.

From the first time you meet the sitter or nanny, establish the L2 as the language you'll use, as it is difficult to change languages once one has been established. If there are certain parts of the language you don't feel comfortable in (for example, compensation, dates and times, and contractual language), then, by all means, use English. Find a polite way to say 'I'm going to say just this part in English', to show that it's only a limited bit of communication.

For those of you learning the L2, time with the sitter provides great opportunities to speak and listen. When your child is present, work hard to use only the L2. If you are a novice in the language, talk with the sitter using body language and pointing to learn simple expressions you need with your child. Be humble enough to welcome correction and you'll learn even more.

Au Pairs

Hiring an au pair from the L2 country is an amazing way to share the language with your child. But keep in mind the motivation of the person applying for the position. Is she coming to see a different way of life? Is she hoping to someday move to your country? Does she want to study in a local university? It's imperative to make sure the au pair isn't expecting your home to be a place to practice the L1. This is a perfectly acceptable goal in most households, but you will want to disclose your L2 objectives.

There are several good books to help with the interview process and with the au pair experience in general. For an easy and entertaining guide, go with *Oh My, Au Pair: A Complete Guide to Hiring and Hosting an Au Pair* (Felix, 2009).

Make sure you ask your au pair to bring resources like books, music and DVDs in the L2, making it clear you will reimburse all costs incurred.

Once she arrives, be curious. Remember that most people love to talk about themselves. Ask to see pictures of her family, find out what she likes to do, take her to local places of interests and get her perspective on things. Anyone with the guts to move abroad is probably ready for some adventure, so don't be afraid to try interesting places and activities. Once she's been away from home for a few weeks, take her to a restaurant with the food from her country and asks lots of questions about which of these dishes she eats at home.

If you have an infant and want to learn 'baby talk', spend time with the au pair when she and the baby are interacting. Parents of older children can spend time with the au pair, too, learning kid-friendly language. Ask questions about how to say certain words. If she's into cooking, stock the pantry and fridge with ingredients she needs for making local dishes and learn beside her. Find out what books she's brought from her country and ask about the ones she's reading in her free time. Consider yourself a detective. Within reason, try to glean everything you can from this person you've invited into your lives.

Full-Time Immersion or Dual Language Daycare

Full-time immersion or dual language daycare and school can be wonderful for exposing your children to the L2, especially if your own skills are just budding. Before you register, observe some classes and ask yourself:

- How much of the actual instruction time is in the L2? For immersion programs, you should see 80% or more of the instruction in the L2. For dual language, at least 40%.
- Is the teacher always talking, or is he using activities in the language that get the kids talking? Students will learn more if they are active – not passive – observers.
- Do students interact among themselves in the language? It's rare during free time for kids to speak in the L2 to each other, but during more structured activities with teacher involvement, they should be encouraged to interact in the L2. This helps them learn the language it takes to talk to their peers, as opposed to just what they need for talking to teachers and other adults.
- Are there a variety of fun activities in the L2? Children get bored quickly. The teacher should have a bag of tricks at hand to keep up the pace and make sure the class is interesting.
- Do children look at ease? If children are anxious, they not only learn less, they form negative associations with the foreign language.

Ask the teacher

Find out how the teacher learned the language by asking him questions about himself. He needn't be a native speaker, as long as he can communicate fluidly and encourages kids to do the same. You might also ask the teacher how he feels students best acquire a language. Hopefully, you'll hear that kids need to listen to and speak the language in real contexts.

If the time spent in the L2 is a few rhymes and some songs, recognize that you're not seeing immersion. If teachers are speaking *about* the L2 but not actually using it, again, that's not immersion. Children still learn in these programs, but not as efficiently as they would if they were immersed in the language.

Language classes

Many towns offer some type of language classes for children. Just search for '<L2> classes for children' with the name of your town. If you're using a less commonly taught language, try looking for a tutor instead. Craig's List, the website for classified advertisements, has a section 'Lessons and Tutoring' which can be helpful as long as you are careful to get references, for the sake of both safety and quality. Ask for a preview class or session before committing financially. You want to make sure the instructor and the level of input are a good fit. The most important criterion is that your child is enjoying himself. If it's fun, the positive vibe will ensure motivation.

After-School Programs and Summer Camps

Make the most of children's after-school and summer free time by registering them for language camps. Steven Pinker writes,

> Children care more about their peers than about their parents, so send them to summer camps, after-school programs, or vacations where they will have to use the language with kids their own age. (Pinker, 2007: 9)

You might be surprised by the variety of after-school programs in other languages. Montessori offers after-school programs that teach Spanish, French and Italian, alternating languages each quarter. Taking all three would be beneficial to show kids how to look for linguistic similarities and differences.

Summer language camps are becoming more and more popular. Search online for '<L2> language camp' in your area. Even if these are just a week long, they let children play in the language and learn vocabulary through games and crafts. Your kids can then teach you what they've learned. Expressions like 'Ready, set, go!' become part of your daily life.

Volunteer in class

If you volunteer to help in your child's language class, you'll get first-hand experience of what he's learning. Don't be afraid if you're a novice in the language. Even if you're just straightening up the bookshelves or sorting papers, you will benefit from overhearing the language.

Consider your child's class or after-school program as a springboard, not an end in itself. Notice that when you pick him up from class, his brain is clicked into L2 mode. Continue that mode while you can. Listen to an L2 CD in the car on the way home. As you're looking outside the car windows, point out things of interest, with follow-up questions in the L2: 'Oh, look at that truck! What do you think is inside?' If you're on a bus or the subway, you could play 'I spy' with the colors and objects around you. 'I spy with my little eye something yellow!' Kids can point to things they don't know the word for and you can help.

You can make it a habit to talk about the language class only in the L2, so that talking about the class itself becomes a trigger to speak the language. You can ask before class 'Are you ready for Mandarin class?' and 'What will you do in class today?', all in the L2.

Commitment

This chapter has demonstrated how talking to your child is key to teaching the language. It has also indicated that parents must seek out other speakers and L2 resources. Commitment to sharing the L2 means work, but it will pay off. One mother explains,

> I have been very committed to my decision to raise my children in a bilingual environment. It has not come easily. I have provided them with ... Japanese language books, videos, games, music tapes and Japanese babysitters when available.... I have found that the amount of time I spend talking and playing with my children is directly proportional to the amount of Japanese they speak. (P.R., interview)

Who, Besides You, Can Talk to Your Child?

- Other children – playgroups with parents who speak the L2 can mean your son or daughter has playmates who speak the L2.
- Babysitters – hire a speaker of the L2 next time you need a sitter.
- Nanny – look for a nanny who speaks the L2.
- Au pair – learn the culture while you learn the language by opening your home to an au pair.
- Dual language daycare workers – these L2 speaking instructors offer a popular alternative to traditional daycare.
- Summer counsellors in language camps – these L2 workers help your child combine outdoor fun with playing in the L2.

8 The Play's the Thing: Fun and Simple Resources

The activities that are the easiest, cheapest, and most fun to do – such as singing, playing games, reading, storytelling, and just talking and listening – are also the best for child development.
Jerome Singer, Professor Emeritus of Psychology, Yale University (Singer, 2013)

This chapter offers simple, ordinary resources that give extraordinary results. You don't need to use them all. Just choose a few that fit with your child's personality and your lifestyle.

Let's Start With Books

You cannot open a book without learning something.
Confucius (Goodreads, 2012a)

From a huge variety of resources, we'll start with books because they work on so many levels. Your children learn listening skills when you read to them. They learn from active participation when you ask them about what they see on the pages.

Think of why you read to your child in your L1. They are exposed to worlds beyond what's in front of them. (See p. 123, 'Beyond the parents' L2'.) So instead of just seeing your apartment, the grocery store down the road and their preschool, your child's seeing an open-air market, a basketball game or a magic circus.

And it's fun.

When to start reading to your child

When my daughter was a few weeks old, I learned a valuable lesson from a woman who had an infant the same age. One morning we met up and her baby's stroller was filled with children's books. When I asked about them, she said she started reading to the baby when he was first born. That seemed so early to me. She loaned me Mem Fox's book *Reading Magic*. Fox advocates reading to children from infancy:

> Reading aloud and talking about what we're reading sharpens children's brains. It helps develop their ability to concentrate at length, to solve problems logically, and to express themselves more easily and clearly. (Fox, 2008: 26)

I followed this advice and it's amazing how much my daughter has loved books since she was old enough to pick them up. Even as a two-year-old, she regularly sat, looking at books and 'reading' them to herself.

Read what you like to read

When reading to babies, you don't necessarily have to read children's books. Experiment with what one parent tried:

> In the safe knowledge that a little baby does not really understand the meaning of the words (so long as you speak in a friendly voice), my husband would read them anything – like a … book on history for the goodnight story. Eventually I copied that by reading to the baby novels that I myself wanted to read. (K.D., email interview)

If your language skills aren't yet to the level of reading something as complex as a novel, you can also just peruse a magazine, telling stories in the L2 about the people on the page, or showing and narrating the pictures in the ads. For older children, you can retell the basic stories of books you're reading for yourself or stories you've read in the past. My kids loved hearing parts of *Life of Pi* (Martel, 2003). This adventure, with all its strange animals, provided some rich vocabulary.

Where to find books in the L2

Many local and online bookstores have children's books, CDs and picture dictionaries in other languages. There are also international clearinghouses with books in other languages. Search for 'children's books in <L2>'. Local libraries often house books in other languages or can order books by request from larger libraries.

Let people know of your intentions to expose your child to another language. They might know someone with resources you can use. Or they may be willing to buy books for you if they travel to that country.

If you can find some sort of association of the target country, oftentimes a simple email saying you're looking for books in the language can lead you to parents whose kids have outgrown their children's books. Search online for 'association' plus the country name and the name of your town: 'association Argentina London'.

Dual language books

If you need help with the second language vocabulary, dual language books (also called bilingual or multilingual books) might be perfect for you. They're books with the second language at the top of the page, and the L1 beneath it. Or they may have the L1 on one page and the L2 on the opposing page. Do a quick online search for 'dual language books' alongside the name of your L2.

Many dual language stories deal with social norms that vary across cultures, for example what people in different countries do when a child loses a tooth or what they try when they can't get rid of the hiccups. The curiosity that naturally surges can help your child be more interested in people of many different races.

If you've just read a dual language story about what people in different countries do when a spicy food burns their mouth, encourage your child to ask people they know what they do in these situations. The more kids can discuss difference in a curious and judgment-free way, the better they will feel about being unique themselves and the less angst they'll have about speaking another language.

Note that dual language books work best when parents read them to their children. Bilingual literary expert Viv Edwards explains that if children read them for themselves, they 'only read one language in the book, and ignore the other' (Edwards in Baker & Jones, 1998: 611).

Seek out the familiar

Get books you recognize, ones you know the storyline to. That way you can better guess what's going on and what unfamiliar words mean.

Grimms' Fairy Tales has been translated into many languages. The morals in the stories cut across cultures and are a nice springboard for questions and interaction in the L2. The stories are exciting and feel more relevant to children, since they have characters they recognize.

Perhaps even more importantly, hearing a familiar story in the L2 'normalizes' the language. This is particularly significant if you're teaching a less commonly spoken language. If Cinderella is speaking Lithuanian, then it must be a pretty normal language.

Get visual for higher motivation

Comic books are especially advantageous for language learning because the visuals help in areas where language skills are weak. My kids and I read comic books about a group of Brazilian kids, akin to the comic *Peanuts*. They play and torture one another and serve as a critique of society's norms, just like comics everywhere. And as a parent reading to a kid, you'll be more interested in reading to your child with the added layer of societal and cultural commentary.

Another strong point of comics is that with the many pictures, children are more likely to try to read the book on their own. We'll look specifically at encouraging children to read independently in Chapter 9, 'Right to Read'.

Active participation

As you read, you'll want to involve your children as much as possible. Some books make that easy – the *Where's Waldo?* series, for example (see Handford, 2014). Other books may require more creativity on your part to get kids active. As you read a book, even those you've read before, ask your child to predict what will happen. See if they want to stand up and show what someone will say or do.

It can be harder to learn the word for action verbs because we can't point to pictures of them in a book. But if you ask your child to mimic the action in a book, you can naturally give the vocabulary: 'Oh, he hopped around and then fell to the ground?'

Picture books and vocabulary

For picture books, ask your child to look at a picture and tell you what she thinks about it. It's a chance to feed her vocabulary she doesn't know. She doesn't have to resort to the L1, because she can point to the picture of a sheep and say 'I like this. Soft.' You can expand on her observation with 'Oh, you like the sheep. Yes, it looks soft.'

Reading researchers Isabel Beck, Margaret McKeown and Linda Kucan, authors of *Bringing Words to Life*, encourage teachers and parents to use what they call 'text talk' (Beck *et al.*, 2013: 60). Parents read the story, then look at the picture and pick something out that might be an unfamiliar word for the child. They give a brief definition. 'Oh look, at the *frying pan*. That's for cooking.' Then the parent asks the child something about the picture that requires the new word. 'What can I use to cook my egg?' If the child points to the pan, great! The parent also points out the word again the next time he reads the book. (See p. 127, 'Picture books'.)

Stair-step questions

Another way to get kids engaged in the language is to ask 'stair-step questions'. As you read, you build up kids' confidence by starting with easy questions. These are ones that kids can guess the answer to just based on the pictures or their previous knowledge of a storyline. You can point to a character like Pinocchio and ask 'Who's this?'

As you read, ask more complex comprehension questions, such as 'Why did his nose grow?' To respond, your child will be using explanation-type speech and you may have to help by feeding certain words. 'Because…'

Then, to take it to the next level of difficulty, ask your child questions that require interpretations. One example would be 'Why did Pinocchio lie?' You might need to give a helpful prompt: 'How did he feel?'

When you're trying to form these interpretation questions, ask yourself 'What are questions I don't know the answer to?' These types of open-ended questions encourage children to rely on their imagination and past knowledge. New vocabulary will naturally come up – vocabulary they're interested in because they need it to express themselves.

If you ask 'What else do you think Pinocchio did while he was out of school?', the responses may include all sorts of language, from 'He ate lots of giant cupcakes' to 'He ran around and jumped with bunnies'. This kind of interaction with your child will keep you interested, by seeing how your child perceives the world.

Audio books

Audio books help children and parents with pronunciation. (See p. 127, 'Audio books for listening to native speakers'.) If your child is very young, look for CDs or MP3s that have nursery rhymes, since they give you the sounds and the rhythm of the language. You and your child can learn together hearing the language spoken by a native speaker.

Listen to CDs in the car, while you're getting meals ready, or play them in your child's room while they are falling asleep.

Photo albums as books

Photo albums can become books you 'read' with your children. (See p. 147, 'Photo books'.) It's easy to get their participation in reading because kids will see pictures of themselves and people they know. You can ask simple questions, 'Who's that?', and build up to harder interpretive questions: 'How do you think she feels?' Feed your children vocabulary like 'cold', 'wet', 'happy', 'excited', 'scared' and 'bored.'

Photographs often show people doing interesting things, for example a child kicking a soccer ball or a clown juggling. These pictures can teach action words. As you look at these pictures, use open, pondering questions: 'I wonder what they're doing here.' This inspires children to use their imagination, keeping the reading fun.

'Everything-books'

Transform a three-ring binder into your child's special book. Fill it with protective sleeves. Inside the sleeves, put images your child would like to keep: birthday cards, drawings, photographs of friends or relatives, colorful junk mail catalogue pictures, or pages from magazines. Then 'read' the book by narrating the images: 'Here's a Disney cruise ship, and there is the picture you painted last week – of a spaceship'.

Customize the books to what your kids need to know. Let's say you want to teach colors with them. Put magazine images on the table and hold up a picture that has something yellow on it. 'I like this yellow rain jacket! Do you see anything yellow you like?' Make new pages based your color conversation.

When to read in the L2

Parents ask when they should read books in the second language. Should the reading time be separate from the reading time in the first language? The answer is that the order of reading – L1 or L2 first or second – isn't that important. I do feel that you should read in the L2 as much as possible. Children will read in the first language when they go to school. One mother speaks matter of factly about when she reads in Russian to her daughter:

> I think you should read books and make it a normal part of the day, not [a] special thing like 'now it's time for Russian'. (O.F., interview)

Books that are hard to understand

It may be hard for you to read to your older children in the L2 if the books they want to read are at too high a level for you.

You can make your own dual language books by getting the L1 translation of your L2 book. In my case, my daughter wanted to read *Harry Potter* (translated into 67 languages), but the vocabulary was advanced for me. I checked the English *Harry Potter* out from the library. Before reading a chapter of the Portuguese version to my daughter, I'd skim it in English. That way, the gist of the story was in my mind. It also made my reading smoother because I knew who said what. With the background knowledge, I could help my daughter with meaning by using gestures and facial expressions to explain hard words.

Where to keep books

When it comes to where to store your books, I'd say 'everywhere!' I like to have books in rooms where the children play and definitely where they sleep. Put them in a place at their height so they can look through them on their own.

Separate books in the L1 and the L2 either by shelf, in different baskets, or just in different piles. That way, children become accustomed to choosing a book in the language that fits the reader or the time frame. If you do your L2 times in the evening, for example, keep the L2 books beside the bed.

If you're doing OPOL, having books separated by language helps your child choose the right language for the right parent. Realize that kids who usually switch parents for reading – one night one the L1 parent, another night the L2 parent – may prefer the L1 book because it is easier to understand. To avoid conflict, choose a very motivating book at nighttime for the L2 parent to read – perhaps a (not too scary) mystery.

From the Screen

> *Children are influenced by people they see on television, especially other kids.*
> Carey Bryson, children's advocte and columnist (Bryson, 2013)

Television

Children's television in the L2 exposes your kids to different language than they get from you. Shows with children are highly motivating because children naturally want to know what others their age are saying. Seeing other kids their age talking among themselves normalizes the language. The kids on television go about their typical tasks – eating, playing and talking – all in the L2. The language serves a practical purpose that no one questions. And since native speakers are doing the talking, the language is at its natural speed.

Where to get television in the L2

You can find television in different languages by subscribing to cable television. Find a local satellite network and search its site for international channels. The top two subscribers for the southeast United States alone offer television in Arabic, Bengali, Chinese, Filipino, French, German, Greek, Gujarati, Hindi, Kannada, Malayalam, Marathi, Portuguese, Punjabi, Tamil, Telugu and Urdu.

If you're looking for free options, search online for 'television in other languages'. Some channels from other countries stream live broadcasts and offer schedules of children's programming. Particularly helpful are those sites with archives of children's shows, so you have more than just the live programming to choose from.

Videos

Videos of kids' movies can be found in all different languages. To find them in your L2, search for a large bookseller in your target country. It will most likely sell videos, as well as books. Many parents I've interviewed say they prefer videos to television because they give parents more control over the content.

You can learn heaps of language from watching with your child. You can even opt to use the subtitles, either in your L1 or in the L2. Comedy is especially motivating because you and the kids will want to understand the jokes.

One problem that can arise is that your kids may prefer videos in their L1. To reduce the temptation, offer a wider variety in the L2. Separate the L1 and the L2 videos and keep the L2 ones organized and easy to get to. In our house, I don't buy L1 videos. If grandparents give them as gifts, that's allowed, but our money goes toward the L2 ones. I also have a nice basket to hold them, in the hopes that 'presentation is everything'.

Use DVDs wisely

Everything you read about screens and learning says that kids learn language from real people, not people or animals on a screen. So to get the most out of a DVD specifi-cally for teaching language, parents should watch them with their kids from time to time. Think of questions you can ask after the video. Once it's over – or even later, at mealtime, for example – ask:

- What was your favorite part? Why did you like it?
- Who was your favorite animal/person?

For younger children, try to get them to imitate characters in the video:

- Can you talk like that frog?

Get them to act out what they've seen. Kids who might be shy to speak in the L2 in their own voice may be less reluctant if they are taking on a role.

Commercial DVDs for language teaching

The market is flooded with commercial DVDs claiming to teach children language. I've always been skeptical about language learning videos for children. Why not just get children's videos made in the target country? But I gave them a try when my daughter was four and my son 14 months. These are my reflections:

> I found one interesting video, *Baby Bilingual*. It was very well done as far as the people it showed, computer graphics. You never hear any English which I found refreshing. I loved how it mentioned different words and then showed the word really large in Portuguese and then a small translation in English. I think it's worth having because it helped teach the color names and short sentences. It's fun and happy. Sydney enjoyed it and even James looked at it from time to time. (journal, 4/20/2005)

My daughter, at age four, may have picked up on some of the language in the video. For my son, who was so young, however, it was mainly voices and music. I benefited from seeing the written words paired with the spoken words and images. So parents who watch these videos may come away with baby-talk to use with their infants.

Where to find videos

When you're looking for videos, start with the library. Ask if they have movies in the L2, and see if they can get movies from other libraries.

Even providers like Netflix have videos in many different languages. It helps to already have a title to search for. To get an idea of what videos are out there, search 'DVD' along with the name of the country in the L2: 'DVD Italia'.

Depending on the language, it can be quite easy to buy videos. You may have the most luck finding translated Disney videos. Amazon.com has many that are new, and sometimes has used ones for half the price. You can also go to Disney's website and buy straight from them.

The best way to get videos that aren't dubbed versions of English films, though, is to ask folks traveling to the target country to bring you back some. They are small and light and so easy to carry, especially if taken out of their cases.

Homemade videos

You can make videos of your children and let them serve as ones for entertainment. They'll definitely hold your children's attention. Film your infant or toddler interacting with other children or adults who speak the L2. Babysitters are great for this. Ask them to leave the camera running while they read a book to your child. Later, plop the kids in front of the computer to watch themselves.

Or just use videos you made of your kids playing outside or during a birthday party – but leave the sound off. You'll need to watch with them to give language input. As you watch, ask what people are doing. Remember that whenever you pose a question, you're feeding them vocabulary and giving them an opportunity to use that vocabulary in their response. Imagine seeing your child in the video jumping around and acting silly. Ask 'What are you doing? Are you dancing or jumping?' Your child might say 'Jumping. Up, up!' You can add 'Yes, you're jumping high!'

YouTube

You may feel frustrated at not having the vocabulary to feed your child words. YouTube.com can help, as it shows just about every type of family interaction. Search for 'mother with baby' or 'father with baby' but put the words in the L2.

For example, if you go to 'baby with mother' in French, *maman avec bebe*, you'll see videos of mothers interacting with babies who are eating, swimming, getting a bath and playing outside. You'll hear the natural ways to talk to children as a French mother tells her child it's time to get out of the tub.

You can also search for 'playing outside' or 'cooking with Mommy/Daddy' in the L2. You'll see videos of parents talking to children and asking questions as they play.

Music in Other Languages

Mary Seehafer Sears, columnist for the Scholastic for Parents website, writes 'simply listening to music gives kids joy along with the freedom to express themselves' (Sears, 2007). We parents know from experience the power of music. Songs leave us with more than just rhymes, rhythms and lyrics. They leave an emotional impression. We feel young when we hear songs from our high-school days. We feel romantic when a familiar love song plays.

If you give your children the input of music in the language, including singing along with the lyrics, those positive emotions will infuse themselves into the language.

Choose music you like

The kind of music you choose should be based on what you like to listen to. It does no good to buy children's music if it drives you crazy to hear it. If you're going to have it playing in your car or in the kitchen while you cook, it needs to be something you like. Children can learn from adult types of music just like they learn from children's music.

If possible, choose music with lyrics you can understand. Country music or other rural genres can be found in many languages. The tempo makes it easier to pick up on the words. Love songs tend to be slower and easier to understand. Religious music is sometimes slower as well, and those with a praise aspect tend to have repetition that helps with comprehension.

Lyrics

Regardless of which type of music you choose, know that you won't catch every word. If you'd like to have the lyrics, do a search with the song's name and the word 'lyrics' in the L2 – for instance, *"A Garota de Ipanema" letras'* (Musica.com.br, 2014).

You don't have to get out your dictionary unless you are really curious. If you hear a word repeated over and over, for example 'I like it when you —', soon you'll just have to look it up.

Improve pronunciation

Music teaches pronunciation. There's a faction of folks who think the pronunciation in songs isn't true to how people really talk. While we know that people don't generally sing their way through ordering at a restaurant, the sounds of words in music and in speech are close enough to offer real benefits in pronunciation.

You're also receiving exposure in learning where one word starts and another word ends. As you hear the lyrics, you are training your ears to know how to separate what you hear into distinct, comprehensible words.

Get a grammar lesson

Believe it or not, lyrics provide a grammar lesson. Parts of the refrain may be all that stick with you and your child, but that's enough. Hearing a love song you play often, your child might memorize a phrase like 'I can't get you out of my mind'. This grammar construction is recorded by the brain, so later you might hear your child say 'I can't get the cup out of my lunchbox'.

Sing, even if you're wrong

Benefits increase when you move from just listening to the music to singing along. You don't have to understand the lyrics to sing them.

Even if you pick up on only some of the sounds, you can still sing and feel the sounds of the vowels on your tongue. It's also a chance to compare the sounds coming out of your mouth with those in the mouth of the native singer.

Where to find music

To buy music, find the 'world' section of bookstores and music stores. Used bookstores and music shops often offer a wide variety at a fraction of the cost.

Remember that most public libraries loan out CDs. Find the sections labeled 'international', 'foreign language' or 'world'.

Free online searches can also save you money. Try looking for 'songs in <L2>'.

For new music at no charge, visit Shoutcast.com and search for the L2. You'll find radio broadcasts from the target countries. This way you hear not only the music, but also the advertisements, news updates and the banter between broadcasters.

Finding children's music

If you're looking specifically for children's music, search for 'songs for children' in the L2. For example, for French search *chansons por enfants*. To find slow songs that are easier to understand, search for the word 'lullabies' in the L2. For example, in Spanish it's *canción de cuna*. (Google Translate can help if you're unfamiliar with these expressions.)

Searches for children's music may lead you to YouTube videos of just regular people singing in the L2. This can be great listening practice and, if the singers are children, they will probably interest your kids. To see children singing in different languages, search 'children singing in <L2>'.

Nursery rhymes can also be considered music. Search for 'nursery rhymes in <L2>'. You'll find blogs by parents and professionals full of rhymes. Those with videos are especially nice because you can hear the pronunciation while watching the speaker's mouth.

Motions to music

You've no doubt seen children instinctively move to music. Capitalize on this tendency and encourage motions to lyrics. The connection of the body movement to the action words in the song offers a stronger memory link for the next time your child needs that action vocabulary.

Let your child help you invent the motions. When you don't have the music with you, try singing the song a cappella. You can speed up the song to make the motions go really fast. It's fun. Or slow the motions way down, slurring the words like it's slow motion. The sillier the action, the easier it'll be to remember the lyrics later.

Put on music with lyrics in the car and ask your child to make up hand movements. Encourage her to do motions like drawing a curvy heart over her chest when the word 'love' comes on, or rock an imaginary baby in her arms when the word 'baby' is sung.

Or, instead of inventing the movements, you can use sign language as your motion. Search 'sign language for children' for quick video clips and images for words like 'daddy' or 'milk'.

Games and Toys

Talking toys

Talking toys like Dora the Explorer® instill a positive feeling toward the L2. They also make the language seem real. It sounds ironic that a toy defines reality, but for a child who may hear the L2 only at home, having Go Diego Go® say something in the L2 makes it normal and real.

Games

Playing games in the L2 is often a starting place to learn a language with an older child. They can also be used with very young children. Games lend themselves to language use in situation- or time-based L2 use because they have a definable beginning and end. They are very rich in context – your child can point to a card, for example, when he doesn't know the specific word. This helps children express themselves even with limited vocabulary.

One researcher in education calls learning through games 'stealth learning' since children don't *realize* they are learning (Sharp, 2012). She indicates that playing such games helps children take risks and make decisions in 'new and varied learning environments' (Annetta in Sharp, 2012).

If you don't have games in the L2, just play the games you already have while speaking the L2. Any of them can help children learn turn-taking vocabulary like 'go ahead' or 'my turn'.

Card games

Card games are inexpensive and are easy to set up and transport. Uno or War is great for teaching numbers and colors. 'Memory', 'Slapjack', 'Old Maid', 'Crazy 8s' or 'Go Fish' are simple ways to practice the language while having fun. (See p. 144, 'Other games'.) Search online for the rules to any of these popular games.

Board games

Most board games for very young children have few words on the board itself and can easily be played in any language. Imagine the board for 'Chutes and Ladders'. The language component comes from you encouraging your child to say 'Oh no, down I go' or 'Up you go!'

Kids can learn number words through the game bingo. For beginners, search for 'simplified bingo' for free printable bingo games that have only lower numbers. (See p. 134, 'Bingo'.)

The higher numbers in dominos are interesting for older children. Since doing math in an L2 isn't always easy, children may use their L1 to count in their heads. Then, they'll translate the sum to the L2. Just give them time to make these transitions.

'Guess Who' is a board game that is very language-rich but has no written words on the board itself. It requires players to make educated guesses to find out which colorful character the other player is thinking about.

'Sorry' and 'Trouble' are good for teaching numbers. They use everyday language – 'I'm sorry' or 'You have to go back'.

The game 'Blokus' teaches spatial vocabulary. Useful directional words and phrases such as 'to the right', 'upside down' and 'the other way' will arise as you play. (See p. 134, 'Board games for reading'.)

Strategic games

If your kids enjoy more strategic games like chess or backgammon, you'll want to learn the vocabulary needed in those games. Search 'how to play backgammon' but make the search words in the L2. I searched *Como jogar xadrez* (How to play chess) to learn words like 'pawn' and 'bishop'.

Video games

Children love screen time. Utilize it well by encouraging them to play games in the L2. Search 'free video games' written in the L2. Watch them play some of these games and ask follow-up questions.

Outdoor games

Any sport demands a variety of new vocabulary words. I remember feeling intimidated when my son wanted to play baseball outside with me, because I had no idea how to say 'bat', 'you're out' and such. I made it up as I went along and later looked up *regras pra beisbal* (rules for baseball). Capitalize on your child's interest as a guide for what vocabulary to learn.

No Need To Be Bored

If you're getting bored with incorporating the language into your daily life, stop in your tracks and ask 'Where can I make a change?' Most likely there's at least one of the resources we've discussed that you haven't tried yet. Remind yourself that you have what it takes to enjoy time in the L2.

Reading Rules

- Read to your infant.
- You don't just have to read kids' books. Read what *you* like to read to your baby.
- Tell your friends you're looking for L2 books.
- Read dual language books to learn new words.
- Choose books you know the storyline to.
- Find books with lots of pictures to keep interest piqued.
- Ask your child questions as you read. Find out what she's thinking.

9 Right to Read: Growing Kids' Independence Through Books

No amount of visiting the country where the language is spoken or contact with other speakers can hope to give a child as rich a vocabulary and such a mastery of the nuances of the language as a thorough immersion in its children's literature.
Una Cunningham-Andersson and Staffan Andersson, *Growing Up With Two Languages* (1999: 58)

The Whys Behind Learning to Read

When we discuss knowing a second language, we use the word 'speak': 'I speak a little Spanish' or 'My husband speaks fluent Japanese'. So learning to read may seem non-essential for our kids. I would argue that, on the contrary, reading is a right our children have. With the written word, they can access what they want to learn about and follow their individual interests.

Myles' book *Raising Bilingual Children* discusses this freedom:

The possibility of using the language independently of the parents providing spoken language input can help children find their own interests in the language, and to continue to use it as they move out into the world as teenagers. (Myles, 2003: 161)

Beyond the parents' L2

Many children need reading in the L2 to give them a broader base of the language than the one they hear at home. (See p. 109, 'Let's start with books'.) Parents who are second-language speakers may not have a broad vocabulary. They may know only simplified grammar. Harding-Esch and Riley write 'Reading will... give your child access to styles and varieties of language she would not meet otherwise. Particularly in cases where the family is a linguistic island' (Harding-Esch & Riley, 2003: 141).

Reading builds vocabulary

The written word has longer and more complex sentences than the spoken language. Have you ever read a passage of text aloud and found the language sounded stiff? It's because in many forms of writing we use a more elevated language. So it makes sense that a child will have a bigger vocabulary and formulate more complex sentences if he's exposed to the written word.

Reading makes connections

Being able to read words helps children make connections between their L1 and their L2. When two words have similar roots, they are called 'cognates'. Indo-European languages are a family of several hundred languages, including everything from English, German and French to Swedish, Russian and Greek. You'll find cognates among these languages. You'll also find cognates among languages like Chinese and Japanese (SciForums, 2007).

If your child learns a word in the L2, it can help her know the meaning of an unfamiliar word in the L1. My daughter was pleased to know what the word 'augment' meant on her vocabulary list because she knew the word *aumentar* in Portuguese. When older children study for the university entrance exams, they'll notice how much easier they can recognize words.

Reading is slower

Reading is slower than speaking and gives children longer to process what words or phrases mean. When a child encounters a new word on the page, her eyes can hang on it just a second longer to guess the meaning from context. The spoken words fly by and are gone before there is time to understand.

Good for the brain

Reading in another language challenges the brain, ensuring cognitive benefits. These are many of the same benefits for speaking the second language, only redoubled. One researcher writes 'Reading [in a second language] … is also a challenging brain workout. In short, higher level language skills promote higher level thinking' (Steiner, 2008: 130).

L2 maintenance over time

If you think long term, you want your child to remember the language skills you're teaching even after he leaves home. Imagine writing him a letter in the L2. You want him to keep up his skills to be able to write back and continue interacting in the language. Reading helps with that maintenance of the language. It allows children to become adults while still interacting with the language through the written word.

This is Doable

The task of teaching your child to read might sound daunting, but it's very doable.

Bilinguals have an advantage

Remember, just the fact that your kids know two languages gives them an advantage with respect to reading. (See p. 3, 'Stronger readers'.) Steiner writes 'Young bilingual children are better able than their monolingual peers to recognize the relationship between a letter and its sound (called letter-sound recognition), which is an essential pre-reading skill' (Steiner, 2008: 132).

From there, bilingual children also pick up more quickly the idea that words mean something. One study finds that four- and five-year-old bilingual children recognize earlier than monolingual children do that written language carries meaning (Bialystok et al., 2012). This often puts them ahead in learning to read in their L1.

Skills transfer

For children who already know how to read in the L1, learning the L2 is not like starting over. And learning to read in the second language won't confuse children or interfere with reading in the L1. Children who already know how to read in their L1 have learned skills for gathering meaning from words. They've discovered how to sound out words, for example. A study from the Center of Applied Linguistics notes:

> Children transfer a variety of component skills from their first to their second language, including phonological awareness (understanding different units of sounds), word reading, word knowledge, and comprehension strategies. (August et al., 2002: 13)

One researcher adds to this list 'decoding words as parts and wholes, making sensible guesses at words given the storyline … and moving left to right across the page' (Baker, 2000: 91). For children whose first language for reading is the L2, the decoding skills will transfer to their L1.

Your child can also learn to read his L1 and L2 at the same time:

> In Canada, children from English-speaking homes take their early years of education through French. Hence they may learn to read in French first, and English a little later. This usually results in fully biliterate children. Learning to read in French first will not impede later progress in learning to read in English. (Baker, 2000: 90)

When to Start With Very Young Children

We have succeeded in keeping our children carefully isolated from learning
in a period of life when the desire to learn is at its peak.
Glenn Doman's Gentle Revolution (Doman, 2012)

It's important to pick up on your child's cues for wanting to learn to read. Otherwise you might miss golden opportunities for teaching. Your child could be ready to read when she does the following:

* calls out what a street sign or other posted words say (even if she's just remembering what it says and not 'reading' it);
* demonstrates an interest in words or people who are reading;
* wants to hold a book in her lap;
* points to words on the page;
* is fascinated by older children who are able to read.

Reading experts like Glenn and Janet Doman, authors of *How to Teach Your Baby to Read: The Gentle Revolution* (1993), argue that children can read much earlier than previously thought. They contend that children don't learn to read sooner because the print is too small for them. Their brains develop the ability to read before their eyes are able to focus on small print. If you try reading books with larger print and your child shows an interest in the words on the page, she might be ready to get started, regardless of age.

Teaching reading to older children

Some parents I spoke with worried it was too late to teach reading to older children. I remind them of institutions such as the Emerson Waldorf School, which don't teach reading in the first language until the third grade, choosing instead to build solid pre-reading skills.

So if you have older children who cannot read in the L2, it's not too late. Consider that you actually have an advantage. By now, your kids know the benefits of reading. That helps them be more motivated.

Imagine flexible goals

Whether you're teaching young children or older ones, you'll want to set attainable goals. For very young children, a beginning goal might be the logistics of holding a book. Children don't instinctively know from which side of the page to read or how to turn pages. You model this for them. Then encourage them to curl up on your lap and 'pretend to read' the story, babbling as they turn pages and point to pictures.

For subsequent goals, remember to consider immediate versus long-term goals. For example, I wanted my children to be able to read simple notes or short letters. Longer-term goals include more involved letters, as well as internet sites and books that interest them.

Choosing the Level

Part of setting realistic goals is starting at an appropriate level. Younger children might read parts of bedtime books that are read to them. Expect them to need the context of a picture to read most words.

For older children already reading in their L1, the L2 book might need to be several levels lower than their L1 books. To keep them interested in lower-level books, try to find ones that are funny and whose covers don't appear babyish.

An exception would be asking them to read books to you that you read to them when they were younger. If you capitalize on the sentimentality factor, the lower level of the book will feel natural. And the familiarity of the books will help with any difficult words.

What to Read

An important component of choosing the level is deciding which type of book to read.

Picture books

You might assume picture books aren't for reading since they have so few – or sometimes no – words on a page. But children are learning that symbols carry meaning. Even pointing out and talking about a drawing of a beetle shows that the picture on the page stands for something. Once they have the idea that they are decoding, then it's only a short jump to understand that those squiggly characters on the page have significance, too. (See p. 112, 'Picture books and vocabulary'.)

Target country and translations

Children's and young adults' books from the target country are excellent for learning not only how to read, but also about cultural and social norms. Translations of popular children's series are perfect for children who want to read popular books all the kids are talking about. By visiting sites like Multilingualbooks.com and Languagelizard. com, you can find everything from *Brown Bear, Brown Bear* and *The Little Prince* to *The Adventures of Tintin* and *Harry Potter*.

Audio books for listening to native speakers

Whether they tell a story or have music that accompanies a book, audio books expose your child to a native speaker. (See p. 113, 'Audio books'.)

Listen alongside your child so you can pick up new vocabulary, too. If you have an audio story with an accompanying picture book, read the story later without the CD. Try to imitate the intonation and accent of the native reader and ask your child to do the same.

The internet

The internet hosts many sites for helping children learn to read. For example, I searched for *apprendre a lir en Français* (learn to read in French) and found commercial sites, but also sites set up by parents and educators. Many learning tools were free of charge – including sites with interactive video games and videos to help kids with letters and sounds.

Game sites in the second language that aren't specifically geared toward reading can also have some benefits. Kids will have to read instructions and communications in the L2.

Invent stories

Encourage storytelling with your kids by telling collaborative stories. Include actual events, but add some fun and imagination. For example:

Once upon a time, in our backyard there lived a little frog named —. [Let your child choose the name.] When we saw this frog in the yard, we didn't know that he was completely crazy. He loved to hop backwards and bark like a dog. One day, the frog tried to go to frog school, but —. [Let your child choose what happens next.]

These types of stories teach storytelling conventions, such as those having the opening line 'Once up on a time…'. They teach children about main characters, description, conflict, resolution and story endings. Such pre-reading skills encourage children to predict action by helping them understand how most stories are set up. After kids get the idea, encourage them to tell their own stories. They may need help at first, but invariably, after a few tries, they'll love creating on their own.

Helping Children Want to Read

Parents must serve as marketers of reading, making it appealing to their children.

Books as gifts

No doubt, your child will have more books in his L1 than in his L2. Take some steps to make sure that L2 books he sees as 'cool' make it into your house.

Find a good website that sells books in the L2. If relatives or friends ask what your child would like for a birthday or holiday gift, pass the site along. Be sure to offer guidance for using the site. You might say that the books are labeled by age, or suggest specific titles or authors.

When you buy your child an L2 book, make it a gift, even if it's not a special occasion. Wrap it or put it in a box that your child can open. It sends the message that books in the L2 are special and important.

Commercial characters

As much as we parents may resist it, children love the flashy characters of Disney and Pixar. It may be worth investing in these books if you know your children will be excited to read them. One mom teaching her kids English in Germany describes her daughter:

> Natalie has always been a keen reader and soon I was able to buy her some English books for young readers. However, I became aware that she would cast aside an English book if she had a German book there. This called for a clever plan! I had to lay my hands on some of this overpriced 'literature', featuring some popular TV characters, the kind one simply *has* to read, even if it's in the language that's harder to read. (K.D., email interview)

Limit television and movies

Ensure your child has time to read by limiting television time. The speed at which television moves is counterproductive to reading goals. Television watching in pre-schoolers has been shown to overstimulate their developing brains and can decrease their attention span (Dimitri A. Christakis in Clayton, 2004). Harvard University's longitudinal study of family reading practices found that kids with parents who limit television 'made significantly greater progress in developing both reading and general literacy than in families without [such] rules' (Snow in Kropp, 1995: 16).

Making Reading Relevant

For children to be interested in reading – and continue their interest – reading must be relevant to them. Parents have several ways of showing children this relevance.

Model reading

Kids want to do what you're doing – to be 'grown-up'. They tend to read if they see you reading. Schwarzer notes that multilingual literacy ('multiliteracy') does not happen effortlessly or 'naturally' but instead results from the 'actions, beliefs, and attitudes of the learner's community' (Schwarzer, 2001: 9).

Kids see parents' beliefs about reading through the parents' actions, not through what the parents say they believe. Encourage your child toward literacy through your own everyday reading. When you read the news in the morning or curl up with a novel – that's modeling reading. You don't have to be reading *War and Peace*. Just thumbing through a magazine shows an interest in the written word. Holding your child or having them sit near you as you read will connect a positive, comforting feeling to reading.

Encourage expression

Activities other than reading can still encourage reading. Myles cites lively dinner conversation as a way to positively impact children's reading skills, since it

> has been associated with later literacy achievement, as has encouraging children to talk about their day or interesting events, asking open questions, encouraging them to make predictions or explain their thought processes in coming to a conclusion. (Myles, 2003: 170)

Don't assume this conversation has to wait until your children are four or five. Try asking questions of your two-year-old. These opportunities help children learn to express themselves, prepping them to understand and discuss what they read.

Keep vocabulary relevant

When it comes to words on a page, children need to feel that new words are relevant to them. If you are reading with your child, you can help make the connection between your child and the written word. For example, if you read the word, 'pond', talk about real-life times when you've encountered that word. 'Oh, we saw a pond near Grandma's, with the ducks, remember? That little lake is called a pond.'

You can also ask questions: 'What kind of water is in a pond? Do you want to swim in a pond?' It doesn't have to be anything complicated, just using the word is enough.

The more you connect written words to your child's life, the more relevant they become and the more likely she is to remember them. The opposite will happen as well: she'll relate life to her books. When she sees something for the first time, such as a hot air balloon, she will already have gathered information about it: 'That's like in my book!'

Keep reading aloud

Think back to your childhood – in your own home or in the classroom in elementary school – and try to remember which books someone read aloud to you. I can vividly remember my first-grade teacher with her long pink fingernails turning the pages of *Charlotte's Web* (White, 1952). When Charlotte died, I sat still at my desk fighting back tears, completely enthralled in the story she unfolded before us.

So why do we stop reading aloud to children at home once they get old enough to read for themselves? Children continue to benefit from hearing stories read aloud.

One of the beauties of reading aloud to a child is that you can move them a level beyond what they would read on their own. Steiner (2008: 137) writes 'reading out loud to your child exposes her to a fluent reading style at a time when she is likely to be reading at a hesitant pace'

This ability to read more quickly and smoothly maintains their interest. Reading aloud also keeps it from being a solitary activity that, for extroverted kids, may feel dull or lonely.

Some argue that reading to your child isn't as important as children reading on their own. But if the object is to keep children interested in reading in the L2, hearing a story is a definite motivator. It keeps kids in the game.

Times of day

There tend to be certain times of day that are particularly conducive to reading aloud to children. The obvious choice is before bed, when children are calming down for sleep.

Another time is just after (or even during) a meal. Once an L2 parent has finished eating, he can read to all at the table. It shows children how important books are in keeping people together.

Some parents make use of car rides, letting the passenger-side parent read aloud. The car is also a fun place to do 'invisible reading'. Try spelling aloud a very short and phonetic word in the L2 and see if children can guess which word you're spelling. Continue with other words that make a funny message or one-line story.

Ask your child to read to you

Be mindful, as you read to your child, that he might be ready to do some of the reading to you. John Rosemond, author of *New Parent Power* (2001), tells a story of two mothers who spent time together while their four- and five-year-olds played. One mother noticed that the children were reading to each other. She was surprised and asked her four-year-old why he didn't read to her. He responded 'Because *you* read to *me*'. Given the chance, many children enjoy doing the reading (Rosemond, 2001: 186).

Let children take the lead in telling you how much they want to read. They may want to read just one word. Others might want to read an entire page. To move even further into independent reading, ask if he'd like to read one book while you read the next.

Don't worry if he's not actually reading the words on the page. It's a good start for some kids just to hold the book, turn the pages and tell the story as they remember it.

Child-to-child reading

Children can also read to each other. The recommendation is generally that older children read to younger ones, but that's not a must. Younger children can read to older children. In this case, just make it clear to the older ones that the reading doesn't have to be perfect.

The How-Tos of Reading

Let's examine some general how-tos for teaching children to read in the L2.

Play with the alphabet

Start teaching the alphabet in the L2 to your child while she is still a baby. One educator and researcher writes 'Knowledge of the letter names was found to be the single best predictor of first-year reading achievement' (Adams in Tokuhama-Espinosa, 2000: 142). Use YouTube to find an alphabet song in the L2 and sing it often.

For young children, read simple books and point out which letters begin words. Then play with lettered blocks, matching blocks to the beginning of words in the book. They'll see that M is for 'monkey'. Let kids get the connection between an image on the page and a letter. Then let them play with the letter M while you make the letter's sound.

Children can also experiment with magnetic letters, mimicking what they see in the book or inventing their own words. Help them say the names of the letters and the sounds those letters tend to make in words.

Letter hunts

Do letter hunts with the alphabet. While your kids are riding in the car, ask them to search for letters. If you see the 'M' for McDonald's on the highway, sing the alphabet song up to the letter 'M'. In the grocery store, ask them to find the alphabet in the overhead signs in food aisles.

Older children will easily learn the alphabet, but the sound each letter makes may be more difficult. When you read to them, point out words and encourage children to sound them out.

Alphabet books

Use a three-ring binder or notebook to make an alphabet book, each page dedicated to a letter. Draw pictures of things in the L2 that start with each letter, or cut pictures out of magazines. Show not only the name of the letter, but also the sound that letter makes in words.

Tricky letters and sounds

Older children who already know how to read may, at first, use the rules of pronunciation of their L1 with the L2 words. Be sure to teach the sounds that might get confused with the L1.

In my house, we used flashcards to learn words with confusing sounds and letters. I called them 'tricks'. They were the tricky words and sounds where the L2 sounds and letters differed greatly from the L1 sounds and letters.

Totally different alphabets

For parents who are teaching languages with different alphabets, know that children can learn Chinese and Arabic scripts just as they learned their L1 scripts. The added complexity will be beneficial for cognitive development. Plus, children often enjoy the novelty and the creative nature of learning a different script. Capitalize on the interest in the 'secret code' aspect of the language by writing cryptic messages in the L2 for your child to read.

Whole language versus phonics

Educators warn against placing all our teaching emphasis on the alphabet and sounds, also called 'phonics'. If you're teaching the different sounds letters make so that children can 'sound out' words, then you're taking advantage of phonics.

Some educators argue that focusing too much on teaching letters and their sounds, as opposed to looking more at an entire word or expression, might teach children to read the words but not understand their meaning. If the writing offers no message, your kids might lose motivation to read. Dr Beth Patterson, an expert in language and literacy, argues 'There is little meaning found in "the duck is stuck in the muck in his truck"' (interview). So it's important – as you teach children to recognize bits of language – that you check to see that there's true understanding.

An alternative to phonics is called 'whole language'. It places a stronger focus on the meaning of a word or group of words. When you use cards to label items in your child's room, you're helping her understand chunks of 'whole language'.

Myles (2003) suggests parents see if their children appear to learn more by what they hear. In this case, more sound-based learning would be beneficial, making phonics the preferred method. Visual learners, though, might do well with whole language. So try both ways of teaching and see which your kids gravitate toward.

Information Gaps

Leaving information gaps open for children to explore motivates them to learn to read for themselves. Leave some pieces of information undiscovered and arm children with the tools to do the uncovering of the missing bits. Below are several activities you can try with your child, adapting them for different ages.

Scavenger hunt

Decide where you want to hide a treasure, which could be something like a piece of chocolate or a new pencil. Write simple clues to get kids started. (See p. 143, 'Scavenger hunt'.) The first clue might be 'Look in the kitchen on the table'. Then have a clue on the table that leads to the next location. Go along with them as they hunt and ask that they read the clue aloud to check for understanding.

M&M game

Pour M&Ms or another loose snack into a bowl to serve as prizes. (See p. 143, 'M&M game'.) On notecards, write (in the L2) words or expressions that family members say. Funny or controversial ones are best, like 'I didn't do it!' or 'I lost my lunch box'. After children read the quote, ask them to guess who said it.

Silly sentences

On notecards, write common words your children will encounter on a daily basis: I, Mommy, Daddy, Sally, our dog, table, tall, silly, funny, huge, dirty, etc. Also include some basic connector words and verbs: am, is, are, and. After your child has read the words, spread them on the table and let them make sentences. Add extra notecards for words you need. Remember that the sillier the sentences, the more memorable.

New Twists on Old Favorites

Reading activities don't have to be complicated, and you don't have to reinvent the wheel. Enjoy these games. Many work best with older children.

Bingo

On a square sheet of paper, make a bingo sheet with the same number of large squares across as you have down. In each square, write simple words your child dictates to you. He can look around the room or look out the window to get ideas. Make notecards with the words you put on the bingo sheet and place them in a stack. Have kids choose the top notecard and read the word aloud before finding it on their sheet. Use coins or small rocks to put over the squares. (See p. 143, 'Bingo for writing'.)

Board games for reading

Board games in the second language give natural practice in reading. (See p. 120, 'Board games'.) If you have access to ones from the target country, try to get some that include a lot of written language. Backgammon won't improve reading skills, but a game where kids put word clues together would be beneficial. Games that ask kids to mimic real-life circumstances like buying groceries or property will expose them to everyday vocabulary.

'The Game of Life', for example, has been translated into 20 languages. On each turn, children are instructed on how to move: 'Pay 1,000 for car repair' or 'Lose one turn'. Parents do much of the reading at first, but eventually children remember the instructions and work at reading on their own.

There are other games as well. 'Monopoly' can be found in 27 different languages. 'Scrabble' can be found for sale online in languages ranging from French and Spanish to Bulgarian and Catalan.

Memory

Memory is an easy game to make. Write a word on a card and then make a second card with the same word. Once you have 20 cards total, mix them up and place them face down on a table. Each player turns two cards face up, trying to make a match. Insist that the person flipping the card read the word aloud. If a player finds a match, he keeps both cards and gets to go again. If no match is found, the cards are turned face down again. The player with the most cards at the end of the game wins. To make the level of the game more difficult, use more difficult words and more cards per game.

Charades

Write words (and expressions, movies, etc.) on slips of paper. One player reads the paper silently and tries to communicate the word to his partner using only gestures. Again, after the turn is complete, turn over the paper and ask your child to read the word or phrase aloud.

Magic Cube

Did you ever play with a 'Magic Eight Ball'? You might have shaken it and asked a question like 'Will I have a boyfriend soon?' The little window on the ball gave you a sort of fortune: 'Most definitely' or 'Probably not'.

Use children's blocks to make a cube. Cover all six sides with small squares of paper. Write responses in the L2 like 'Of course!' or 'Maybe' or 'Ask again'. I found that making two of these cubes was fun because my kids could roll them both, then choose the answer they preferred.

You can also make action cubes with short activities to do. (See p. 144, 'Action cubes'.) One side might say 'Quack like a duck' and another 'Jump ten times'. Continue to play until children get a chance to read every side.

Keeping It Real

To keep reading relevant, use authentic materials, such as maps, recipes and letters.

Maps

Use Google Maps to find a town in the target country, searching for the town's name in the L2. Print out the map or look at it on the computer screen. Ask questions of your child: 'I'm at Crooks Crossing. Can you point to where I am?' They will have to scan the map and read the location names to find you. You can also tell them you are 'by the library' or 'at the bus station'. Practice directional vocabulary as you play – in front of, beside, close to/far from, east/west, left/right, or up/down. Once kids get the idea, let them ask the questions.

Real messages

After trying many complicated things to get my kids to read, I found it very effective to just leave them a message on a small piece of paper. I try to have a real meaning to convey, so that if they don't understand, they come to me to see what they are missing.

Your messages can be simple: 'I love you. Good night.' They can also be miniature scavenger hunts. A simple note on their pillow might say 'I left you a candy in your bottom drawer'. They love it!

Touch!

For young children, play a simple game called 'Touch!' Label different objects in your home: window, table, clock. Put the words on large cards in big, colorful print. When you're in the room, ask your child to touch certain words.

After you've played, leave some labels in place for several days. Make them as relevant to your children as possible. Instead of just putting the name of the item, 'chair' on the child's chair back, add some relevant information, 'Karen's purple chair'.

To make the game more challenging, use descriptive words like 'tall' and 'red'.

I wrote about some labeling we did when my daughter was three:

> My husband traced around me on butcher paper and we cut out a body to put on the wall. Then I labeled it with the poster board cards of 'man' and 'head' 'arms,' etc. I didn't stick the words up immediately though, instead we played with the cards, danced with them (this sounds ridiculous now that I'm writing it up, but with a kid it wasn't so weird) and talked about them. Later I heard Sydney 'reading' the words to 6-month-old [brother] James – she was really enunciating. First she read the 5 words we'd worked on, then moved on to those already hung on the playroom wall – sometimes translating them to English but still acting as if she were reading them. (journal, 11/8/2004)

Mystery notes

Also for young children, Merrill (1984) writes that she leaves mystery letters from different fictional characters. One night it might be the Easter Bunny, the next the Tooth Fairy. Capitalize on that and have Superman leave your child a note.

Calendar

Give your children opportunities to read by writing things on the calendar in the L2. It doesn't have to be a big 'lesson'; just get the calendar out while kids are talking about upcoming events. (If you have a whiteboard calendar that allows you to write in the names of the months, it's particularly educational.) Print the name of the activity in bold letters in the L2. Later, when you refer to those same activities, let your child read the activity name. If she has have trouble reading it, offer hints by pointing to the day of the week or the time of day. 'Remember what we have on Thursday afternoons?'

Try to be descriptive in your activity names: for example, 'children's museum downtown'. To give clues to meaning, use people's names in the L1, since being able to read the 'Susan' of *visita de Tia Susan* (Aunt Susan's visit) is a confidence booster that'll make your child more willing to read.

Grocery lists

Write your grocery list in the second language. (See p. 145, 'Grocery list'.) It's good practice for you to learn the everyday names of foods, ingredients and paper goods. Read over the list to your child, pointing to items that might interest him.

When you go to the grocery store, let your child hold and read the list. He can then help you find the items. Of course, the food names on the packages will be in the L1, but just having the list in the L2 will allow kids the chance to practice food names.

If possible, try shopping in an international grocery store. Even if the products are not from your target country, your kids will see the words and products from abroad. It reaffirms that other non-L1 languages are real and valid.

Recipes

Use the L2 for your recipes. Go to online cooking sites in your L2, or, for child-friendly recipes, search 'recipes for children' in the L2. You can also translate simple L1 recipes. Involve children when you cook with the recipes. Kids will be reading and using math in the L2 in a natural way.

Children's chores

Do your children have chores to do around the house? Make a list of your kids' jobs in the L2. Without calling attention to the list, post it on the refrigerator or other central location, with their name above the jobs. Kids' curiosity will lead them to read what is connected to their names. And, if they forget a job – clearing their place at the table or feeding the dog – instead of telling them what they left out, point it out on the list.

Morning message

I got the idea for a morning message from my children's elementary school. Each morning they are greeted by a message on a whiteboard. It explains what they'll be doing that day and asks a question.

Buy a small whiteboard and markers. You might write 'Good morning! What day is today?' You can ask your child to respond orally to the question. For more advanced readers, you might write 'It's test day. Eat a good breakfast. Are you nervous about the test or are you feeling okay?'

As your children get older, you can incorporate higher-level messages and have students respond in writing on the whiteboard. (See p. 137, 'Morning message'.)

Conclusion

If you're reading this chapter and feeling overwhelmed by the difficulty of teaching your child to read, know that you're not alone. Teaching reading is a job even professionals in education wrestle with.

Do not let these feelings of doubt hinder your efforts to try. You don't have to set your reading goal at fluent perfection. Decide what bits and pieces you'd like your child to pick up. See what fits your lifestyle. Know that you can make changes once you get going.

Why Learn to Read in the L2?

- Children can surpass their parents' knowledge of the language through the written word.
- Children will be more motivated to learn the language if they can make choices about what to read.
- Reading feeds children words they would not have been exposed to in their daily lives.
- The spoken word can go by too quickly to process. Reading allows children more time to process language.
- Reading is a cognitive workout that stimulates children's brains.
- Reading helps children maintain the second language as they get older and spend less time at home.

10 Delight to Write: Sharing Ways to Create and Tell

The pen is the tongue of the mind.
Miguel de Cervantes (Book Mania, 2013)

Why Teach Writing?

The most compelling argument for teaching kids to write is that it empowers them to express themselves in a new way. We don't just teach our kids to understand the L2, we want them to speak it. Likewise, we want them to not only read, but to write. Writing is creating.

Writing is similar to reading in that it is slower than speaking. It allows children to describe what they want to say in their own time, on paper. They also get the satisfaction of seeing what they've written and watching others glean meaning from it.

Realistic goals

Writing goals for your child must fit the environment. Recognize that since he is not exposed to the L2 as much as to the L1, his L2 writing may not be as advanced. Set manageable objectives and be flexible enough to re-evaluate these as time passes.

As you choose your goals, it's important to remember that for children to express themselves, we have to give them some control over what they write. Baker says writing must be 'relevant to the child, belonging to the child's experience, allowing choice by the learner, giving children power and understanding of the world' (Baker, 2000: 93).

Confusion

Parents worry that teaching their child to write in the L2 will slow down their progress in L1 writing. And it's true that, early on, you might notice children confusing the spelling of certain words as they transfer the spelling from one language to another. However, no long-term problems have been shown to be connected to bilingualism.

Skills transfer

In fact, skills in writing, just like skills in reading, transfer from one language to the other. If your child has learned to write in the L1, she already has the mechanics of writing – such as how to move a pencil from one side of the page to the next. She knows how to express a message using words. And research asserts that children who write well in one language will do so in another, given they have enough vocabulary in the L2 (Tokuhama-Espinosa, 2000: 149).

You can encourage this transfer of skills by pointing out any words that are similar in the L2 and the L1. Show them an easy-to-read book in the L2 and ask them to point to words that look like the L1. If they choose *leçon* (lesson) and *liste* (list), for example, ask them about what letters are different.

Start by Modeling

Start any writing activity with modeling. This is important whether or not your child already knows how to write in their L1.

Take away a sound

Use magnetic letters and find a simple word that is relevant to your child ('peach' if she loves peaches) and make the word with the letters. Let her take letters away one at a time and subtract that sound. For example, if she takes the 'p', say 'each'. Ask for the letter back and say 'Can you help me make the word "peach"?' To continue the play, ask your child for a couple of handfuls of letters and try to make a word from what you're given. Again, let your child take away letters. Then ask her to rebuild the word.

Eventually, your child will want to do what you're doing and she'll try making her own words. Praise her words, even if they are misspelled and even if she has to tell you what they are. Encourage follow-up words. If she writes 'dog', ask 'What do you like about dogs?' Try to write with magnetic letters or pen and paper some of the words in her response – 'sweet' or 'fun'.

Rhyming words

Modeling with rhyming words can entertain while it teaches. Use a quick online search for rhyming words in the L2. (Search online for '<L2> rhyming words'.) Come up with a list of three to five words you can imagine your child writing. You might choose 'hand', 'band' and 'sand'.

On a whiteboard, write some sentences with the three words, but leave out the repeating sound: 'I burned my h___ when I touched the stove' and 'At the beach, we played in the s___'. Ask your child to fill in the missing parts, offering hints if necessary.

For further expression, ask him questions to connect the words to him personally. 'Tell me something about your hands.' Or, 'When have you played in the sand?' Then ask him to choose some words in his answer to write down. For example, if he says 'My hands are sticky', he might choose to write the word 'sticky'.

Tongue twisters

Another way to practice words with similar sounds is to do tongue twisters. They expose children to clusters of similar consonants. Every language has tongue twisters. Search 'tongue twisters in <L2>'. Or, with the help of Google Translate, search for the expression 'tongue twisters' in the L2.

Recognize that tongue twisters don't always make sense. They may be just a list of words with the same sound. Say the tongue twisters with your child. At first slowly, then more quickly. On the whiteboard, write one of the tongue twister words that has other words with similar spellings. For example, 'seashells' and 'seashore'. Ask your child to write words from the tongue twister that are spelled like the one you've written.

Finger paint

Using finger paint as a way to write is an inviting environment where children can experiment with words and easily erase them or turn them into other words. Spread finger paint thinly all over a piece of white paper or a large plate. It will serve as your 'paper' for writing. Ask guided questions. For example, 'What will you write?' or 'Can you write the word for something you see nearby?' The colors and the textures will motivate your child to keep trying, and the novelty of the experience will help her remember what she's learned.

The same activity can be done with shaving cream spread thinly over a flat – preferably dark-colored – surface.

Sidewalk chalk

Use sidewalk chalk to write messages or practice words and expressions. Like with finger paint, children may need some initial encouragement. Start with 'Let's make messages and words today in Spanish. Let's leave a message for Mommy/Daddy/ brother.' Your child may prefer you write the message. Just make sure that afterward he writes the words himself. Even if he's just copying what you wrote, he gains confidence in writing that can motivate him to write more later.

Model with your own writing

Set some goals for yourself with writing, as well. As with reading, children are more apt to write if they see parents writing. When do you write in your L1? Would it be possible to write in the L2 for some of these situations? What about Post-It Notes to yourself that are stuck here and there? I found that in making lists of to-dos in the L2, I was forced to learn everyday vocabulary like 'recycle' or 'call the insurance company'. And when your language skills improve, you'll pass them on to your child.

Morning Message

As your children get older, you can incorporate higher-level communication and have children respond in writing on a whiteboard. One big whiteboard works, or a couple of smaller ones.

For my own children, I started out with very simple messages. 'Happy Tuesday! Do you have PE or art today?' It was easy to write the answer, because it was just a matter of copying 'PE' or 'art'. As the children grew, I wrote more complex messages: 'Good morning. I had a great weekend, especially the fall festival. What was your favorite part?'

Be careful not to overcorrect their responses. If you can easily understand what your child wrote, even if words are misspelled, do not correct his work. If you have to ask for clarification to understand, show your child how to write the word and find a way to bring up the word again in the next morning message.

Extended message

If your children have summers off from school, or on their breaks from year-round school, spend time each morning on an extended message. Ask a question that requires more time to respond and needs more help from parents. Read a children's book or part of a young adult book and discuss what you read. Then help children write the most interesting part of what they heard.

Or read a book aloud, pointing to the words as you read. Ask them to choose favorite words – the ones they don't understand or just ones they want to write. Have them write the word on the whiteboard. Extended messages can also include playing any of the games suggested in this chapter. The idea is to get kids interested in the printed word and get them writing.

Short questions

An alternative to the morning message is to write a brief question on a piece of paper and put it with a pencil at your child's place at the breakfast table. Make the question relevant. I've asked, 'Is your science quiz today or tomorrow?' and 'Are you eating the school lunch or a packed lunch?' Form the question such that the answer can be found within the sentence. For example, in the lunch question, they can look at the sentence to get help with the answer: 'school lunch' or 'packed lunch'.

Link Writing to Reading

One way to have meaning-rich writing is to link writing to reading. Any of the reading games from Chapter 9, 'Right to Read', can connect to a writing game or activity. You just have to ask yourself 'How can my child be active in *making* the game?'

M&M game

The M&M game, for example, has children reading slips of paper with quotes of phrases said in their household: 'Did you do your homework?' or 'This dinner's delicious!' (See p. 134, 'M&M game'.) To expand this into a writing activity, let children dictate the sentences they want on the slips of paper and have them watch you write. Eventually, the children can do the writing, starting with the first few letters and building up to words and expressions.

Scavenger hunt

Scavenger hunts motivate kids by playing to their love for codes and secrecy. (See p. 133, 'Scavenger hunt'.) They work best when you have a sibling to hide the treasure for, but kids can do it for parents as well. Decide what the treasure will be – a rubber ball or a piece of chocolate – and where you want to hide it. For the clues, begin with a simple command like 'Go to the kitchen. It's on the table.'

Encourage children to write some of the subsequent clues. Help them find vocabulary on their writing level. If they are frustrated by trying to write a full sentence – for instance, 'The clue is on the sink in the bathroom' – ease them into the writing by suggesting they simply put 'bathroom'.

Don't worry if they misspell words, as long as they can express the main idea. Encourage children to try to write clues without your help so that you can be the seeker. Siblings can work as a team and help each other with the writing. It will give them confidence in their writing to see you follow their clues correctly.

Silly sentences

Children reading words on cards that the L2 parent wrote is the basis for Silly Sentences. They place together cards to form sentences that are nonsensical and fun. To make this a writing activity, get children involved in writing the cards. Children will want to write independently to make you surprised at the silly sentences.

Bingo for writing

The bingo game involves a board made by the L2 parent. (See p. 134, 'Bingo'.) The words on the board have corresponding cards used in the calling. For a writing activity, let the children be involved in making the boards. Have them give you a word for the board. Write the word for them, but let them copy the word onto the corresponding card. If they seem ready to write on their own, let them take over, or give them some direction: 'Write the names of things you see in this room' or 'Write down your favorite foods'.

Don't stifle children's creativity by insisting that each word be spelled perfectly. The idea is to get practice in putting what they know on paper.

Action cubes

The game 'Action Cube' lends itself beautifully to a writing game. (See p. 135, 'Magic cube'.) Find a small box to make a six-sided die. A square kitchen container or an empty square cardboard box will do. Cover it with paper you can write on with a marker.

First, encourage your child to choose an action, such as 'jump up and down three times' or 'clap your hands'. Write the command on one of the faces. Show how the cube can be rolled and explain how the game works. This will get the juices flowing. Encourage your child to do some of the writing, even if she is writing only the simplest words while you write the more complex ones. Set the rule that the actions must be done in the L2, so that 'count to 20 as fast as you can' means you're counting in the L2.

You can also construct a 'Magic Cube', where each side makes a prediction. You then ask the cube a question like 'Will I win my soccer game?' or 'Am I going to get my test back today?' Kids can invent the answers on the block's faces: 'Definitely!', 'No way!', 'Ask again later.'

These games are fun to play just after mealtime while some people are still finishing and the family is relaxing.

Pictionary

Pictionary works best with three players or more. Enlist your child's help in writing cards with common words. Stick with people, places and thing, especially when you're first starting. Place the cards in a pile face down. Have one person take a card and, without showing it to anyone, draw what is on the card. Other players try to guess what it is. Once a correct guess is made, turn over the card for everyone to see, and ask the child to read the word aloud. The artist who gets the most correct guesses from other players wins.

Other games

Other games – like memory and charades from Chapter 9, 'Right to Read' – can all be used for writing. Instead of you doing the writing, the child makes the cards and the hints. (See p. 120, 'Card games', and p. 135, 'Charades'.) To give your child words to choose from, bring out language-rich children's books. Let him know it's not cheating to borrow words from the books.

Calendar

Filling out the family calendar can become a regular writing activity. It starts with the L2 parent committing to writing in the calendar in the L2. Children are encouraged to write activities that involve them – band concert, dance lesson. Parents can help with the first time they write the new words, but when the activity needs to be written on a new date, children write on their own. They are motivated because it is something they see adults doing. They are attracted to the activity because it's authentic and necessary.

Grocery list

Children are motivated to write when it has positive consequences for them. The family grocery list can become the means to that positive outcome. If children write what they would like on the list (in the L2), they have a higher chance of getting the food item they desire. Model these food items by writing your grocery list in the L2. (See p. 137, 'Grocery lists' and 'Recipes'.) Enlist children's help with the list at the grocery store. That way the words are familiar and children can make educated guesses about how to write them.

Errors Are Part of the Process

Your instinct might be to correct your kids whenever you see mistakes in their writing. Instead, give them the time and tools to self-correct.

And if they don't see the mistake, don't get too hung up on it. David Schwarzer is a researcher who taught his first-grade daughter to write in Hebrew, Spanish and English. In his book *Noa's Ark: One Child's Voyage into Multiliteracy*, he notes 'Using language totally free of errors is not an effective way to perceive development. Miscues are the window to the … process' (Schwarzer, 2001: 45). (See p. 88, 'Correction'.)

The first thing my son wrote to me, all on his own initiative, was on a tissue, in big black letters: *Eu adora você*. It translates as 'I loves you' and though I really wanted to correct the verb ending, I resisted. I even hung the tissue on a kitchen cabinet to remind myself that some is enough for now.

Keeping Writing Creative

Remember, you are not a boring classroom teacher and your child isn't sitting in a little wooden desk. Keep it fun! These sample activities can help.

Color and paint

Recognize that drawing and painting may be springboards for writing. Steiner notes that 'Drawing a picture can help the writing process because it helps kids become aware of and develop their thoughts and ideas, a necessary step before you can write them down' (Steiner, 2008: 146).

When you're first starting out, ask your child to draw or paint a picture to make a story about. Then encourage him to tell you the story of the drawing. What are the children doing in the picture? Where are they going next? Where is their mother, father, brother? Let him make up the stories, and *you* do the actual writing on the page once he's finished coloring. Use the story as a bedtime reading to validate it as a *real* story. Once children get the idea, have them write some of the words to the next story.

Label decor

To help children read, we know that labeling things in the house can be fun and effective. Let children decide which items to label. Write the labels in pencil for them to trace in crayon or ink. Or write partial words, leaving out the first letter. This eases children into writing. Eventually, they can write the labels themselves.

After the game, encourage children to look around the room and see their original writing. This serves as a confidence booster. Having the labels in the kids' handwriting gives them more of a sense of ownership, which increases their motivation for the next writing activity.

Collage

Making word collages prepares your child for more advanced forms of original writing. Find magazines or newspapers in the L2, or online magazines you can print. Parenting magazines are particularly effective because they have pictures of families and products that relate to households.

Point out headlines with accompanying images and guess at the meanings. Let children choose words or sentences they recognize and paste them on paper or poster board. Encourage them to add their own illustrations, as well. Some children might draw one illustration for every word. Others might be interested in making a sort of comic strip. The idea is to let your child jump ahead a level or two by 'borrowing' the printed words that might be difficult for her to write on her own. Being able to express more complex ideas shows your child how powerful words can be.

Happy box

Find a cardboard box you can designate as the 'Happy Box'. Use L2 magazines, newspaper or stickers and find images that make your child happy. Then cut out words that have to do with happy things. The word could be 'dog' or 'sun'. Paste the words and images on the box, or put them inside. Children may think of words like 'Grandpa' that aren't in magazines. Help them write the original words on the box.

Fill the box with actual items that make your child happy: a ball, a coin or a toy car. Encourage him to write the word for each item to glue to the outside of the box.

Photo books

Use a blank book or spiral notebook for a scrapbook of photos. (See p. 113, 'Photo albums as books'.) Begin with your child telling you what descriptions to write below the photos. As you write, make sure your child is watching. Ask questions like 'Do you see the humps of the "M"¿' Once she learns to recognize familiar words – 'Daddy in the yard' or 'Me swinging' – see if she wants to do the writing.

For more enriched vocabulary, ask her to describe what people are doing or how people are feeling below the pictures: running, fishing, happy, or sleepy. You can also write captions of what people in the photo might be saying. Cartoon bubbles would be fun: 'I love it here!' or 'I'm tired, let's go!'

Connecting Through Writing

There are many opportunities for your child to connect to others though writing.

Making board games

With games like 'Monopoly' and 'The Game of Life' as models, children can make their own games. (See p. 134, 'Board games for reading'.) The board can be made of a large piece of butcher paper with a trail drawn through it. Children put directions along the trail: 'Go back three' or 'Draw a card'. Then they make the actual cards to be drawn. Give assistance where needed, but let the bulk of the ideas come from the children. Being able to use the game will be a big confidence builder for their language abilities.

Secret letters

Write simple letters to your child and leave them on her pillow. Tell her that if she responds, you'll write back to her. Initially she may write back in the L1, but encourage her to write back in the L2. Ask her questions that contain many of the words she'll need to respond.

In my case, I made little survey-type questions for my daughter to answer. That way, she had all the vocabulary she needed. She often had multiple-choice responses, like 'Which was your favorite thing we did this weekend? a. skating b. the dog park c. watching the video'.

Native speaker letters

Contacting a native speaker by letter or email can help writing feel natural. Do you know a native speaker to write to? (See p. 15, 'Native speaker as a tool, not a goal'.)

The first correspondence could be one your child dictates to you. That lets him create the ideas while you do the actual typing or writing. Or, for simple messages, you can write the words and have him color them in – 'HAPPY BIRTHDAY!' in block letters, for example. Eventually you'll want your child to do some of the writing too. Consider sending a card to an L2 speaker, with just a few words added to it, such as a get-well-soon card. Remind your child that the words don't have to be perfect to be meaningful.

Computer games and videos

Search 'learn to write' or 'activities learn to write' in the L2 and you'll find free online games where kids can play with letters and words. You'll see an abundance of educational sites with online worksheets you can download free of charge. Passive games like word searches are a good place to start because children look at and play with the word they are searching for before being asked to actually write the word.

Many sites have crossword puzzles to print out. You may need to fill in some of the blanks to get your child started.

Add 'games' to your search and you may find sites that have interactive ways to move letters around. You'll also see talking words that activate curiosity, giving children control over which words to learn.

Go to YouTube and search 'learn to write' in the L2. You'll find help for children and adults with music and interesting images.

Social networking

For high-school students, social networking is an excellent way to practice writing. Different counties use different social networking sites. Search for 'social networking other countries' in English to find which one is most used in the target language country. It is easy to assume Facebook is the only option, especially given how it's translated into so many languages, but look around. RenRen.com, in China, closely follows Facebook's model and has 120 million users. Sonico.com is popular in Latin American, while Mixi.jp in Japan has 30 million users worldwide.

Just logging on to a foreign social networking site exposes kids to new vocabulary. Filling out preferences offers writing practice. Your child will utilize descriptive words as she makes her own page. When adding pictures to the page, she will write captions. The advertising is even educational, because images are accompanied by words.

A pen-pal-type relationship can develop through this networking, offering constant practice with a native speaker. (See p. 15, 'Native speaker as a tool, not a goal'.) And since the page is a reflection of your child, she will be motivated to be accurate in the language she uses.

Make writing assessable

Just like it's easier to do carpentry if you have the right tools around you, it is easier to write if you have easy access to writing tools. This is as simple as having sharpened pencils available, but can be enhanced by brightly colored pens and nice notebooks that entice children to write.

Try to keep your writing utensils and paper for the L2 separate from those in the L1, and go the extra mile in making the L2 ones interesting. Change the materials you use from time to time to keep things novel.

You Can Do This

If you still feel in doubt about teaching your child to write, remember, you're not teaching your child to write everything. You are working to attain a certain realistic writing goal – modeling each step as you go. Give the reins little by little to your child, watching him become more and more confident. The errors that you see show what to do for future writing practice.

Seven Reasons Why Teaching L2 Writing Makes Sense

- Writing gives kids another form in which to express themselves.
- Writing offers children the chance to further practice their fine-motor skills.
- Kids who write can create characters and situations that keep them interested in the L2.
- Writing slows communication down, allowing for a new level of processing.
- Writing gives children the satisfaction of being able to see what they've written down. They get pleasure out of seeing others glean meaning from what they've written.
- Kids who write can try on different voices as they write in different genres: personal emails, texts, instructions for games, recipes or business-type letters.
- Writing means recording stories to go back to another day.

11 Take Off! Finding Ways to Actually Go There

One language sets you in a corridor for life.
Two languages open every door along the way.
Frank Smith (Live Mocha, 2014)

Just Do It!

You've been thinking of going to the target country for years. When do you finally take the plunge? The answer is, do it when your children are still little. Merrill writes 'The temptation is always to delay – until the house is renovated, or your bank account is healthier ... until the children are old enough to appreciate the Alhambra' (Merrill, 1984: 174). But it's important to go while children are still young and not intimidated by trying something new. As they see first-hand how a whole country speaks the L2, they understand that the language that seemed 'extra at home is essential abroad' (Merrill, 1984: 174).

I'm at a disadvantage

If you're a non-native speaker deciding on travel to the target country, you may feel at a disadvantage. After all, native speakers can have extended stays, visiting relatives and friends. One non-native mom laments,

> I had friends who were doing it [teaching their children French], but they were actually French so they were more legit and they had more success. The reason is that they would take the child to the place where the language was spoken. (J.F., interview)

Non-native parents might also feel behind culturally. They know the right words, but not the right customs behind what they're saying. What better reason, then, to expose yourself to the culture of the target country, to experience firsthand how people live.

This chapter will highlight how a non-native can best benefit from travel to the target country. It offers tips on how to avoid the tourist trap and instead meet people and participate in day-to-day life.

Speaking to other children

A good place to start is to help your child meet other children. One mother teaching French to her son writes,

> He would only use French with me for about a year. Whenever anyone else, native or no, spoke to him in French, he always replied in English until that trip to Paris in March. It was brilliant! He met a little girl in the park the first day and ran up to me, face aglow, shouting *'Maman, Maman, elle parle Français aussi!!'* [Mommy, Mommy, she speaks French too!!'] It was a total light bulb moment. Since then, he has been happy to speak to others in French. (M.G., email interview)

Passive to active

The beauty of travel for language learning is that language skills that may be passive (listening skills) can become active (speaking skills). (See p. 74, 'Is understanding enough?') So for parents who are frustrated that they're speaking the language but their child's not responding in the L2, traveling can tilt their child toward speaking.

Myles says 'Children are pragmatic and they will learn what they perceive as necessary, interesting, and fun' (Myles, 2003: 3). Speaking a language while you're in the country is necessary – you must order food at a restaurant. It is interesting and fun because you're in a different environment, puzzling out what to do and how to behave. You have built-in motivation to actively use the L2.

There is also a normalization phenomenon occurring. It is the norm to speak Serbian in Serbia, whereas when you speak Serbian at home in Australia, people look and stare. One man I interviewed had, as a child, refused to speak the L2 his parents spoke to him: 'I guess it was too weird and I was weird enough. I think I just wanted to fit in' (E.O., email interview). He said, though, that when his parents took him to visit the country, he soaked up the language and used it much more.

How to not be tourists

> *Go where people are talking, since you haven't come abroad to commune with the trees.*
> Jane Merrill, *Bringing Up Baby Bilingual* (1984: 174)

You are not a tourist on this trip. You may have had trips in the past to historic places where you were sightseeing. You may have gone to the beach where you read novels and caught some waves. This is a different sort of holiday, where you'll focus less on the places you'll see and more on the communication and culture you'll be exposed to.

This trip is more for being with people in their daily lives and trying to use the language in real situations. Before you leave home, communicate with your children how this trip will be different from other vacations. Let kids know they'll be taking an active role in deciding how to spend the time, in reading maps and in talking to locals. Get their input in setting goals early on. They are not along for the ride; they are sharing the driving.

Setting goals

Setting goals for your trip is just as important as packing your suitcase. One mother felt that the promise of a trip kept her motivated to speak the language, but as to the reality of a trip, she says 'Unfortunately, I would be a bit slack unless I had a set goal' (H.G., email interview).

Make plans for events ahead of time, if possible, so you can know what to expect. That way you can use the language effectively in the activities. For example, if you know you're going to tour a military fort and the changing of the guards, discuss what you'll see ahead of time. Ask your child what she thinks she'll see at the base. Look at the fort online in the L2. Come up with some L2 questions to ask the tour guide.

Keep in mind that you may do only one or two things a day to have time for interaction with other people. Merrill warns against 'inflicting a slew of postcard-like scenes on your bored children' (Merrill, 1984: 175). Instead, keep your plans kid-friendly and simplify whenever possible.

Language Prep

To get the most out of your travels, prepare ahead of time for what language you might need along the way. Give your kids practice in communicating with others by acting out typical interactions they may face: asking for a cup of milk at a restaurant, buying a map at a newspaper stand or inquiring about a restroom. Keep the interactions light and comical so children look forward to talking with native speakers. (See p. 15, 'Native speaker as a tool, not a goal'.)

Tell bedtime stories that have the target country as the backdrop. Use city names that children will later see on signs. Ask your child to repeat the names of towns and places to practice the pronunciation.

Travel information

Much of this information can be found from online travel guides. Frommers.com has many destinations and LonelyPlanet.com has budget travel ideas. Or search 'travel in Ecuador' written in the L2. You'll find websites and guidebooks in the L2. You can guess at the meanings, since pictures are often attached to captions and short blurbs of information.

Using the guides, you can mention to your children important places you'll spend time in, like a popular park or shopping area. Discuss famous people you might learn about and why they're important. Look into different modes of transportation and decide how to get to places of interest.

Find pictures and descriptions of typical dishes and ask your child which ones he is looking forward to. (And which ones he's nervous about.) Search online for 'restaurants in Quito', in the L2. Menus of some restaurants are posted online. Decide what you'd order and practice speaking to the waiter.

You can also go to YouTube.com to see videos of the country. Search for *viajar a Buenos Aires* (travel to Buenos Aires). You'll see everything from television sound bites to people's individual travel videos in the L2. Focus on one or two of the things said in the video and replay them several times until the children can mimic the accent. Being accustomed to natives' speech will give children confidence when they hear the L2 on the trip.

Safety prep

Be sure your children have the language they need to find you if they get lost. Explain who to ask for help – a family with children, an elderly woman. If applicable, practice saying your cell phone number in the L2. Go over the addresses where you'll be staying.

Pack some fun

As you pack, think of things that will attract other children. Those crazy high bouncy balls, stickers and yo-yos. Your children playing with toys – especially unusual ones – will draw other kids to play and interact in the language. On our trip to Brazil, we found kazoos to be a fascination among adults and children.

Travel smart

Be smart about money and your documents. Have a money belt to keep your money and documents close to your body. Keep the phone number of your credit card company in a separate place from your credit card. Have the emergency number of the embassy and a copy of your passport in a safe place, separate from your passport.

Keep travel as stress free as possible. In your carry-on bag, pack one change of clothes for everyone in case your luggage is delayed or lost. Carry all medications on the plane with you. Band-Aids® and an allergy medicine like Benadryl® can be a last-minute lifesaver. (Take the chewable Benadryl® to pass through security.)

In your bag, have a pen and notepad, since they aren't usually offered in smaller hotels. You may want them for writing down new words.

Check with airlines about meals and snacks. You can request special food, like children's meals, if your kids are picky eaters. Have plenty of granola bars, nuts and dried fruit in your carry-on.

Remind yourself that if you leave something at home, there's no need to despair. It'll give you more chances to interact with people as you purchase, for example, a hat or a large bag. And it'll be a nice souvenir for after the trip.

Connect to media

Once you are on your trip, connect to the media. Listen to the radio or watch television. Ask your child to listen and report one thing he heard. It could be on anything, from a child's program to the weather. Let him be the expert, explaining what he's learned.

Work with your child to read headlines from newspapers or headings from magazines. Read the comics together.

Stay for a Month or More

One of the most expensive parts of travel is getting to and from your destination. If possible, therefore, try to stay for several weeks. Many families I interviewed found three weeks to one month to be ideal, because it was financially feasible and gave their children a good amount of time to be surrounded by the language.

One parent I interviewed by email lives in the UK and speaks Flemish to her daughter. She visits Belgium frequently to see visit old friends. She writes in an email:

> I know that Myra has some problems to talk with me in Flemish, but I also know that, when she comes back to Belgium and plays a few days with her Belgian friends, her Flemish vocabulary comes back quickly. I do think that this kind of contact on a regular basis is very favourable. (D.E., email interview)

Frugal lodging

A longer stay may mean more frugality. Go on the off season. (Be sure to check the weather to make sure it's not the rainy season, since you want to spend time outdoors.) Stay in budget accommodation. Many countries have family hostels that are clean and comfortable – not like the youth hostels of the past. The communal amenities (shared bathroom, kitchen) may appeal to your children because they'll have more contact with other children. Online photos and reviews let you know what to expect.

Search 'international homestay' or 'house/home exchange' to find families abroad interested in hosting families for pay, or in a house swap. To learn about kid-friendly places to rent, sites like AirBnB.com have specific sections for families.

Think outside the box. Some countries like Italy offer ready-to-stay-in tents that you can rent quite cheaply. Do some research ahead of time to see what type of area you will be in, to make sure it's safe. You will also want to avoid being surrounded by tourists who speak your L1.

The most frugal lodging is to stay with friends. Search out personal connections in the target country. Perhaps you can room with relatives of friends you've met who are living in the target country. If you can stay with someone, you will hear the language so much more and be exposed to more of the local culture. The emotional bonds formed when staying in close quarters with people of the culture will tie you more firmly to the country and the language. You can maintain contact and offer to reciprocate the lodging if they travel to your country. If they come to visit you, you'll get to practice your L2 all over again.

Eating well on a budget

You can save money by finding alternatives to eating out. Make a meal of local produce, cheeses and breads. Find spreadable proteins made from ham, beef, cheese or nuts. Bring a can opener and consider purchasing an inexpensive food warmer to heat canned items like soup, especially if you're traveling during cold weather, when hot food is more appealing.

Don't assume because you're 'eating in' that you won't have contact with locals. Ask questions of the butcher, the man at the bakery or the woman selling you wine.

Consider food as you choose your lodging. You might be interested in a pension – a guesthouse that serves meals. Or a bed and breakfast-type lodging might suit your needs, especially if it means having access to a refrigerator and microwave.

Engaging native speakers

To engage native speakers, think small! Small hotels, small grocers and small restaurants. You'll get more personalized service. And for you who are native English speakers, you'll limit your exposure to English being spoken by tourists and staff. For people you'll see more than once, like hotel workers, mention that your family is very interested in learning the language. If people respond in your L1 to your attempts to speak the L2, pleasantly continue speaking in the L2 and they'll probably get the hint.

Engage strangers in simple conversations. Seek out the butcher or waiter who doesn't appear to be in a rush, and ask questions. Follow up on these conversations later with your children. Children love to mimic others. Ask 'How did the grocer answer your question?' Encourage funny voices and faces.

Get outside

Don't worry if you don't climb the highest mountain or visit every museum. Just get outside, because it can lead to interactions. Eat lunch outside. Go to playgrounds in residential neighborhoods. Find popular parks.

Do kid-friendly things like feeding the ducks at a pond. Offer to share your bread with a child who is looking at the ducks. To facilitate making friends, return to the same places at the same time of day. You'll begin to recognize other families and it'll be easier to start up a conversation.

Go to local festivals, sporting events and outdoor markets. Keep your rain ponchos handy for outdoor shows. Ask questions of other families at the event. Even something as simple as asking another parent 'Where are the restrooms?' can start a conversation and give your children time to play with their children.

Be a detective

Find out what is happening in the community by playing detective. Be a part of the culture around you. Here are some hints:

- Find out what the local community center offers.
- Tap into churches, since they typically have ongoing activities for children. Imagine how much authentic language you would hear at a church barbecue!
- Libraries and universities have listings for everything from local speakers to play-groups.
- Go to a visitor help center. Tell them why you're in the country and ask for ideas for ways to meet up with local children.
- When leaving stores or cafés, pick up brochures on local happenings.
- Buy a local paper for its calendar and search for gatherings involving kids.

For anything you read and don't understand, ask a local. Remember that most people are happy to answer questions. Take a risk and meet someone new.

Call attention to yourself

Most of the time when traveling, you want to blend in. But there is a time to call attention to yourself – to draw in children to play with yours. Bring the interesting toys you packed for the kids, or buy some bubbles. Take them to places like the post office or a café. This will catch the attention of other children and a conversation can begin.

Don't be shy with other children's parents – remember, this is your opportunity to converse as well. Prepare questions ahead of time so you can ask 'How old are your children?', 'Have you lived here long?' and 'Where are the kids in school?' Once you've established a rapport with a parent, ask about local activities you might attend.

Transport

Choose public transportation over taxis when possible, because you have more chances of meeting other children. When you enter a bus or train, scout out a good location – near children of your kids' ages. Again, bring some sharable toys so they can easily start playing.

Whenever possible, walk. It gives you time to stop, listen and connect to others. Remember, you're taking this vacation slow. There's no race to hit all the hot spots.

Kids Take the Lead

While on public transportation or out around the town, encourage your child to read the signs. Give him the map and let him do the navigation. He can also read subway guides, storefront signs, the bread types at the bakery, etc. If you go to a supermarket, let him find the canned goods, so he can read the labels. Ask him about the prices of different produce so he'll read the names of the fruits and vegetables. Get his help deciding on the best deals on cheese and meat so he'll need to look at names and prices. Encourage him to use the money, ask about cost and say the pleases and thank yous.

Once you're back at your hotel, let your child take the lead on communications. If you need extra soap, let him make the phone call. If you need a parking pass, let him ask at the front desk. These little interactions will build your child's confidence in the language and he'll be more apt to use it with strangers in the future. (If your child tends to be shy, you might practice similar interactions in the L1 and then in the L2 before leaving on your trip.)

Gifts and resources

Let your child take the lead in buying gifts and resources in the language. If she's in charge of which gifts are bought to take back home, she's more likely to agree to ask questions about products. Use this time to buy resources in the language to take home: books, games and DVDs.

Document what's happening

Blog or keep a journal about your experiences, making entries at the end of each day. Let children think back on the day and come up with titles in the L2 for different activities. If you had dinner purchased from a street vendor, they might title it 'Street Food'. Let children illustrate your book, or use postcards as illustrations.

Taking the time to write allows for reflection on cultural differences. Mention the people you came in contact with: the little girl in the pharmacy who wanted to know where you were from, the woman asking for alms in the open-air market. Writing about your experiences makes them real and encourages future interaction. Read passages from journal entries and use what you learn to help make plans for the next day. Do we want to return to the square nearby? Did you want to see any more of that arboretum with the unusual plants?

Ask if there were times your child felt strange or uncomfortable. Encourage a positive interpretation of these feelings. Avoid judgmental statements. Instead, say 'That was so different for me when I saw…' or 'I wasn't used to someone doing…'.

Discuss what it means to be the foreign one. Open children up to the perspective of Robert Louis Stevenson, who says 'There are no foreign lands. It is the traveller only who is foreign' (No Foreign Lands, 2013).

Alone time

If you're traveling in close quarters with your family, you'll need some alone time. Taking time to rest will rejuvenate you for later. Everyone's definition of rest is different, so discuss as a family how each of you will relax: taking a nap, reading in the hotel or indulging in a long bath.

Extended Stay

Twenty years from now you will be more disappointed by the things that you didn't do than by the ones you did do. So throw off the bowlines. Catch the trade winds in your sails. Explore. Dream. Discover.
Mark Twain (Goodreads, 2012b)

If you have the chance to live in the target country for several months, or years, it'll make an amazing difference in your language skills, and in your life as a whole. If you are looking for a short-term job, you can find everything from an internship in a company to a 'farm stay' in a rural area. Check out Overseasjobs.com for thousands of job listings around the globe. Or use a job site like Monster.com, which has 40 countries to choose from. You'll also get tips on how to manage changes in the family dynamics as you move abroad and when you return. Keep options open by being willing to live in a smaller town off the beaten path. The more rural and less commercial, the fewer tourists you'll see and the more you'll hear the L2.

Search 'expats in [city name]' and you'll find expatriate resources all over the world, tips on moving to the country and how to get established, and blogs of veteran parents with free advice. You can also contact the target country's embassy. It will have information on children's activities and school enrollment. The staff can also help with paperwork you'll need for travel.

Connect through faith

If applicable, take steps even before your trip to connect with others of your religious affiliation. Use denominations or religion names paired with the town you're visiting to find churches, synagogues or mosques. Contact the office or leader by phone or email to let them know you're arriving with your family and would love to get to know other people with young children.

Network with parents

A journey is best measured in friends, rather than miles.
Tim Cahill, adventure travel writer (Goodreads, 2012c)

Join a parenting network. Many blogs are available to help parents make the transition to a new place. Talking with other parents can help with details, like how to best register your kids in school. Ties you form can help you break into society and make friends. Don't be shy about asking for new friends' email addresses or phone numbers to contact them during your stay and keep in touch after your trip is over.

Short-term classes

Many countries have short-term classes for adults and children. Parents and children who study together in school can share a real bonding experience. I spoke with one American mother who was having trouble getting her elementary school-aged son to speak Spanish with her. She decided to enroll him and herself in classes in Honduras. That way, she reasoned, upon returning, they could continue speaking Spanish. The Spanish would become an extension of the interesting and fun trip they experienced.

To find short-term classes for children, search for '<L2> classes for children <target city or country>'. It's best to start looking for kids' classes before the adult ones, because adult classes are easier to find. Some private language schools offer classes that adults and children take together.

Kids in school

If you're in the country for several months, you might enroll your child in a full-time school or preschool. The extra exposure will help with cultural connections. One Australian family I interviewed had enormous success putting their two children in preschool in Japan for a month:

They fit in and became little blond blue-eyed Japanese boys. It was so incredible. I was surprised at how they fit in, not only in terms of speaking and things, but behavior and bowing and the whole cultural thing, it was very powerful. (P.R. email interview)

Find out details about schools through expat sites and blogs. Contact the target country's minister of education for schedules and details about paperwork. As you decide where to enroll your kids in school, remain as flexible as possible about location and dates.

If possible, arrive in the country several weeks before school starts for your children to acclimatize to the newness of the area. Buy school books and supplies early. If your children feel intimidated by any of the subjects, find a high-school or college student to tutor them. The work with a native speaker will greatly improve their L2 skills. (See p. 15, 'Native speaker as a tool, not a goal'.)

Bilingual schools abroad

Across the globe, children are educated in bilingual schools. (See Edna Murphy's *Welcoming Linguistic Diversity in Early Childhood Classrooms* – Murphy, 2011.) Parents who are moving abroad might enroll their children in such bilingual programs. For example, a British family might choose an English/Spanish school while living in Madrid. Some sources I've read discourage this plan, since these schools are designed to teach English to local children, not Spanish to foreign students. I think, however, that they expose your kids to curriculum in the L2 and to other children who speak the L2. On the playground, there will be no 'bilingualism': kids will speak Spanish.

Delayed results

Have you ever taken your child to an activity and, at the time, they seemed uninterested? It may have appeared they weren't enjoying themselves or weren't taking anything in. Then, months later, they describe the experience to a friend or remember a little detail you've forgotten and you realize they absorbed more than you thought. Traveling is a lot like that. In the moment, there's often too much going on to process, and children may appear distant or not as responsive as you'd like. It's best to relax and know that the trip will have an influence past what you see in the moment. This point was well illustrated by a mother who responds to my question 'What advice would you offer other parents raising bilingual children?'

> Go to the place. There's nothing that I think will substitute for going to the country. And to make it as child oriented as possible. When they were little we went to Paris and they went to a park and we had to pay a lady to push them on the swings....

And that was extraordinary for the kids to have a lady take over and not the parents who pushed the swings…. And looking at the funny money you pay with…. At the time it didn't seem to have such an impact on them, but the way they talk about it now makes me realize how much they got from it. At the time, I was disappointed from the lack of reaction from them, but it was all absorbed, so there's a delayed proof of the experience. (S.B., email interview)

Travel's not a must, but…

As parents, we have to give ourselves some grace in case we just cannot travel. Financial and health-related issues may mean it's not feasible. You don't need to travel to learn another language. It's the icing on the cake. A non-native English speaker writes,

> Some people prefer to go to Italy to learn Italian but I learned English in the Soviet Union, so I know it's possible because my teachers didn't speak proper English and had horrible accents. I think you can learn, but it's more free when you get to the environment. (O.F., interview)

So go to the country if possible. Immerse yourself. Find children to play with and adults to talk to. If not, try to do these same things in your own country, spending time with native speakers and using the hints you've learned in past chapters.

In either case, enjoy the ride.

Seven Tips for Travelers

- Go small. Small hotels, small shops, small restaurants. You have a better chance of talking to native speakers and of avoiding tourists who speak your L1.
- Try new foods but procure some old favorites too. That way kids are willing to be adventurous, knowing that there's a safety net. Prepare them for the unfamiliar foods by showing pictures of local fare.
- Make connections before you go. Contact a house of worship of your religion or make a connection through your university.
- Ditch the taxi and take the bus instead. Stake out a seat by a family with kids of similar age to your own.
- Get outside. Swing in local playgrounds. Spend time in parks and on benches outside public places. Return to the same spots in hope of meeting the 'regulars'.
- Walk and listen. Whenever you can, get from place to place on foot. Stop as you go, to listen to those around you.
- Let kids lead the way in the shops. Let them decide what to buy as souvenirs and gifts. Encourage them to ask questions about quantities or prices.

12 Meeting Challenges: Skillfully Riding the Ups and Downs

Accept challenges, so that you may feel the exhilaration of victory.
George Patton (quoted in Daugherty, 2011)

In my interviews with families and my readings of the literature, I've found three over-arching concerns about raising bilingual children in homes with non-native speakers:

(1) It's not right.
(2) It won't work.
(3) It won't last.

Many of these assertions stem from outside pressures from people and groups I call 'naysayers'. At this point, we'll look at naysayers' arguments and how to combat them. Some of these statements come from parents' own lack of confidence in teaching a language. With a few hints, you'll feel more at ease in carrying out your language plan. And through the words of bilingual teenagers, you'll get a glimpse into results that last.

It's Not Right

Naysayers include complete strangers, educators, doctors and even our own kids. Their negativity is often based on mistrust and misinformation. Annick De Houwer writes 'Many parents, schoolteachers and child health professionals believe that bilingual input can be a threat to children's development' (De Houwer, 2009: 69).

We're not telling secrets

There is the fear, common to all English-only speakers, that the chief purpose of foreign language is to make fun of us. Otherwise, you know, why not just come out and say it?
Barbara Ehrenreich, columnist, *The Worst Years of Our Lives* (Ehrenreich in Eilers, 2011)

Some people equate speaking another language with passing along a secret message. This makes speaking the L2 secretive and rude, though that is probably not the speaker's intent at all.

One woman who tries to speak exclusively Flemish to her children says 'We don't pay attention to it [to speaking the L2]: it's something so natural'. But she quickly adds that when she spoke Flemish to her children around other monolinguals, people looked at her 'as if we want to say something they are not supposed to hear' (D.E., interview).

What can parents do to show they are not speaking a code language? One mother who speaks Japanese to her children offers some great advice:

> The most difficult thing for me to overcome is speaking the language in public.... If people overhear me, I just say, 'I'm teaching my children to be bilingual – I hope it doesn't make you feel uncomfortable. I'm happy to tell you what we're saying if you ever want to know.' If you put yourself in this humble position, people are really respectful and think it's great, but if you don't make people feel comfortable, they'll think, 'Gosh, she thinks she's so great' or they think you're talking about them behind their back. (P.R., interview)

Exclusion

Another common problem is that people overhearing the L2 feel left out of the conversation. I have to share my personal experience in this area. My parents have been supportive of my raising the children bilingual, but were frustrated when they found out that I would be speaking Portuguese even when I was around them, not just when I was alone with the children. My journal entry from when the children were two and four years old reflects their angst.

> Today, Momma said I'd changed from what she thought was my original plan which was to speak Portuguese to Sydney when English speakers weren't around. She said, 'We miss some of her personality because we don't understand what you two are talking about.' I can see her point. Not ready to make a change, though. I do translate when Sydney says something cute. (journal, 10/26/2006)

This problem got worse as the children grew. The following journal entry was written five years later, when the kids were seven and nine. We spent a week in my parents' house and this entry was written toward the end of the week.

> Today my parents said they didn't like how we were speaking so much Portuguese [around them].... Diddy [Daddy] said it was rude and that he didn't raise me to speak in a language that some people don't understand. I couldn't get across that we've established Portuguese as our language and we can't just change it when we're around people. (journal, 7/25/2011)

I found myself very frustrated for the next couple of days, because I knew in my heart that it's very difficult to teach children a language when you're basically the sole person doing it. We need every chance we get to practice. Otherwise, it's like someone who goes on a diet, but then at every turn – the office party, a birthday, holidays – they splurge and go off the diet. It just doesn't work as well as eating well overall. Trying something worthwhile takes effort, and sometimes sacrifice. It was worth it to me, but I love my parents and wanted them to be happy. Was it right for me to insist they sacrifice?

For days after the journal entry, I handled the problem by translating everything the kids and I said. In the end, I think we realized that some flexibility on all our parts was needed. Since that time, I've asked the kids to direct the conversation toward my parents, instead of speaking directly to me. It allows for more English, while keeping the 'Portuguese-only with Mommy' rule intact.

Grandparents and expectations

One reason extended family such as grandparents might not be on board with hearing so much of the L2 is that they have expectations for what their grandchildren will be like and how their relationship will be. Children speaking a language their grandparents don't understand is rarely a part of these expectations.

Virginie Raguenaud's book *Bilingual by Choice* (2009) suggests that grandparents want to see themselves in their grandchildren and that children rattling off a language totally incomprehensible to them makes them feel distant, not close. She also notes that grandparents may have found learning a foreign language difficult, and assume their grandchildren are having the same difficulty. One mother writes of her in-laws, 'We've had it said to us by family members – not mine, Tony's [my husband's] family members who are devoted to English … [that] we might burn out our children's brains' (S.B., interview).

Authors of bilingual guidebooks have a variety of opinions on this circumstance. One recommends using the L1 more around people who seem uncomfortable with the L2. Carolyn Gibson writes:

> If you cannot minimize contact with such people, for instance the difficult mother-in-law who comes over for Sunday lunch, and you still want to minimize the conflict that it might cause either between you or between those people and your children, then it might be necessary, as a last resort, to (slightly) alter your learning plans to avoid such conflicts. (Gibson, 2011: 135)

Or you can go the way of one of the authors of *Bilingual Is Better*:

> I even have a few family members who get angry with me because we can't have a three-way conversation since I only use Spanish with my daughter and refuse to switch to English regardless of where we are or who we are with. Observing how

well my girl communicates in both languages at three years old, I'm learning better how to not care what others think. (Flores & Soto, 2012: 89)

Similarly, Steiner remains firm in the face of these negative attitudes. She writes,

Don't cave in if people around you express disapproval or concern that you are 'forcing' your child to speak another language. It can sometimes be difficult for a monolingual person to understand that raising a child to learn to speak two (or more) languages is in some ways like raising a child to learn to eat a healthy diet. (Steiner, 2008: 109)

Discuss with grandparents how this healthy diet works. Explain how the process of early acquisition differs from learning a language later, in the classroom. Raguenaud suggests asking grandparents to express 'their own frustrations at not speaking a second language' (Raguenaud, 2009: 63) to the grandchildren. This could be a wonderful way to show children the value of learning a language early in life.

Tone and volume

One of the most important things you can do to bring family and others on board with your language choice is to watch your tone in the L2. Keep your tone positive when you're around others. Your kids know they have a code language with you, but discourage them from using it to make derogatory comments. Never talk negatively about someone in the L2 when you're in their presence; people generally get the vibe, even if they don't understand the meaning.

Also, try speaking in a quieter tone if you're around people who are sensitive to the L2. It's similar to talking more quietly on a cell phone in public as a way to respect people around you.

Naysayers who are strangers

Negative feelings about our speaking the L2 can also come from people we don't even know. As parents, we must remind ourselves that negative comments sometimes come not from malice, but from ignorance. One woman I interviewed spoke Japanese to her children and was shocked by the comments made when other people overheard Japanese:

I'm bi-cultural and have dark skin, so I look sort of Mexican or Spanish or something, so people have even looked at me and said, 'That's not Spanish, what are you speaking?' or 'Shouldn't you be speaking Spanish to them?' (P.R., interview)

We can't protect ourselves and our children completely from odd or negative comments, but we can control how we react to them. Part of that reaction is to keep the comments in perspective. Most families I've interviewed will attest to the fact that they receive more positive feedback from people seeing them raise bilingual children than negative. One mother writes,

> Usually I get good feedback, except for once there was a woman at Layla's dance studio who heard us speaking it and got all mad and was like, 'This is an ENGLISH speaking country. Speak ENGLISH!' (F.R., email interview)

As is often the case, the negative comments seem to burn more deeply into our consciousness. That's because 'the brain handles positive and negative information in different hemispheres', according to Professor Clifford Nass, cited in the *New York Times* article 'Praise is fleeting, but brickbats we recall'. He goes on:

> Negative emotions generally involve more thinking, and the information is processed more thoroughly than positive ones…. Thus, we tend to ruminate more about unpleasant events – and use stronger words to describe them – than happy ones. (Nass in Tugend, 2012)

To stop the rumination, make the negative comment about the speaker, not about you. A friend of mine says that, in public, when her four-year-old is being loud and active, if someone keeps giving her dirty looks, she says to herself 'They must have very bad gas.' Know that you're not alone when it comes to negative comments, and try to come to the most benign conclusion.

Strangers and language confusion

Strangers may have a sincere worry that you'll confuse your children with a second language. One woman I interviewed said people who heard her taking to her infant in another language warned 'Don't do that, you'll confuse that baby!' (J.S., interview).

Some of the fear of overloading children's brains is based on antiquated research that said children could be cognitively confused when introduced to two languages at once. These studies have since been dismissed for poor methodology, but they still influence some people's opinions about bilingualism. (See Chapter 1, 'There Is a Free Lunch!', for more information on language confusion.)

Look for positive models of bilingualism around you to assuage your doubts. A case study by Stephen Caldas and Suzanne Caron-Caldas (1992) follows the authors (husband and wife) as they teach their L2, French, to their children in the United States. Though both were teachers of French, they were worried about confusing their son by speaking two languages to him. The one thing that kept them going was the inspiration received from a little boy they saw while traveling in Europe. He was three years old and spoke French to his father and English to his mother, speaking perfectly to both. Even with Caldas and Caron-Caldas' language background, having a real situation in mind was more helpful than anything else.

Language delay

Onlookers and well-meaning friends or professionals may blame bilingualism for more than just 'confusion'. They may notice that your child is slower to start talking because she is bilingual. This extended time period or slower rate of linguistic development is referred to as language delay. King and Mackey discuss a silent period that sometimes occurs as bilingual children develop, wherein you don't see much language progress – a 'plateau or stabilization' (King & Mackey, 2007: 213).

Instead of giving up on bilingualism when a lull in progress occurs, parents should increase the linguistic input by expanding on what the child does say, even if it's only one word. For example, if your child says 'juice' in the L2, add 'Oh, you would like juice. Say, "juice, please!"'

Parents of boys who are getting the L2 from their mothers notice a longer delay. Some argue that's because boys are less verbally communicative. One mother says 'In general, girls have a wider vocabulary and tend to be more chatty, so [they] pick up the language more rapidly' (P.R., email interview). In such cases, parents may need to do extra work to find topics of conversation or stimulating questions that relate to their son's interests. Ask open-ended questions to discover what these subjects are. Once you know, ask specific questions that show you're paying attention and genuinely curious. Avoid general yes-and-no questions like 'Was preschool fun today?' Ask instead, 'What did you make in art?' or 'What games did you play on the playground?' and follow up with 'Tell me more'.

Parents with children who show any of the following signs of challenges to language development may need to discuss their language plan with a clinician, particularly one who is familiar with childhood bilingualism: these include but are not limited to prolonged language delay, stuttering or stammering, dyslexia, deafness, Down syndrome, autism, or other behavioral and educational challenges. See the following resources for suggestions of interventions:

- Barbara Zurer Pearson's *Raising a Bilingual Child* (2008), pp. 221–238.
- Carey Myles' *Raising Bilingual Children* (2003), pp. 189–198.
- Kendall King and Alison Mackey's *The Bilingual Edge: Why, When, and How to Teach Your Child a Second Language* (2007), pp. 207–219.

Hormonal studies have shown that testosterone at a certain point of male development inhibits the use of the language part of the brain. It can seem to parents that their boys are slower to communicate. Parents should beware, however, of the self-fulfilling prophecy of the belief that daughters are more communicative than their sons. Barron-Hauwaert, in her look at siblings and language learning, writes 'girls might excel linguistically because mothers talk more to their daughters than their sons.... Therefore, it would make sense that girls acquire more vocabulary at an earlier age' (Barron-Hauwaert, 2011a: 94).

Saunders puts it sensibly: 'even when growing up in the same family under basically the same conditions, children do not necessarily acquire bilingualism in exactly the same way' (Saunders, 1988: 96). (See p. 177, 'Why won't they speak?') So recognize that your children have biological reasons to be different, but do not compound the differences with changes in your own behavior.

Expressing love

Some of the most cutting naysayer comments come from people who can't imagine 'loving' in another language. I met some parents who were perfectly able to speak the L2 to their children, but didn't do so because they heard they could not adequately show love in a language that wasn't their own. Two women I interviewed give a glimpse into this kind of thinking:

> I was thinking of doing Spanish with Jeremy, but there was this speech therapist who said it wasn't 'natural bilingualism' and that I wouldn't be able to convey love to the children in the best possible way. (S.P., interview)

> There's a researcher in Cary who's head of Babies French Club and Baby Spanish Club and she said I didn't have a perfect accent in French so I would mess Mary Kate up. (J.F., email interview)

For parents who have already made the bilingual decision, these ideas about inadequacy may cause them to second-guess their decisions. Or they may feel anxious or guilty. Meg, a British woman raising her children to speak French (her L2), emailed me about how sick she was of people's surprise at her speaking exclusively French to the kids. She writes about one incident in particular:

> I was explaining to a mom I'd met about why I spoke French to my children. She furrowed her brow and said, 'Well, I lived in Moscow for 5 years and am totally fluent in Russian but would never *dream* of talking to my children in Russian. That would be really weird and we'd never have a proper relationship.' (M.G., email interview)

Meg said she had even cried over this encounter. She wanted to avoid such negativity in the future. I love her dramatic solution:

> So, the next time I got the 'So are you French?' question, I lied. Like an Oscar-worthy actress, I smiled and said 'No, I'm English but they have an aunt who was French and I want my kids to speak French too.' The lady smiled back and said 'I think that's wonderful!' It was such a RELIEF not to have to launch into an epic defense of my linguistic and parenting views, so LOVELY to have a simple, positive acceptance. And now I am wracked with GUILT. What kind of self-delusional lunatic am I turning into? (M.G., email interview)

I wrote her back with the highest criticism for the misinformed and condescending comments she'd received. I tried to ameliorate her guilt by telling her 'Sometimes you just do what you have to do to protect yourself. White lies included.'

Being different, when it comes to our kids, can make others feel awkward. Family members and friends who don't speak the L2 can be challenged to step out of their comfort zone. An open discussion allows you to acknowledge that what you are doing is not the norm, but is another way to communicate, and deserves respect.

Sour grapes

Keep in mind some people may be negative about your language choices because they wish they had tried bilingualism. A Hungarian father teaching his son English said,

> I have a friend who lived 6 years in the US and the kids lived in the US till they were 4 and when they came back to Hungary they didn't consider speaking English to the kids, and they look at me and hear my son answering me in Hungarian [instead of the L2, English] and they say with a smile 'See it's useless, why are you trying?' (E.O., email interview)

Knowing why people are making negative comments can help you take what they say with a grain of salt and continue with your language plan.

Find an ally

Perhaps the best solution to the negativity you may confront is to find an understanding friend you can confide in. Just having someone to laugh with can take away the sting and give positive motivation to press on. One mother who speaks her second language, English, to her child while living in the Czech Republic writes,

> I have met a girl from Russia who speaks Russian to her baby girl. Well, she tries.... We have become friends, and I support her in speaking Russian to her daughter. Apparently, I am about the only one.... It feels really good for both of us to be around someone who understands our situation and is supportive. (J.A., interview)

In this case, the friend wasn't a non-native speaker, but she understood the bilingual situation. Likewise, you don't have to find someone who is exactly in your situation, just someone who understands and lends an ear.

It Won't Work

Many parents face the daily challenge of wondering 'Will this work? Can I really teach my child to speak my L2?' A variety of factors cause parents to call their decisions into question.

Feeling imperfect

To confidently speak our L2, we must believe it's okay not to speak it perfectly. Research on language teachers' fear of imperfection can help us here. Tim Murphey and Tsuyoshi Sasaki's study of high-school teachers of English in Japan found many were speaking English less than 10% of the time because they bought into what the authors called 'the perversion of perfectionism' (Murphey & Sasaki, 1998: 21). This perversion made them avoid speaking the language because they might not do it perfectly. Linguist Peter Grundy discusses a similar phenomenon he calls the 'uncertainty avoidance' of instructors teaching their second language. He found teachers overused repetition and allowed little freedom of expression, to avoid questions they might not be able to answer (Grundy, 2001).

If you're feeling worried about teaching your child a language that's not your own, ask yourself where the fear comes from. Oftentimes it's based on comments from someone else – someone who doesn't have a clear picture of what's involved in language learning. One parent writes,

> Sometimes feel my English as inadequate! My grandmother used to tell me that as long as I had an accent, I wasn't really speaking the language properly, so whenever I make stupid grammar mistakes in English I can still see her smiling face! (L.G., email interview)

As parents – and learners – we have to shake off the views others might place on us, knowing that we are indeed good enough.

I feel fake

Some parents I work with said they felt they were being fake when they spoke the L2. One mother who I spent considerable time interviewing and observing feared her son would never really know who she was if they did not speak in her first language. In her second language, she not only felt unsure of herself, she didn't feel 'like herself'.

These doubts reflect the results of a study in foreign language education in which students and teachers felt they couldn't represent themselves well in the L2.

Language anxiety researchers put it this way:

> Their perceptions of genuineness in presenting themselves to others may be threatened by the limited range of meaning and affect which can be deliberately communicated. (Horwitz et al., 1986: 128)

Remind yourself that your language abilities will get better with time. With this improvement, you will better represent yourself. Early on, when your child is very young, you don't have to orally show him your personality in profound ways. If you are starting later in a child's life, discuss with him your reticence over speaking a language you are still learning. You can be a good model for how learners don't have to be perfect.

If you are truly willing to admit you are an amateur, the pressure to be fluent won't be a burden, and you open yourself up to new learning possibilities.

Weaker in one language

If your child's L1 is stronger than his L2, you may feel your bilingual plan is not working. But, in fact, this imbalance is very common. And if you're doing more than two languages, the balance can be tipped even more.

Educators are partly to blame for parents' fears over how balanced the languages are. Well-meaning instructors, administrators and evaluators may form their definitions of bilingualism on outdated bilingual childhood research. Newer research has shown that even children who were significantly weaker in one language are still truly bilingual and still achieve higher scores than their monolingual counterparts on various competency tests (Myles, 2003).

Doctors and speech therapists

Some parents' doubt stems from what they learn from medical professionals. Negative comments from these trusted professionals may cause you to worry if bilingualism is possible for you and your child. But remember, just because a doctor is an authority figure on your child's health doesn't mean she knows about bilingualism and how best to proceed with a language plan. One mother shares her story:

> I also had a very difficult conversation with my parents who disagree with our language model. They think that a child should first master his/her native language before starting to learn a foreign one. My mom's friend who happens to be a pediatrician supports my mom's theory, and that makes things all the worse. I am glad for the amount of research I have done because it allowed me to stay calm and focused. Gosh! But was it hard! (J.A., email interview)

A 16-year-old girl I interviewed had a similar experience as a child being raised to speak an L2 in an English-speaking country.

> I did rebel and refuse to speak it when I was very little, 3 years old. My parents thought I had speech or communication problems and sent me to a speech therapist. The therapist said the only problem I had was that I was stubborn and my parents would have to let me speak English [the L1] in order [for] me to speak at all. (F.E., email interview)

Harding-Esch and Riley explain why it's best to seek language advice from someone other than a health professional.

> Bilingualism does not appear on the training syllabus of doctors … nurses, social workers, or even psychologists and speech therapists. It makes as much sense to ask

your doctor for advice about bilingualism as it would to ask him about your car. (Harding-Esch & Riley, 2003: 147)

So if your doctor is blaming an issue on bilingualism, remember that if bilingualism becomes the scapegoat for an issue that's actually unrelated, you might not be finding the true root of the problem.

Siblings

Another bit of evidence naysayers may use to say bilingualism isn't working is to point out how your children do not speak the L2 with each other. The advice I give parents on siblings is to encourage them to speak the language to each other, but don't feel too dejected if, as time goes on, they start speaking the L1. Parental efforts toward sibling use of the L2 are rarely successful. Suzanne Barron-Hauwaert authors an entire book on the sibling dynamic, entitled *Bilingual Siblings: Language Use in Families* (2011a). She writes,

> Parents ... noted that it was harder to control the language the siblings choose to use together, especially when they played together, away from the parent. (Barron-Hauwaert, 2011b)

Cunningham-Andersson and Andersson's book *Growing Up with Two Languages* studied siblings who used the L2 among themselves, but only when there were trying to sound more parent-like.

> The language chosen by brothers and sisters to talk between themselves is usually the majority language if this is their dominant language (as is usual, at least for children of school age).... Sometimes older siblings address a younger one in the minority language if they believe it might get better results perhaps sounding more authoritative. (Cunningham-Andersson & Andersson, 1999: 27)

Parents can insist their children speak the L2 to each other, but that will work only if the parent is present. Pearson writes of a mother who wanted her children to always speak the L2 around each other, but who was meeting strong resistance. She says the compromise they finally reached was that the children 'would speak Spanish with each other in her presence because they could see it meant so much to her, but by themselves, they used English' (Pearson, 2008: 152).

I do something similar. I gave up on forcing the kids to speak Portuguese to each other, but if they are telling a story with just them and me present, the story must be told in Portuguese. If they have something to say exclusively to each other in my presence, that's fine, I don't correct them, but I also don't acknowledge having understood what they've said to each other. This means they tend to stay in Portuguese so they don't have to repeat themselves.

Each family is unique. Find the plan that maximizes the L2 without forcing rules on your children that may not be respected or are very difficult to enforce.

Non-L2 partner

> *In a successful marriage, there is no such thing as one's way. There is only the*
> *way of both, only the bumpy, dusty, difficult, but always mutual path.*
> Phyllis McGinley (quoted in Chang, *Wisdom for the Soul*, 2006: 541)

You may worry your bilingual plan won't work due to issues with your non-L2 partner. Let this section put those fears to rest.

Non-L2 parent learns over time

When parents were asked in interviews about problems with partners, responses ranged from feelings of being left out of the conversation to having actual misunderstandings. One parent who spoke Japanese to her children writes about her husband's feelings:

> Well, he took a [year's] class at the junior college … of Japanese, so that helped out a lot because not only was he learning, but he was actively paying attention to verb tenses and that kind of thing, but he felt he missed out on jokes like when the kids would say something funny and I would laugh and he would say, 'What'd they say?' and I'd tell him, but he felt he missed it. (P.R., interview)

Not only could feelings get hurt, but misunderstandings could arise. This same mom goes on,

> He'd miss the verb tense so I'd say [to the kids], 'Oh it's great that you picked up your toys' and he'd say [to the kids], 'Did you hear your mother? Pick up your toys.' He's only getting the gist and his intention is good … but it's counterproductive. It's exhausting. (P.R., interview)

A mother whose husband didn't speak the L2 worries that he will feel distant from their children if she speaks the L2 to them:

> [My husband] James doesn't know it [my L2], and I would hate for him to be like, 'What are they saying? I can't even understand my own child!' I wouldn't want that to happen. (M.O., interview)

Imagine this, though. If you start a bilingual plan while your child is an infant, by the time they're five, your partner has heard many repetitions of vocabulary and expressions. Even if he doesn't get to the level where he can speak the language, the passive knowledge will help him understand. You won't have to translate everything you say and he will feel more on board with the bilingual plan.

Steiner's interview with a man whose wife spoke Swedish to the children shows how adults living in the house with another language can pick it up little by little.

> To be honest, baby talk is not very difficult to pick up – especially for an adult. When I realized that I was 'getting it,' I was really proud and it made me want to learn the language so I started to learn Swedish…. I've continued to speak to our kids in English, which is what we had planned all along, but when they speak to Anna in Swedish, I understand everything that is said! (Steiner, 2008: 124)

Partner accountability

Some parents I interviewed said they had trouble speaking the L2 around the L1 husband out of laziness. The L1 was just easier. One mom says,

> With Mary Kate I spoke with her in French except when it was awkward around my husband. Most of the time I just spoke French around her but sometimes on the weekend I would get lazy because I was speaking English with him and it was awkward to switch and he was there and didn't understand. (J.F., email interview)

In this case, the L2 parent can enlist the help of the partner as someone to gently hold her accountable. Discuss how you'd like to be reminded to speak the L2. Then, make sure to offer thanks, not retribution, for his assistance.

Partner's respect

If you are the L2 parent, you'll want to insist that your child's use of the L2 be respected. Teasing or mimicking aimed toward the children should be avoided, since it puts a negative slant on the language.

> Another mistake my husband made. He started teasing us about French, and I told him not to. He would imitate it in a funny voice, and almost immediately, she stopped making any effort. She was two and a half and knew what he was doing and didn't like it. (J.F., interview)

Raguenaud expresses how important it is to take the L2 learning seriously. 'Your partner's respect and enthusiasm for your … language will have a direct effect on your child's willingness to learn it' (Raguenaud, 2009: 64).

Communication and compromise

Regardless of the challenges you and your partner face, you have to talk about it. Ask questions such as 'Could you give me some examples of when this is difficult?' and 'What would make this more comfortable for you?'

If the exclusive use of the L2 with your child really is causing problems, make some concessions that leave both partners happy. In my case, when my husband looks lost,

I explain briefly what we're saying, or offer a full translation. You can also give an explanation before you talk to the kids, especially if you have a partner who can follow along somewhat. If we're at dinner and I have something to say exclusively to the kids, I might mention to my husband right before starting to talk: 'I need to tell them real quick about tomorrow's pick-up-from-school plan'. Then we switch to the L2, and he's usually fine not knowing all the details.

It may be that your partner isn't comfortable with this scenario. In that case, you might need to rethink when you speak the L2. The bottom line is that you need your partner's support. Without it, it'll be hard to stay motivated and happy.

Recognize your partner's sacrifice

> *You can sacrifice and not love. But you cannot love and not sacrifice.*
> Kris Vallotton, author and moralist (Goodreads, 2012d)

There is more than one way to help partners feel connected. One mother who speaks Japanese to her son handles her husband's frustration by reminding him of future changes:

We had a nanny for a year and it wasn't until I stayed home till he [my son] started speaking Japanese at like 18 months. So then my husband started feeling insecure and he would say, 'Gosh, I don't feel like I can communicate with him' so it would've been easy for me to quit..., but instead I said, 'I'm so sorry, this has got to be so hard but once he goes to school it'll be the opposite'. (P.R., email interview)

In this case, the L2 parent recognized the sacrifice of the husband and reminded him that, soon, she would be the one sacrificing. Since this shift would be several years away, she might also have offered to make concessions to bring him on board. For example, she could offer to use the L1 on specific occasions when he felt lost. Or, she might have helped make it possible for him to spend more father–son time, where the time would be in his L1.

It Won't Last

Parents worry that they may start speaking the L2 but that they won't be able to keep speaking it as the children get older. They fear their children, as they turn into teenagers, will rebel against speaking the language, or that they'll stop speaking it due to the level of difficulty.

These fears are not unfounded. Many families I interviewed said that even when their kids were very young, it was a struggle, at times, to get them to speak only in the L2. For many, this became even more difficult as the children grew older. We'll examine some of the specific forms that children's 'rebellion' takes and see what measures can be applied.

The brain

But first, let's look at how little rebellious brains work.

The efficient brain

Recognize that what is seen as rebellion in children may not be intentional resistance. Remember from Chapter 5, 'Many Methods', that the biological impulse of the human brain is to seek the quickest path between two lines. We humans are hardwired to get what we need or want with the least amount of effort. Generally, this efficiency is helpful and rewarded. In fact, research shows that when you put people of many different languages in a room, individuals will find others who speak the same language within a matter of minutes, because they're trying to communicate in the quickest and easiest way possible.

As we look at the reasons why children rebel, we'll examine different forms of incentives for speaking the language. These will make speaking the L2 worth the effort.

The brain relearns

You may feel like your child has asked the same question a million times: 'Why do we have to speak German?' Steiner (2008) suggests that as children age and enter new developmental stages, they reevaluate their environment and themselves to see where they fit in.

So try not to get frustrated that you're having to repeat yourself. To your child, the answer sounds different from before, because of their newfound perspective.

The brain seeks novelty

Recent research shows us that the brain seeks out novelty. Russell Poldrack, in his article 'Multitasking: The brain seeks novelty', writes 'The brain is built to ignore the old and focus on the new' (Poldrack, 2009).

This explains why our children tend to rebel against L2 materials that have been around a while, be they books, games or movies, etc. Ask yourself where you might find new materials. Having a new book arrive in the mail, a new DVD brought over from a traveling friend or finding a new friend who speaks the L2 might curtail the 'I'm bored' reason for rebellion.

Why won't they speak?

If you find that all of a sudden, despite your efforts to keep learning fun and new, your child is refusing to speak the language, search for underlying reasons. Did someone on the playground hear him speaking the L2 and make fun of him? Is he wanting to speak the L1 because it's easier? You can't address these concerns unless you get your child to disclose them.

If possible, ask direct questions about why your child is reluctant to speak the L2. Ask if there's anything you can do to help. If you don't think they'll respond to direct questions, start by telling them a story about a time you didn't want to do something. Sometimes just making yourself more vulnerable will help your kids open up.

Parents may wonder why one of their children refuses to speak the language while the other complies. Consider the birth order of your child, since the first child gets more one-on-one time with the parent. (See p. 167, 'Language delay'.) You may have the older child in preschool bringing home the L1 to the younger child. King and Mackey write,

> Parents naturally have the most one-on-one language and interaction time with their first-born. Subsequent children, in turn, spend much more time in conversations not just with their parents, but also with their older siblings. (King & Mackey, 2007: 24)

Avoid the 'dog and pony' show

Children may hold negative feelings toward the L2 when people ask them to 'perform' in the language. It may seem that they're being asked to show off. One teenager I interviewed responds to my question about whether she ever rebelled against speaking French:

> The only time I can think of rebelling against it is when someone at school asks me to say something in French. It happens a lot and I never know what to say. (F.E., email interview)

A mom speaking French to her daughter has a simple solution:

> People would say [to my daughter], 'Say something in French' … and she just says 'Oui' and that's it which I think is funny because she can say more, but that sort of ends the discussion. (J.F., email interview)

Harding-Esch and Riley take a strong stance against putting children on show:

> When visitors ask children to 'say something in French,' parents should shield children from having to answer. Several children in our study chose this as the only disadvantage they could think of in being bilingual … 'saying something' [was] excruciatingly embarrassing and totally unnatural. (Harding-Esch & Riley, 2003: 160)

So if someone asks your child to 'say something in <L2>', dodge the response with 'That's tough to do' and change the subject. If your kid isn't bothered by the question, let him come up with a brief response. My kids find it a strange request and ask, in the L2, 'What do you want me to say?'

Identity

Children may show a reluctance to speak the L2 if they are struggling with aspects of their identity.

Identities children wear

Think of something your child likes to do – play soccer, for example. For her to buy into the time and effort it takes to play soccer, she must identify with it. She is a soccer player.

King and Mackey liken children's relationship to language with their relationship to clothing. Language has a 'functional component' – we speak it to express ourselves – but it also has an 'identity component' – how we talk shows who we are and how we perceive ourselves. Clothing is similar in that it has a function – to keep us covered and warm – but it also reflects how we want people to see us (King & Mackey, 2007: 239).

If we continue this analogy, we see that when children are very little, they are generally happy to wear the clothes we choose for them. As they grow older, they like to choose their clothes for themselves. What they wear shows us the image they want to portray. If language is similar and we want them to choose the L2, we must make the L2 not only functional, but also help connect it to an image they want to emulate.

To encourage your children to make this connection, help them find icons – from Disney characters to pop stars – who speak the L2. Find ways to visit the target country, literally or virtually. And help them make friends with L2 speakers. Most important, continue to offer praise even if the L1 creeps in from time to time.

Sex and identity

For families using the OPOL method, there can also be a disconnect in language and identity when the sex of the child is different from the sex of the L2 speaker. This is especially true for sons learning the L2 almost exclusively from their mother. A male child may identify more with his father, but is asked to speak a language he hears only from his mother.

There also may be an external pressure on boys to speak their father's language. One mother said her daughter didn't rebel against speaking Portuguese to her, but her son did. In an interview, she says of her son 'His grandfather is very against the idea of me speaking Portuguese to him. And his father speaks English to him even though he knows Portuguese' (G.F., interview). This boy was getting the message that Portuguese is not for boys.

Questions of identity are not ones that you can 'solve'. However, you can work on finding people your child relates to that will help him identify with the language. If your son is struggling with speaking the mother's L2, find a male L2 babysitter or 'mother's helper'. Point out to your son that the babysitter speaks the L2 just like Mommy.

When you read a book, point out the male characters. You might say 'Mateo speaks Spanish just like Mommy. But his voice is very low.' Do the same with television or movie characters. Watch YouTube with your child, choosing characters he identifies with, and searching for them in the L2.

'Less freaky'

As children get older, they tend to rebel against things that make them feel different from other people, particularly their peers. Spending time with international people, even if they aren't from the target country, helps normalize the L2. Saunders tells of how his son was proud to speak German to him after seeing other bilingual children in the schoolyard speaking Greek, Turkish and Italian to their parents:

> He showed considerable interest in this and obviously took some pride in the fact that he, too, could speak a language other than English. Wendy [my wife] and I capitalized on the situation to portray bilingualism as something natural but special. (Saunders, 1988: 118)

Similarly, one mother I interviewed who was teaching English to her daughter says 'I think, in a way, even having Finnish friends helped our kids stick to their second language. This way they never felt like freaks, speaking another language' (K.D., interview).

Into the L2

Parents have many tools at their disposal for shifting their children from the L1 to the L2. Some are more direct than others. It's important to have a variety since every child is different. They also go through different phases and moods.

A point system

Use a point system as a lightweight game to move children from the L1 to the L2. Some families use coins given at the beginning of a day or week and kids lose them whenever they speak the L1.

A more positive spin on this is to have a point system where children gain points for speaking only in the L2. You and your family can decide the value of the points. They can be 'bundled' for a dinner out or traded for money.

To really get your kids on board, let them help make the rules of the points game. If they're involved in the planning, they'll be more likely to stay motivated to play. I asked my kids 'Do you have any ideas of how to remember to speak in Portuguese?' At first, my son suggested that I make the loud *errrrrrk!* sound (one you hear on game shows when someone says the wrong answer). They then decided that a less annoying sound would be a tiny *beep* when someone says a word in English. *Voilà*, a new plan was in place that came from the children, and therefore wasn't so top down.

You can compensate

A game isn't always the answer to more serious L2 problems. For example, some L2 parents complain that their children prefer to speak to the L1 parent. Cunningham-Andersson and Andersson cite an interview where an L2-speaking mother said:

> Whenever both of us go to pick our daughter up from the childcare, she wants to go straight to my husband and absolutely refuses to come to me.... She might not like to be spoken to in Japanese. Even at home, she wants to be with him rather than with me, especially when she is tired. (Cunningham-Andersson & Andersson, 1999: 37)

A woman I interviewed who also speaks Japanese to her children tells of similar woe:

> If I do insist [they speak Japanese] they'll roll their eyes and say it in Japanese with a funny voice like, 'I'm being made to say this so there you go, Mom' and they have an attitude about it because they they're at the age where they have an attitude about things and think they're so big. (P.R., email interview)

To these frustrations I would first say, notice if you're perhaps exaggerating the situation. Are your children always avoiding you, or only sometimes? Could it be they are avoiding you the most when they're tired? Try not to take it personally, since it obviously has to do with having to speak the 'harder' language.

Consider just riding it out. Your kids will eventually need something from you that only you can give them. Praise them profusely when they do come to you and speak the L2.

You can also win more L2 from your kids by becoming the über-enthusiastic and engaged parent. Susanne Dopke's study in Australia notes that the most successful parents use

> a child-centered mode of interaction, i.e. [they] actively work at sustaining a conversation with the children by being responsive to the children's contributions to the conversation, by working at maintaining a topic once it has been introduced, and [by] being more interested in conversing with the children than in exerting control over them. (Dopke in Saunders, 1988: 133)

To give a personal example, when my kids first get out of school each day, they have trouble speaking the L2. Sometimes when I insist on Portuguese, they just drop what they were saying, as if it's too much effort. Or when they are telling a story and get to a word that's hard to say in Portuguese, they'll start telling the story to their father, even if he's busy doing something else. I compensate by becoming the more excited parent, the extremely interested parent.

I really, really listen, stopping what I'm doing to make eye contact. If they slip in an English word because the vocabulary is unfamiliar or they forgot the word, I ask a question using what they *were* able to say in Portuguese 'So you were playing a fun game on the playground that used a what? Describe it to me.' Or 'Do the motion' or 'Show me what it looked like'. If they can't think of a word and it's something in the room, I say 'Point it out to me'. I use anything possible to show their message is important to me.

Eat your peas, speak the L2

If you've tried some indirect methods of steering your child into speaking the language and are not getting results, consider more direct reactions.

What if you treated bilingualism like other typical requirements and responsibilities: polite manners, homework, or setting the table without complaining? (See p. 95, 'Is non-reacting cruel?') Then, when children rebel against speaking the language, you can you ask yourself 'How do I enforce these other jobs?' It's not a punishment per se, but, as with other requirements, there must be an understanding that 'This is non-negotiable'. Discuss directly how homework requirements are like language requirements: they are just what we do. This might help you not have to fight the language battle over and over again. Or it can shorten the battle to a reminder: 'Remember how language is like being polite?'

False monolingual strategy

One mother says enforcing these rules means pretending she can't hear her children until they speak in the L2:

> One of my friends thought I was being mean to the children when I told her this. However, I find it no different than insisting on politeness. I won't get them juice if they yell at me, 'JUICE!!' I ask them to say 'Juice, please' before I comply. Forcing children to speak a language by begging, pleading, or insisting nearly never works. However, setting ground rules and sticking to them does. (P.R., interview)

Here we should come back to an idea from Chapter 6, 'Marketing Strategies' – try a little pretending. (See p. 94, 'Non-reacting'.) Pretend you don't understand what your kids are saying until they use the L2. It's also called the 'false monolingual strategy', since the L2 parent feigns understanding only the L2.

This strategy is recommended for use with children who are over two or three years old. Suzanne Barron-Hauwaert, in *Language Strategies for Bilingual Families*, writes that children over this age 'can be rebellious and aware of the effect of language' (Barron-Hauwaert, 2004: 39). If they are aware, for example, that at dinner they should speak the L2 and they are aware that they are instead speaking the L1, then they can make changes to their behavior.

You can help with these modifications by simply asking the child to repeat what she has said, but this time in the L2: 'What was that? In German, please.' If only part of the utterance is in the L1, as so often happens, repeat back the part said in the L2, and ask for the rest to be in the L2. A child in Spain learning English from his mother might have this encounter:

> Child: Where is my *mochila*?
> Mother: Where is your what?
> Child: My book bag?

If your child seems not to know the vocabulary, encourage different strategies. To ask her to show what she wants through actions, say 'Can you point to something that might help?' or 'Can you act something out?' Or, encourage her to circumnavigate: 'Use other words to describe it', 'What does it do?' or 'What does it look like?'

It is imperative to temper your insistence on the L2 with an upbeat attitude. Saunders encourages parents to insist children speak the L2 and feels that resistance to this plan 'can be successfully overcome provided the parents are persistent, yet show understanding and good humour' (Saunders, 1988: 126). He does add, however, that, depending on some children's personalities, parents should be careful not to push kids to the point of frustration, because it could cause 'an adverse effect on their willingness to speak the language' (Saunders, 1988: 126). Just as when dealing with children's anxiety in general, take stock of a situation and the level of emotion.

Handling the emotion

There are other ways to deal with children's negative emotion toward the L2.

Follow your instinct with anxiety

Even parents well versed in the current language learning literature struggle with their L2 convictions if they see their children getting upset. It is important that you pay attention to your intuition, particularly when it comes to your children's anxiety levels. This doesn't mean switching back to the L1 at the first sign of difficulty. It means, instead, that you are taking their feelings seriously and acting to help.

For example, one mother I spoke with tells me that when she speaks the L2, 'the youngest of ours is 3 years old and he says, "Quit talking that, I don't understand anything.... Stop with all that!"' (M.R., email interview). She might need to slow down her speech or repeat something with easier vocabulary. It might also mean using an expression her son doesn't understand in a context he's more familiar with.

Again, you know your child best and may need to 'fudge' and use the L1 in certain circumstances. Speaking the second language shouldn't become a battleground. If it does, make a new plan – even a mini-adjustment for a specific situation.

One mother has an interesting outlook on L2 expectation changes:

> Decide what you consider success because if you consider success only that [your] child speaks like a native at age 3 and that doesn't happen, you'll be setting yourself up for a lot of disappointment ... at some point you have to be responding to that child's needs which may not be in that language right then, so keep in mind various degrees of success. (J.F., email interview)

Teasing

Parents must help their children sort through the emotions that go hand in hand with teasing. Baker writes about children who tease bilinguals: 'Their poking fun may be a sense of their inadequacy in communication, their underlying jealousy, [or] their worries about exclusion from the conversation' (Baker, 2007: 94).

Teach your kids that if you laugh it off and don't take offense, the teaser isn't gratified because she'll not have gotten the desired reaction. Sometimes people seem to be teasing, but in fact they're just amazed they can't understand a word you're saying.

A boy who heard the kids and me speaking Portuguese said 'It sounds like you're speaking gibberish'. His surprise was ironic, because he spoke French at home to his native French parents. Even so, the very different sounds of our language baffled him.

Teach your child to explain your bilingual situation simply. Discuss how to say 'It probably sounds funny to you, the sounds of German, but I speak it to my dad because I want to have another language and be able to talk to more people'.

If you're tried these and other methods but the teasing is still a problem, you may want to change how or when you speak the L2.

Finding a voice

Parents must listen to children, particularly when they feel they do not have a voice. Cunningham-Andersson and Andersson write of a frustrated child who, 'at age four, rejected the whole idea [of speaking French] by yelling, "The words, they're stuck in my throat, they won't come out"' (Cunningham-Andersson & Andersson, 1999: 110).

It is crucial to pay attention to children when they feel, as one teenager did, 'like somebody was silencing me' (M.S., email interview). One journal entry illustrates my four-year-old's interpretation of what it feels like not to know certain words:

> Sydney: *Mamãe*, someone took my voice *em português* [in Portuguese] and I can only speak in English now.
> Me: *Alguém roubou sua voz? Como pode ser?* [Someone stole your voice? How can that be?]
> Sydney: *Sim, roubou, Mamãe não deve!* [Yes, someone took it, they shouldn't have.]
> Me: *Que pena! ... Tem gente que só tem uma voz – eles so sabem falar inglês. É uma pena. Mas você, você tem sorte – você tem DUAS vozes!* [What a shame! ... Some people only have one voice – only speak English. That's a pity! But you, you're lucky – you have TWO voices!]
> Sydney: *Sim!* [Yes!]
> (journal, 4/15/2005)

In my response, I focused on how special she is to know two languages. Let's examine other ways to talk to your child about rebellion.

Keep your cool

Staying relaxed but firm is a balancing act that helps deal with rebellion. If your child is not speaking the language, remember that being militant can cause her to dig in her heels. Stubbornness breeds stubbornness in some situations. If you appear on your child's side, she may be more compliant and want to please you.

Pearson suggests doing this by using 'I-messages' when you ask your child to speak in the L2. For example, 'I feel so good when you answer me in our language' or 'I understand so much better when you speak our language' (Pearson, 2008: 150) as opposed to 'you-messages' that are negative about the child: for instance, 'You know better than to speak English'.

Letting your child be the boss will also help him feel more empowered. Lower the intensity when you really want him to speak the L2 by playing a quick game. One example is 'Okay let's play a game. Point to anything in the room and I have to say the word seven times fast!' This will surround your child with the language in a non-threatening way. Just lightening the moment can help your child remember his words better. The game will also remind him to point to objects for vocabulary help.

Feed the word

Sometimes children are not rebelling so much as they are just feeling stuck in the language. When they resort to the L1 just to get their message across, give them a hand with a quick translation. This strategy is helpful if used very sparingly. (If your kids see you're willing to do it a lot, they'll let you do all the L2 speaking for them.)

When I employ this method, I insist my kids repeat back the translation. So if your L1 Spanish-speaking daughter is asking for your help in finding her doll but says *'Me pueden ayudar?'* (Can you help me?) Respond with 'Say, "Can you help me?"' Once she has repeated the expression, go about helping immediately to show just how powerful her L2 voice is.

Recently my son tossed me some keys yelling, in the L1, 'Catch!' I let them fall to the floor without even trying to catch them, which made us both laugh. I then asked

him in the L2, 'Was I supposed to catch those?' I asked him to repeat what he'd yelled in Portuguese, and he did so without a problem because I'd fed him the word 'catch'.

Surround the word with the L2

It is maddening not to be able to remember a certain word when we need it. When your child is having trouble with word recall, jog his memory by surrounding the word with other L2 vocabulary. For example, if he can't remember the word for stick, use a short humming sound for the word 'stick' and try saying 'Remember, we used a long (hum) last night to roast our marshmallows?' Surrounding the unknown word with other L2 words helps his brain to click out of the L1 and into the L2.

Correction: No nit-picking

Parents trying to avoid negative emotions with their children should watch how they correct them. Harding-Esch and Riley advise that 'There is no need for the parents of bilingual children to feel that they should go in for incessant nit-picking' (Harding-Esch & Riley, 2003: 145). (See p. 88, 'Correction'.) Constant, overt correction discourages children from speaking the language. They prefer to tell their stories without all the interruptions. Baker writes,

> A constant focus on language correctness and form is unnatural for the child, who is more interested in facts and ideas, stories and activities. For the child, language is a means to an end, not an end in itself. (Baker, 2000: 64)

As long as your child stays in the L2, avoid much direct correction. (See p. 145, 'Errors are part of the process'.) Children in their L1s learn correct forms from hearing other speakers model correct grammar. Your child will eventually follow suit.

Stressed out parents

Parents also have to deal with their own emotions. They may have difficulty speaking the L2 if they're feeling upset. Flores and Soto asked non-native parents about their biggest struggle. One parent, whose L1 is English, says 'In emergencies or stressful situations, or ones I hadn't planned for, my instinct is always English' (Flores & Soto, 2012: 89).

It is important in these moments to take a few deep breaths and continue in the L2. I will never forget once, I was very angry at my son and I yelled at him in English instead of Portuguese. The fact that I changed languages was scary to him, as if I wasn't the mommy he knew.

Teenagers

Let's face it, some of the highest emotions we face from our kids is when they are teenagers. They bring a new set of challenges.

Curtailing rebellion

Starting early helps. Keep your L2 use consistent over the years so that children, as they get older, will be in the habit of speaking the L2 and won't be as likely to rebel. Myles writes,

> It is not uncommon for adolescents to use language choice as a way of expressing their increasing independence. Although it may seem manipulative, from the parents' point of view, the less a teenager thinks about making a choice regarding which language to use, and the more the family minority language becomes habit for them, the better for their continued language development. (Myles, 2003: 11)

Teenagers' passive bilingualism

Parents may feel frustrated, as their children grow, that they are speaking the L2 less and less. I advise parents to continue speaking the L2 even if their children respond in the L1. The continued input is often enough to plant the seed for later. Baker writes,

> Should the teenager reject one language, the parent has still provided sufficient growth in the sturdy young plant for passive bilingualism to change into active bilingualism later ... a person who has not actively spoken or read the language for 10 or 20 years will still find it relatively easy to relearn and become an active bilingual again. (Baker, 2000: 76)

Claire Thomas, in her book *Growing Up with Languages*, agrees: 'It is certainly much easier to go from the ability to understand a language to being able to speak it than having to learn it almost from scratch' (Thomas, 2012: 87).

It's important to keep in mind, as well, that oftentimes teenagers quickly move from one phase of their life to another. They could easily move back into speaking the language again. So don't consider their slacking off a done deal. Keep the lines of communication open to facilitate the coming back to the L2. Teenagers may even reveal there's a reason why they prefer to speak the L1.

Teenagers' perspectives

Research shows that teenagers who do stick with the L2 feel a sense of pride. Caldas's study of his three children learning French while living in Louisiana writes of his son,

> Even a teenager who had complained for years that he only wanted to speak English, not French, said, when asked if he was glad to be bilingual, 'Yes, because I can understand tourists, and they don't know I hear everything they say.' (Caldas, 2006: 155)

One 16-year-old girl I interviewed says that when growing up she sometimes felt self-conscious and even 'dumb' speaking the L2, but that changed in her mid-teens:

Now being bilingual is something I am proud of. Whenever people remark on my bilingualism now, it's always positive and they always seem to be curious and interested. Also, people will often be jealous of being able to speak two languages.... Some colleges take bilingualism into account for applications. Also, I will probably be able to enhance my experience of living. (M.S., email interview)

These sentiments echo those of a student Dr Steiner interviewed,

Sometimes I would be embarrassed that my parents would speak to me in Russian in front of my friends. Then at some point, I kind of gave up that they would ever speak to me in English. I wrote about my bilingualism in all of my college applications. I realized that I'm proud to speak Russian ... and that I wanted to tell the world. (Steiner, 2008: 111)

Curve Balls

Often the way forward is through a detour.
Susan Rothenburg, minimalist artist (in Wallach, 1997)

We all know that even the best plans may not work out just as you'd foreseen. And sometimes your situation just changes. You might move countries, make major job changes or face a change to your family dynamic. Only you know what your circumstances are and what has to be adjusted. Keep close communication with your children over any modifications. Get their input, even if it's only a minor tweak.

Whenever possible, minimize the changes to the language environment and avoid dropping the bilingual idea altogether, making small adjustments instead.

I'll close with a quote from a woman who faced certain challenges with respect to language learning:

As a child it was difficult for me to move to a new place, make new friends, and not speak the same language as the kids around me. For example, after my family left Raleigh ... to Brazil, I attended preschool in a Catholic school. My classmates didn't like me because I didn't know how to pray in Portuguese ... stuff like that! But now ... I thank my parents every day for raising me bilingual. The benefits definitely outweigh the costs, and I feel like I am a more rounded person thanks to my parents' early actions! (A.D., email interview)

How to Avoid the Naysayers

- Reassure people you know that when you speak the L2 you are not talking about them. Offer to translate anything they want to know.
- Let family and friends know you appreciate their cooperation in speaking the L2 to your child. Make solidarity comments like 'I know it can get tiring hearing a language you don't understand'.
- To avoid criticism from strangers, keep your tone and volume in check when out in public.
- If you do receive a negative comment about raising your children bilingual, ask yourself how many positive comments you've received. Chances are the positive outweigh the negative.
- Be sensitive to those who may be intimidated by your language use. To level the playing field, try a self-deprecating remark like 'We speak French together, but we make lots of mistakes!'

Parting Words

You must do the thing you think you cannot do.
Eleanor Roosevelt (Goodreads, 2011b)

If you've reached the end of this book, you're probably serious about learning another language and teaching it to your child. Just some final reflections and reminders before we part.

As you expose your child to another language, take courage in the knowledge that you don't have to be perfect to get started. I'll never forget the reaction of a public school teacher when I told her about the topic for this book: 'If I had kids, I'd teach them my second language even if it was all dilapidated' (L.S., interview). You will make mistakes along the way, but your language skills will improve as your children age. James Joyce writes 'A man's errors are his portals of discovery' (Goodreads, 2010). Use what goes awry as teaching tools for you and your child.

Keep your language plan set in play dough, not stone. That way, you can always tweak it to fit your needs and the needs of your children. I love Dr Naomi Steiner's wisdom, as both a linguist and a childhood development specialist:

Remember, in many ways raising your child is not different than many other parenting goals. And as most of us parents quickly find out, parenting in general does not lend itself to goals written in stone, one-time fixes, or single solutions! (Steiner, 2008: 172)

Give yourself some leeway when you're setting goals. Gibson writes,

Remember full fluency is not necessary for our communication with anyone: how often is it that a simple conversation about the weather is enough to enjoy being with a friend or acquaintance? (Gibson, 2011: 145)

Recognize that you're doing more than just teaching a language. You're opening your children's eyes to the world. One mother speaking Russian in Australia says that her daughter may not be a perfect speaker of Russian, but 'she knows that one subject can have 2 names and ... that English isn't the only language and Australia isn't the only place in the world' (O.F., email interview).

Know that you're building confidence by helping your child learn something new and different that can become an important part of her identity. One father speaks of his multilingual six-year-old who shows off her language skills: 'She is also highly language aware and confident about it. She thinks that it is "cool" to speak extra languages. She likes to switch between them' (D.G., email interview).

And remember that if the going gets tough, children pass in and out of phases in all areas of learning. I asked one mom what advice she would give parents embarking on this journey:

> Be persistent! A majority of children and young kids will be stubborn. They don't see the point in learning a language they won't be able to speak at school or with their friends. Only when they start to mature or develop will they see the usefulness and worth in knowing two languages. Their lives will only be benefited by it. (H.G., email interview)

Remind yourself that you're not a one-man show. You may be the only one speaking the L2, but there is still a community around you. Your children's teachers at school, coaches, leaders in daycare or after-school programs, or authority figures at your place of worship can help validate your child's learning. Encourage these leaders to ask questions about the L2 and show an ongoing interest.

When you feel anxiety about the future, keep in mind that you will learn as you go. A mother confides in me,

> When he was born, I worried 'How will I potty train him in French?' then 'How will I prepare him for the arrival of his little sister?' etc., but then it just happened fine. Now I try and foresee us discussing the facts of life in French, when he's older, or talking about girlfriends, drugs, drinking, etc., and it's hard to imagine, but it may all just happen naturally ... we're both learning! (M.G., email interview)

And finally, be aware of how much richer your time with your child is. For me personally, that's been a great 'side-effect'. I have my favorite people speaking a language that I hold dear.

It is my hope that the accounts you've read in this book and the research that stands behind it will encourage you to pursue your dream of sharing a language you love with the child you love. Proceed with confidence!

References

Ackerman, D. (2005) *An Alchemy of Mind: The Marvel and Mystery of the Brain*. New York: Scribner.

Amazon (2014) Accessed March 17, 2014. http://www.amazon.com.

Amica (2014) Accessed March 17, 2014. http://www.amica.de/.

Andruss, P. (2008) *iSeek: Minnesota's Career, Education, and Job Resource*. Accessed March 10, 2014. http://www.iseek.org/news/fw/fw6715FutureWork.html.

Ariely, D. (2011) *The Upside of Irrationality: The Unexpected Benefits of Defying Logic at Work and at Home*. New York: Harper Perennial.

Association for Behavior Analysis International (2013) Dissemination of behavior analysis. Accessed March 2, 2013. http://aboutbehavior.webs.com/bfskinner.html.

August, D., Calderón, M. and Carlo, M. (2002) *Transfer of Skills from Spanish to English: A Study of Young Learners: Report for Practitioners, Parents, and Policy Makers*. Washington, DC: Center for Applied Linguistic. Accessed December 12, 2012. http://www.cal.org/acquiringliteracy/pdfs/skills-transfer.pdf.

Babbel (2014) Accessed March 14, 2014. http://www.babbel.com.

Baker, C. (2000) *A Parents' and Teachers' Guide to Bilingualism* (2nd edn). Clevedon: Multilingual Matters.

Baker, C. (2007) *A Parents' and Teachers' Guide to Bilingualism* (3rd edn). Clevedon: Multilingual Matters.

Baker, C. and Jones, S. (1998) *Encyclopedia of Bilingualism and Bilingual Education*. Bristol: Multilingual Matters.

Baker, T. (2010) The native speaker myth: death, wake and funeral of a fallacy. *Professor Baker's Worldwide English Blog*, December 11. Accessed January 25, 2013. http://profesorbaker.com/2010/12/11/.

Bales, D. (1998) Building baby's brain: Learning language. Accessed April 25, 2014. http://spock.fcs.uga.edu/ext/pubs/chfd/FACS01-6.pdf.

Barron-Hauwaert, S. (2011a) *Bilingual Siblings: Language Use in Families*. Bristol: Multilingual Matters.

Barron-Hauwaert, S. (2011b) *Bilingual Siblings: Fine Tuning Family Language Strategies*. Accessed January 1, 2012. http://www.multilingualliving.com/2011/11/08/bilingual-siblings-fine-tuning-family-language-strategies/.

Barron-Hauwaert, S. (2004) *Language Strategies for Bilingual Families: The One-Parent-One-Language Approach*. Clevedon: Multilingual Matters.

BBC (2014) Accessed March 14, 2014. http://www.bbc.co.uk/languages/.

Beck, I., McKeown, M. and Kucan, L. (2013) *Bringing Words to Life*. New York: Guilford Press.

Ben-Zeev, S. (1977) The influence of bilingualism on cognitive strategy and cognitive development. *Child Development* 48 (3), 1009–1018.

Berg, E. (1998) *Joy School*. New York: Ballantine Books.

Berlitz (2014) Accessed March 14, 2014. http://www.berlitz.com.

Bialystok, E. (2002) Acquisition of literacy in bilingual children: A framework for research. *Language Learning* 52 (1), 159–199.

Bialystok, E., Fergus, C. and Luk, G. (2012) Bilingualism: Consequences for mind and brain. *Trends in Cognitive Science* 16 (4), 240–250. http://www.ncbi.nlm.nih.gov/pmc/articles/PMC3322418/.

Book Mania (2013) The pen is the tongue of the mind. Accessed January 17, 2013. http://bookmania. me/post/12210793355/the-pen-is-the-tongue-of-the-mind.

Braine, G. (1999) *Non-Native Language Educators in English Teaching.* London: Routledge.

Brown, D. (1994) *Principles of Language Learning and Teaching.* Englewood Cliffs, NJ: Prentice Hall.

Bruer, J. (2002) *The Myth of the First Three Years.* New York: Free Press.

Bryson, C. (2013) TV can be good for kids! *Kids, TV, and Movies.* Accessed March 22, 2013. http:// kidstvmovies.about.com/od/healthytvhabits/a/tvgoodforkids.htm.

Busuu (2014) Accessed March 14, 2014. http://www.busuu.com.

Caldas, S. (2006) *Raising Bilingual–Biliterate Children in Monolingual Cultures.* Clevedon: Multilingual Matters.

Caldas, S. and Caron-Caldas, S. (1992) Rearing bilingual children in a monolingual culture: A Louisiana experience. *American Speech* 67, 290–296.

Caretas (2014) Accessed March 17, 2014. http://www.caretas.com.pe.

Carlson, A. (2009) Why pictures speak louder than words, *The Big Picture,* July 26. Accessed January 16, 2013. http://ddunleavy.typepad.com/the_big_picture/2009/07/why-pictures-speak-louder-than-words.html.

Cenoz, J. (2003) Are bilinguals better language learners? *Bilingual Family Newsletter* 20 (1), 2–6.

Chang, L. (2006) *Wisdom for the Soul: Five Millennia of Prescriptions for Spiritual Healing.* Washington, DC: Gnosophia Publishers.

Clayton, V. (2004) What's to blame for the rise in ADHD? *NBC News: Growing Up Healthy.* Accessed October 12, 2012. http://www.nbcnews.com/id/5933775/.

Connecticut Council of Language Teachers (2013) Accessed November 19, 2013. http://www.ctcolt. org/pages/welcome.asp.

Craig's List (2014) Accessed March 17, 2014. http://www.craigslist.org.

Cunningham-Andersson, U. and Andersson, S. (1999) *Growing Up With Two Languages.* London: Routledge.

Daugherty, A. (2011) Climb your mountain. *The Examiner,* January 25. Accessed March 4, 2013. http:// www.examiner.com/article/climb-your-mountain.

Davies, A. (2003) *The Native Speaker: Myth and Reality.* Clevedon: Multilingual Matters.

Davis, C. (2000) In Florida, it pays to be bilingual, University of Florida study finds. *University of Florida News,* January 31. Accessed March 10, 2014. http://news.ufl.edu/archive/2000/01/in-florida-it-pays-to-be-bilingual-university-of-florida-study-finds.html.

De Houwer, A. (2009) *An Introduction to Bilingual Development.* Bristol: Multilingual Matters.

Deubel, D. (2011) 4 keys to learning English: Input, input, input, noticing. *EFL Teacher Talk,* March 29. Accessed March 2, 2013. http://ddeubel.edublogs.org/2011/03/29/4-keys-to-learning-english-input-input-input-noticing.

Deutsoher, G. (2011) *Through the Language Glass: Why the World Looks Different in Other Languages.* London: Picador Publishing.

Doman, G. (2012) Glenn Doman's Gentle Revolution Library. Accessed November 2, 2012. http:// www.amazon.com/Glenn-Domans-Gentle-Revolution-Library/lm/R100H0FN7294SZ.

Doman, G. and Doman, J. (1993) *How to Teach Your Baby to Read (Gentle Revolution).* Garden City, NY: Avery Publishing.

Dougherty, D. (2001) *How to Talk to Your Baby.* New York: Perigee Publishers.

Dreifus, C. (2011) The bilingual advantage. *New York Times,* May 30. Accessed November 29, 2012. http://www.nytimes.com/2011/05/31/science/31conversation.html.

Dubey, A. (2013) Widen your career choices. *Language Must.* Accessed February 19, 2013. http://www. knowledge-must.com/language_must/why_learn_languages.html.

Eilers, C. (2011) 23 great language-learning quotes. *Dauntless Jaunter*, August 27. Accessed February 4, 2013. http://www.dauntlessjaunter.com/2013/08/27/23-great-language-learning-quotes/.

Eliot, L. (1999) *What's Going on in There? How the Brain and Mind Develop in the First Five Years of Life.* New York: Bantam Books.

Everyday Language Learner (2012) Language learning tip: Use music to learn a foreign language. Accessed March 19, 2014. http://www.everydaylanguagelearner.com/2012/01/30/language-learning-tip-use-music-learn-foreign-language/.

Facebook (2014) Accessed March 17, 2014. http://www.facebook.com.

Falk, D. (2009) *Finding Our Tongues: Mothers, Infants, and the Origins of Language.* New York: Basic Books.

Farber, B. (2000) *How To Learn Any Language: Quickly, Easily, Inexpensively, Enjoyably and on Your Own.* New York: Citadel.

Felix, N. (2009) *Oh My, Au Pair! A Complete Guide to Hiring and Hosting an Au Pair.* Indianapolis, IN: Dog Ear Publishing.

Flores, A. and Soto, R. (2012) *Bilingual Is Better: Two Latina Moms on How the Bilingual Parenting Revolution Is Changing the Face of America.* Madrid: Bilingual Readers.

Floyd, P. (2011) Presentation to the Foreign Language Association of North Carolina, Marriott Hotel, Winston-Salem, October 13–15.

Fluenz (2014) Accessed March 14, 2014. http://www.fluenz.com.

Fox, M. (2008) *Reading Magic: Why Reading Aloud to Our Children Will Change Their Lives Forever.* Chicago, IL: Mariner Books.

Frommers (2014) Accessed March 18, 2014. http://www.frommers.com.

Geisler, M. (2012) Larry Summers is wrong about languages. *Inside Higher Education*, March 6. Accessed March 10, 2014. http://www.insidehighered.com/views/2012/03/06/geisler-essay-why-larry-summers-wrong-about-languages#ixzz23insfmo9.

Gibson, C. (2011) *Catching Tongues: How to Teach Your Child a Foreign Language, Even If You Don't Speak One Yourself.* Lexington, NC: CreateSpace Independent Publishing Platform.

Goldstein, E. (2012) Neuroplasticity isn't necessarily an ally, but understanding it is. Accessed October 3, 2012. http://blogs.psychcentral.com/mindfulness/2012/03/neuroplasticity-isnt-necessarily-an-ally-but-understanding-it-is/#more-2571.

Goodreads (2010) (James Joyce). Accessed November 18, 2010. http://www.goodreads.com/quotes/13800-a-man-of-genius-makes-no-mistakes-his-errors-are.

Goodreads (2011a) (Robert Henri). Accessed January 10, 2011. http://www.goodreads.com/quotes/43394.

Goodreads (2011b) (Eleanor Roosevelt). Accessed March 9, 2011. http://www.goodreads.com/quotes/3823.

Goodreads (2012a) (Confucius). Accessed October 15, 2012. http://www.goodreads.com/quotes/2057.

Goodreads (2012b) (Mark Twain). Accessed March 18, 2014. https://www.goodreads.com/author/quotes/1244.Mark_Twain.

Goodreads (2012c) (Tim Cahill). Accessed December 15, 2012. http://www.goodreads.com/author/quotes/25126.Tim_Cahill.

Goodreads (2012d) (Kris Vallotton). Accessed March 12, 2012. http://www.goodreads.com/quotes/335357.

Goodreads (2013) (Dale Carnegie). Accessed March 20, 2013. http://www.goodreads.com/quotes/tag/enthusiasm.

Google Images (2014) Accessed March 14, 2014. http://www.google.com/imghp.

Google Translate (2014) Accessed March 14, 2014. http://translate.google.com/.

Grundy, P. (2001) Listening to ourselves. *Humanising Language Teaching* 3 (6). Accessed March 14, 2014. http://www.hltmag.co.uk/nov01/.

Handford, M. (2014) Where's Waldo. Accessed March 17, 2014. http://www.whereswaldo.com.

Harding-Esch, E. and Riley, P. (2003) *The Bilingual Family: A Handbook for Parents.* Cambridge: Cambridge University Press.

Hill, A. (2013) The multilingual dividend. *Financial Times*, March 13. Accessed March 10, 2014. http://www.ft.com/cms/s/0/3fd31c1a-85b6-11e2-bed4-00144feabdc0.html#axzz2vZi538Tp.

Horwitz, E., Horwitz, M. and Cope, J. (1986) Foreign language classroom anxiety. *Modern Language Journal* 70, 125–132.

Jaquith, W. (2013) The state decoded: Don't let perfect be the enemy of the good. *PBS Idea Lab*, October 9. Accessed November 12, 2013. http://www.pbs.org/idealab/2013/10/the-state-decoded-dont-let-perfect-be-the-enemy-of-the-good/.

Jokes All Day (2014) Accessed March 14, 2014. http://jokesallday.com.

Kaplan, L. (2010) Language – the mirror of our soul. Accessed May 17, 2013. http://www.macmillanglobal.com/blog/global-bloggers/language-the-mirror-of-our-soul.

Kennedy, J.F. (1962) Commencement address at Yale University. Accessed January 13, 2013. http://millercenter.org/president/speeches/detail/3370.

King, K. and Mackey, A. (2007) *The Bilingual Edge: Why, When, and How to Teach Your Child a Second Language*. New York: Harper Perennial.

Kluger, J. (2013) The power of the bilingual brain. *Time Magazine*, July 29, pp. 44–47.

Krashen, S. (1973) Lateralization, language learning, and the critical period: Some new evidence. *Language Learning* 23, 63–74.

Krashen, S. (2008) The din in the head, input, and the language acquisition device. *Foreign Language Annals* 16 (1), 41–44. http://web.pdx.edu/~fischerw/courses/advanced/methods_docs/pdf_doc/wbf_collection/0601-0650/0646_FLA83_Krashen_D.PDF.

Kropp, P. (1995) *How to Make Your Child a Reader for Life*. New York: Broadway.

Lambert, W. (1977) The effects of bilingualism on the individual: Cognitive and sociocultural consequences. In P. Hornby (ed.) *Bilingualism: Psychological, Social, and Educational Implications* (pp. 15–27). New York: Academic Press.

Lang-8 (2014) Accessed March 17, 2014. http://www.lang-8.com.

Language Lens (2012) Accessed June 15, 2013. http://languagelens.wordpress.com/2012/10/15/.

Lanza, E. (1992) Can bilingual two-year-olds code-switch? *Journal of Child Language* 19 (3), 717–722. http://journals.cambridge.org/action/displayAbstract?fromPage=online&aid=4236416.

Lauchlan, F., Parisi, M. and Fadda, R. (2013) Bilingualism in Sardinia and Scotland: Exploring the cognitive benefits of speaking a 'minority' language. *International Journal of Bilingualism* 17 (1), 43–56.

Lavers, C. (2010) *The Natural History of Unicorns*. New York: Harper Perennial.

Lawler, J. (2001) Ask a linguist. *International Linguist Community*, January 12. Accessed September 12, 2012. http://linguistlist.org/ask-ling/message-details1.cfm?asklingid=200315949.

Lawless, L. (2012) How French has influenced English. Accessed November 1, 2012. http://french.about.com/od/vocabulary/a/frenchinenglish.htm.

Le Point (2014) Accessed March 17, 2014. http://www.lepoint.fr/.

Lewis, T. (2013) How bilingual babies keep languages separate. *Live Science*. Accessed February 18, 2014. http://www.livescience.com/27186-how-bilingual-babies-keep-languages-separate.html.

Little Pim (2014) Accessed March 14, 2014. http://www.littlepim.com.

Livemocha (2014) Accessed March 14, 2014. http://www.livemocha.com.

Livemocha (2014) Accessed December 6, 2014. http://livemocha.com/blog/2012/03/07/inspirational-quotes-why-learn-a-language/.

Lonely Planet (2014) Accessed March 17, 2014. http://www.lonelyplanet.com.

Mango Languages (2014) Accessed March 14, 2014. http://www.mangolanguages.com.

Manitoba Government (2013) Key elements of behaviour. Accessed March 2, 2013. http://www.edu.gov.mb.ca/k12/specedu/behaviour/key_element6.pdf.

Marcos, K. (1998) Center for Applied Linguistics. Accessed February 18, 2013. http://www.cal.org/resources/archive/rgos/bilingual_children.html.

Martel, Y. (2003) *Life of Pi*. Wilmington, MA: Mariner Books.

Martin, D. (2011) *Elementary Science Methods: A Constructivist Approach*. Independence, KY: Cengage Learning.

Mayo Clinic (2014) Positive thinking: Stop negative self-talk to reduce stress. Accessed March 12, 2014. http://www.mayoclinic.org/healthy-living/stress-management/in-depth/positive-thinking/art-20043950.

Meetup (2014) Accessed March 12, 2014. http://www.meetup.com.

Melvill, H. (2009) *Thoughts Appropriate to the Season and the Days, Lectures.* Whitefish, MT: Kessinger Publishing.

Merrill, J. (1984) *Bringing Up Baby Bilingual.* New York: Facts on File Publications.

Montgomery, L.M. (1915) *Anne of the Island.* Accessed January 5, 2012. http://www.goodreads.com/quotes/24859-humor-is-the-spiciest-condiment-in-the-feast-of-existence.

Morsch, L. (2009) Why it pays to be bilingual. *AOL Jobs*, January 26. Accessed March 12, 2014. http://jobs.aol.com/articles/2009/01/26/why-it-pays-to-be-bilingual/.

Multilingual Living (2011) Bilingual siblings: Fine tuning family language strategies. Accessed June 2013. http://www.multilingualliving.com/2011/11/08/bilingual-siblings-fine-tuning-family-language-strategies.

Murphey, T. and Sasaki, T. (1998) Japanese English teachers' increasing use of English. *The Language Teacher* 22 (10), 21–27.

Murphy, E. (2011) *Welcoming Linguistic Diversity in Early Childhood Classrooms.* Bristol: Multilingual Matters.

Musica.com.br (2014) Garota de Ipanema. Vinicius de Moraes. Accessed March 12, 2014. http://musica.com.br/artistas/vinicius-de-moraes/m/garota-de-ipanema/letra.html.

Myles, C. (2003) *Raising Bilingual Children.* Parent's Guide Series. Los Angeles, CA: Mars Publishing.

Navracsis, J. (2003) An interview with François Grosjean. *The Bilingual Family Newsletter*, 1–7.

Nelson, A. (2013) 30 excellent quotes from content marketing experts. *Exact Target*, September 12. Accessed January 2, 2014. http://www.salesforcemarketingcloud.com/blog/2013/09/content-marketing-experts/.

Newfoundland and Labrador Department of Education and Early Childhood Development (2014) Teaching with puppets: A video resource for teachers. Accessed May 1, 2014. http://www.ed.gov.nl.ca/edu/earlychildhood/puppets.

Nickeldeon (2014) Dora the Explorer. Go Diego Go. March 19. http://www.nickjr.com/dora-the-explorer/.

No Foreign Lands (2013) August 24. Accessed October 12, 2013. http://macaulay.cuny.edu/eportfolios/other/.

Okrent, A. (2013) How many languages is it possible to know? *Mental Floss*, February 27. Accessed March 12, 2014. http://mentalfloss.com/article/49138/how-many-languages-it-possible-know.

Olson, D. (2014) How does being bilingual affect learning? Accessed March 11, 2014. http://www.ncld.org/types-learning-disabilities/executive-function-disorders/bilingualism-advantage-benefit.

Oxford Dictionary (2014) Accessed November 1, 2014. http://oxforddictionaries.com.

Palabea (2014) Accessed March 17, 2014. http://palabea.com.

PBS Home (1990) *John Garner's Writings*, November 10. Accessed March 12, 2012. http://www.pbs.org/johngardner/sections/writings_speech_1.html.

Pearson, B.Z. (2008) *Raising a Bilingual Child.* New York: Living Language.

PhysOrg (2009) New study may revolutionize language learning. PhysOrg.com, January 27. Accessed December 1, 2012. http://phys.org/news152292870.html.

Pimsleur (2014) Accessed March 14, 2014. http://www.pimsleur.com.

Pinker, S. (1995) *The Language Instinct.* New York: Harper Perennial Modern Classics.

Pinker, S. (2007) *The Language Instinct: How the Mind Creates Languages.* New York: Harper Perennial Modern Classics.

Pinsky, T. (2003) *Homedaddy: Little White Lies and Tales from the Crib.* New York: Push Pull Press.

Poldrack, R. (2009) Multitasking: The brain seeks novelty. *Huffington Post*, October 28. Accessed 5 2015, January. http://www.huffingtonpost.com/russell-poldrack/multitasking-the-brain-se_b_334674.html.

Power, C. (2005) Not the Queen's English. *Daily Beast*, March 5. Accessed November 13, 2012. http://www.thedailybeast.com/newsweek/2005/03/06/not-the-queen-s-english.html.

Pressfield, S. (2012) *The War of Art: Break Through the Blocks and Win Your Inner Creative Battle.* New York: Black Irish Entertainment.

Raguenaud, V. (2009) *Bilingual By Choice.* Boston, MA: Nicholas Brealey Publishing.

Reschke, K. (2002) *Family and Consumer Sciences: Baby Talk.* Accessed June 15, 2013. http://archive.is/EtofL.

Risley, T. and Hart, B. (1995) *Meaningful Differences in the Everyday Experience of Young American Children.* Baltimore, MD: Brookes Publishing.

Rosemond, J. (2001) *New Parent Power!* Kansas City, KS: Andrews McMeel Publishing.

Rosetta Stone (2014) Accessed March 14, 2014. http://www.rosettastone.com.

Sacred Text Archive (2012) Accessed March 12, 2012. http://www.sacred-texts.com/cla/ari/nico/nico014.htm.

Saunders, G. (1988) *Bilingual Children: From Birth to Teens.* Clevedon: Multilingual Matters.

Schwarzer, D. (2001) *Noa's Ark: One Child's Voyage into Multiliteracy.* Portsmouth: Heinemann.

Science Daily (2012) Bilingualism can increase mental agility. *Science Daily*, August 3. Accessed March 8, 2013. http://www.sciencedaily.com/releases/2012/08/120803082915.htm.

SciForums (2007) The cognate thread. Accessed January 3, 2014. http://www.sciforums.com/showthread.php?63555-The-cognate-thread.

Sears, M.S. (2007) Extracurricular extras: What kids learn from music. *Scholastic*, August 13. Accessed January 3, 2014. http://stage30.scholastic.com/browse/article.jsp?id=3747351.

SharedTalk (2014) Accessed March 17, 2014. http://www.sharedtalk.com.

Sharp, L. (2012) Stealth learning: Unexpected learning opportunities through games. *Journal of Instructional Research* 1, 42–48. http://www.gcu.edu/Academics/Journal-of-Instructional-Research/-Unexpected-Learning-Opportunities-Through-Games-.php.

Shoebottom, P. (2004) Grammar Notes: Frankfurt International School. Accessed January 8, 2014. http://esl.fis.edu/grammar/rules/index.htm.

Shute, N. (2012) Speaking multiple languages may help delay dementia symptoms. *Shots: Health News from NPR*, April 4. Accessed November 15, 2012. http://www.npr.org/blogs/health/2012/04/04/149995850.

Singer, J. (2013) Quotes about play. *Child's Play Magazine.* Accessed June 4, 2013. http://www.childsplaymagazine.com/quotes/index.htm.

Skwarecki, B. (2013) Babies learn to recognize words in the womb. *Science Magazine* online, August 26. Accessed April 25, 2014. http://news.sciencemag.org/brain-behavior/2013/08/babies-learn-recognize-words-womb.

Snow, C. and Hoefnagel-Höhle, M. (1978) The critical period for language acquisition: Evidence from second language learning. *Child Development* 49 (4), 1114–1128. http://www.jstor.org/stable/i247316.

Steiner, N. (2008) *7 Steps to Raising a Bilingual Child.* New York: Amacom.

Stengel, J. (2013) *WARC: News and Opinions.* Accessed June 15, 2013. http://www.warc.com/Pages/NewsAndOpinion/Quotebank.aspx?Category=Marketing.

Steves, R. (2014) Accessed March 17, 2014. http://www.ricksteves.com.

Swayne, M. (2011) Juggling languages can build better brains. *Penn State News*, February 18. Accessed March 12, 2014. http://news.psu.edu/story/160653/2011/02/18/juggling-languages-can-build-better-brains.

Te Kete Ipurangi Ministry of Education (2012) *LEAP: Language Enhancing the Achievement of Psifika.* Accessed December 15, 2012. http://leap.tki.org.nz/Is-bilingualism-an-advantage#.

Thomas, C. (2012) *Growing Up with Languages: Reflections on Multilingual Childhoods.* Clevedon: Multilingual Matters.

Tokuhama-Espinosa, T. (2000) *Raising Multilingual Children: Foreign Language Acquisition and Children.* Westport, CT: Praeger.

Trimnell, E. (2005) *Why You Need a Foreign Language and How to Learn One.* Cincinnati, OH: Beechmont Crest Publishing.

Twombly, R. (2012) To teach is to learn twice. Georgetown University Medical Center. Accessed November 1, 2012. http://gumc.georgetown.edu/news/to-teach-is-to-learn-twice.

Tugend, A. (2012) Praise is fleeting, but brickbats we recall. *New York Times*, March 23. Accessed December 4, 2012. http://www.nytimes.com/2012/03/24/your-money/why-people-remember-negative-events-more-than-positive-ones.html?pagewanted=all&_r=1&.

University of Guelph (2010) Bilingualism translates into higher earnings, study finds. http://www.uoguelph.ca/news/2010/08/bilingualism_pa_1.html.

Upegui, O. (2008) Do you think puns are funny? *Lingua Franca*, April 26. Accessed December 18, 2011. http://epiac1216.wordpress.com/2008/04/26/are-puns-funny/.

Wallach, A. (1997) At midcareer, an artist switches gears. *New York Times*, October 26. Accessed December 7, 2011. http://www.nytimes.com/1997/10/26/arts/art-at-midcareer-an-artist-switches-gears.html?pagewanted=all&src=pm.

White, E.B. (1952) *Charlotte's Web.* New York: Harper Collins.

Vinson, J. (2014) The deliverance of bilingual education: Translanguaging. Accessed March 3, 2014. http://bilingualeducationtranslanguaging.bravesites.com/translanguaging.

Xiha Life (2014) Accessed March 17, 2014. http://www.xihalife.com.

YouTube (2014) Accessed March 14, 2014. http://www.youtube.com.

About the Author

Christine Jernigan instructs foreign language teachers at North Carolina State University in Raleigh, NC, and is a language coach for parents who want to raise bilingual children. She holds a PhD in foreign language education, and her main research interests include motivation, expectation and authenticity in the language classroom. She has contributed to the book *Raising Children Bilingually in the US* and to *The Bilingual Family Newsletter*. Her own children speak English and Portuguese. Visit her YouTube channel for videos on several of the chapter topics: youtube.com/getbilingual and Twitter @getbilingual.

Index